THE LIMITS OF RAWLSIAN JUSTICE

THE LIMITS OF
RAWLSIAN
JUSTICE

ROBERTO ALEJANDRO

The Johns Hopkins University Press

Baltimore and London

© 1998 The Johns Hopkins University Press
All rights reserved. Published 1998
Printed in the United States of America on acid-free paper
07 06 05 04 03 02 01 00 99 98   5 4 3 2 1

The Johns Hopkins University Press
2715 North Charles Street
Baltimore, Maryland 21218-4319
The Johns Hopkins Press Ltd., London

Library of Congress Cataloging-in-Publication Data
will be found at the end of this book.
A catalog record for this book is available from the British Library.

ISBN 0-8018-5678-7 (pbk)

But one who is genuinely of the popular sort should see to it that the multitude is not overtly poor; for this is the reason for democracy being depraved. Measures must therefore be devised so that there will be abundance over time. Since this is advantageous also for the well off what ought to be done is to accumulate what is left over of the revenues and distribute accumulated [sums] to the poor. This should particularly be done if one could accumulate enough for the acquisition of a plot of land, or failing this for a start in trade or farming. If this is not possible for all, it should be distributed on the basis of tribes or some other part [of the city] by turns; and in the meantime the well off should be taxed to provide pay for necessary meetings, while at the same time being released from pointless sorts of public service.

—Aristotle, *The Politics*

Contents

Acknowledgments

Writing a book entails a plurality of debts. This book is no exception. Over the years, as I have been thinking, teaching, and developing the arguments that are now this book, I have incurred many obligations to teachers, colleagues, administrators, and institutions. The Ford Foundation Fellowship for Minorities provided a fellowship in 1993–94 which gave me ample opportunity to research Rawlsian justice. Philip Green was very generous in arranging the institutional support of Smith College during my tenure as a Ford fellow. Dean Seymour Berger of the Faculty of Social and Behavioral Sciences at the University of Massachusetts provided financial support during the same year. Several people read earlier versions of some chapters and offered generous comments and criticisms. Patrick Neal (University of Vermont), Will Kymlicka (University of Ottawa), and Edward Portis (Texas A & M University) stand out as three theorists who encouraged my efforts without failing to fulfill their roles as colleagues and teachers. In different ways I have incorporated many of their suggestions by either modifying or expanding my arguments. The criticisms of the anonymous reader for the Johns Hopkins University Press were very helpful and allowed me to see my work from a different perspective. I owe a larger portion of my debt to Professor Sotirios Barber (University of Notre Dame), who was very kind in his advice and support when I was completing and later revising this project. The works of George Kateb, Anne Norton, and Sheldon Wolin have always been sources of fresh perspectives which have nourished my own interpretations. As always, Linda Chatfield's suggestions when proofreading the manuscript were invaluable. Linda Bembury helped me to prepare the electronic version of this book.

My deepest gratitude goes to my wife, Carmen, for her kindness during these years.

THE LIMITS OF RAWLSIAN JUSTICE

1

Liberal Tribulations
and Modern Malaises

History is full of surprises.

—John Rawls, *Political Liberalism*

John Rawls's *A Theory of Justice* has been the dominant conception of justice in contemporary liberal theory for more than two decades. Since its publication in 1971 it has sparked a new interest in theoretical arguments and practical designs that gave philosophical justifications to the institutions of the welfare state. Its influence, though, went far beyond the issue of justice and reached to areas encompassing what I might call a *liberal ontology*. Rawls's arguments touched upon subjectivity, moral psychology, and epistemology, as well as the role of societal norms and contexts in shaping those issues. The debate between liberals and communitarians, which flourished in the 1980s languished in the 1990s through a displacement toward issues of identity and is still an unavoidable referential point in any attempt to understand the liberal project in the last decades of the twentieth century, was spawned to a large extent by Rawls's philosophical reflections.

A Theory of Justice is a work that elicits as many surfaces as the undercurrents informing it. The book bears witness to a long process of development reflecting different influences and even different emphases. As an architectonic project, the Rawlsian model draws its clues from a variegated array of fields which includes philosophy, economics, psychology, and even so mysterious an area of knowledge as eugenics. In a clear prose, Rawls managed to put together arguments coming from disparate sources and assembled what he took to be a coherent conception of justice. Critics and sympathizers alike have seen in the Rawlsian project a strong egalitarian urge that infuses all of the intellectual resources Rawls brought to his endeavors.

The present investigation seeks to shed a different light not only on the egalitarianism so often attributed to Rawlsian justice, but also on the whole philosophical and political project inaugurated by *A Theory of Justice.* The path I intend to travel should be demarcated through an initial distinction between genealogy and archaeology. By *genealogy* I mean the quest for origins, the search for the intellectual and political traditions that could be seen as a subterranean well nourishing the Rawlsian view of justice. In *The Metaphysics of Morals,* for example, Kant wrote about a perpetual contract, the principle of reciprocity, and the centrality of choice in his idea of right.[1] These three principles occupy a prominent role in Rawls's views, and they could be read as signs of the genealogical links between Rawls's philosophy and the Kantian tradition. By *archaeology*, I refer to the arguments suggested by Rawls's texts themselves and how they weave a web of arguments whose end result is a paradigm traversed increasingly by a gap between its goals and its solutions.

In this chapter, I begin by offering a sketchy genealogical portrait of the traditions underlying the idea of justice which Rawls named *justice as fairness.* But the emphasis of this book will be on an archaeological approach, namely, on an examination of Rawls's texts to probe both their theoretical and political arguments.

I should warn the reader about something that, depending on his or her sympathies, will soon become evident. Although some of the propositions advanced in this genealogical sketch may be controversial, they are not arbitrary. I provide reasons to support them. But the reader should not lose sight of the larger project, which is a critical inquiry into the rich complexity of Rawlsianism. With these caveats in place, I hope that students of contemporary liberal philosophy will be in a better position to understand why I have chosen to paint in broad strokes the genealogical question before devoting my attention to the archaeology of justice as fairness.

Worn-out Warriors and Order

The contractualism informing the Rawlsian conception of justice has never been an invigorating philosophy. It is hardly a doctrine that inspires people to assault a decrepit prison or to make barricades against a Winter Palace. Quite the contrary, liberal principles are an effort to show why those assaults are unnecessary (they lead to bloodshed) and how those barricades ought to be avoided (they are harbingers of death and cruelty). It was so in the past; it is so in the present. A Hobbesian description of the state of nature would cool down any insurrection; a Dworkinian speech would kill any nascent revolution.

It is true that the banner of liberty mobilized people to stand up against the feudal order and its aristocratic principles. But liberty was then conceived metaphysically as part of a larger whole—liberty as God given or as nature's purpose—and that metaphysical reading inspired masses to overthrow an existing order. It did not move individuals to enter into the liberal social contract. Inspiration and deliberation are two different things, and liberal theory does not seek to inspire with passion, but to convince with arguments.

This might explain why liberal manifestos are rare. The Declaration of Independence stands out, but it was superseded quickly by a constitution that, with its articles, sections, "herein" and "thereof," is emblematic of the liberal discourse. Legal and administrative memorandums, not manifestos, are the defining moments of liberal reasoning. For the founding moment of liberal theory, that juncture in which chaos vanishes and coalesces into a universal agreement is a social contract between rational parties which is arrived at through deliberation and persuasion.

The contractarian tradition underpinning contemporary liberalism is not an invigorating philosophy because its paramount goal has been a dry and pasteurized order that seeks to make citizens out of soldiers and to create tranquility out of civil disturbances. Tocqueville's syndrome is its sign: a fear of the people (who are referred to as "the masses"); a fear of majorities; and a deep-seated, and not necessarily misguided, suspicion of democratic practices. The Tocquevellian fear of the people and a Hobbesian-Kantian abhorrence of revolution are the landmarks that have historically mapped out the liberal universe. (Locke is nothing more than a straying heretic.) It could not be otherwise since liberalism appears as the last gasp of worn-out warriors in search of a last-minute compromise.

Which, after all, stands to reason. For, as a systematic theory, liberal contracting creatures arrive when the dangers of social conflicts wane because the enemies are too tired to keep fighting. In the vast landscapes of the last five hundred years, it is possible to find scattered fragments pointing toward some revolutionary origins of liberal ideas. One can almost hear the voices of the Levellers at Putnam and be amazed at how they insisted, on the basis of their comprehensive metaphysical doctrines, on the principle of consent and saw the political body as a metaphor for the human body. One can also see the revolutionary language of the American Declaration of Independence and the French version of the Declaration of the Rights of Man. But those revolutionary fragments are the exception. Liberalism, as a systematic exposition of political principles, is a cry of fatigued souls inhabiting a worn-out century.

I do not pretend to derive philosophy from chronology, but certain dates carry a nagging symbolism. Hobbes's *Leviathan* was published in 1651, when the ashes of the civil war were still smoldering but no longer incendiary. Cromwell was the sovereign. Locke's *Two Treatises,* which contained an explicit defense of the right of revolution, came to light when the prospects of revolutionary mobilization against the monarch were nil.[2] The paradigmatic principle of the liberal discourse, tolerance, is the best example of liberal fatigue. It is a compromise, a modus vivendi, arrived at by tired fighters who realized, rather late, that the wars of religions were a waste of time and human lives.

Bills of Rights are born when revolutions fade. In the United States, the liberal country par excellence, the sequence is clear: revolution—a constitutional order that substitutes nation building for nation founding—and a bill of rights that keeps the state at bay and thus prevents another revolution. Yes, Jefferson talked, anticipating Trotsky, of an almost permanent revolution.

> We have had 13. states independent 11. years. There has been one rebellion. That comes to one rebellion in a century & a half for each state. What country before ever existed a century & half without a rebellion? & what country can preserve it's liberties if their rulers are not warned from time to time that their people preserve the spirit of resistance? Let them take arms. The remedy is to set them right as to facts, pardon & pacify them. What signify a few lives lost in a century or two? The tree of liberty must be refreshed from time to time with the blood of patriots & tyrants. It is it's natural manure.[3]

But, in the liberal canon, those Jeffersonian outbursts border, if they are not already in, the domain of insanity. Hobbes's *Leviathan* is a monument to order. Kant's political philosophy seeks order, which is conceived as a moral state that contributes to the development of the individual's higher faculties. Tocqueville's political theory is a paean to the dangers that unfettered and untutored majorities represent to order.

Yet, when seen against the backdrop of contemporary liberal philosophy, the modern and by now classical expositions of liberal theory seem like remote and foreign texts. Although the classical texts addressed pervasive but aging conflicts, the tiring confrontations of tired combatants, those texts were creatures of heroic times, and their theoretical formulations partake of that heroism: Hobbesian selves struggling and toiling in the state of nature until one day their collective fear overcomes their universal right to everything, and, after deliberating in that jungle of private meanings arising from private definitions, they redefine individual interests and institute the commonwealth. It is a heroic saga that goes from a cacophony of voices leading to a nasty, brutish, and short life, to the unity of a state devoted to protecting the lives of its members.[4]

The Kantian vision of history is no less heroic.[5] No one should use or treat a person as a means: this is a principle of reason. But in the realm of human history, nature may use some generations as a means for future generations. It may even use violence to show the futility of war, and one is left with the sense that Kantian reason and Kantian nature inhabit two different universes. Reason demands an unconditional loyalty to moral principles, whereas nature may use immoral means—violence—to achieve a moral end—perpetual peace. The Kantian individual is heroic in his devotion to deontological principles. He does not need an outside redemption. He creates himself by following principles declared by his own will, and yet he is or should be aware that, regardless of his efforts to act as an end, forces that are beyond his control may treat him as a means.

This does not matter much, though. Kantian selves ought to act as moral agents regardless of what others might do. To do this requires a moral environment, a state ruled by the principles of right. It also requires a sense—how fragile or strong is up to the individual to decide—of heroism. To pursue morality without any regard for happiness: not even the Son of God demanded that. The Kantian self is also heroic in the competitive environment he needs for his moral and intellectual development. He is like a tree. And by competing with other trees for sunlight, he does not grow twisted, but straight, reaching toward the sun and the starry sky.

For all of his trembling before any sign of revolutionary tremor, Tocqueville's heroic efforts are not only present in his masterful descriptions of the tensions haunting the democratic project: the citizen versus the individual; the public versus the private; the state versus civil society; mores carrying the weight of tradition versus laws that are unstable and unreliable; public associations as schools of communality and citizenship versus the tranquility of private gatherings of friends and families.[6] His entire theoretical project is heroic: to teach a new political theory to a new age that is too ready and too hasty to abandon the wisdom of the aristocratic past.

Not even the pessimism of the second volume of *Democracy in America* is able to defeat the heroic sentiment informing his agenda. Yes: democracy may end up in a powerful and centralized state, crushing local authorities and stultifying individuality. Yes: the boisterous and active citizens of the first volume, the ones who impressed him the most when he landed on the New England agoras, may become a passive herd following the state's commands. Yes: the tyranny of the majority may deny or make moot the existence of individual rights. And yet, democracy may learn from the legacy of an aristocratic past in which, according to Tocqueville's story, municipalities resisted the crown and carved out a niche for local and free institutions. Democracy may construct local and public spaces where individuals may learn to be citizens and to keep the state and its encroaching nature at a safe distance. It just needs to look at the mirror of aristocratic practices to check its own defects.

The heroism of modern liberal theory sought to create a stable order by expunging the public sphere from any trace of ideas or doctrines that might even remotely trigger conflicts (Hobbes); or by defining the public realm around citizens committed to common pursuits and guided by a common faith that served as a moral anchor in the midst of universal uncertainty (Tocqueville); or by encouraging an active deliberation among male citizens (Kantian reason is universal, but Kantian citizenship is masculine) willing to engage in free discussion about any topic, including legislation, since no matter how deep their disagreement with the executive or the legislative authority might be, they were willing to obey (Kant).

There is no heroism in contemporary liberal theory. Nor is there the sense of fragility which accompanied the classical account of the liberal argument. Nowhere in contemporary exemplars of the liberal view will one find the heroic landscapes of a Hobbesian state of nature with its open acknowledgment of fear as a driving force of the social contract and its universalistic tone about obedience.[7] Nowhere will one find the fragility of the Hobbesian commonwealth, which has the state of nature as a permanent, dark companion.[8] Nowhere will one find the Tocquevellian claim that a universal adherence to religious mores is a socializing factor for democratic citizens. Hobbesian selves and their agonizing struggle for order have been replaced by faceless shadows inhabiting an original position from which any trace of contingency, presumably, has been cleared up.

Nor will one find Tocquevellian citizens who are caught up in conflicting loyalties. Rather, one will find the tired survivors of a capsized ship (the metaphor is illuminating) who land on an island and decide to found an egalitarian community and then begin by organizing an equal distribution of clam-shells—their money—before going on a shopping spree.[9] "Suppose a number of shipwreck survivors are washed up on a desert island which has abundant resources and no native population, and any likely rescue is many years away."[10] This ominous mixture of shipwreck survivors and shoppers describes liberal theory at its best. Readers will find one Adrian, one Bruce, one Deborah, all Dworkinian characters engaged in the "heroic" process of counting costs and benefits, or the costs represented by the choice of expensive tastes, and after all of the pluses and minuses are considered, the philosopher is ready to announce that philosophy requires accounting.[11]

In *A Theory of Justice*, there are, perhaps, three sentences that bear the mark of a heroic age.

Being first virtues of human activities, truth and justice are uncompromising.[12]

Thus to see our place in society from the perspective of this position [the original position] is to see it *sub specie aeternitatis:* it is to regard the human situation not only from all social but also from all temporal points of view. (587)

For given favorable conditions, it is by maintaining these public arrangements that persons *best* express their nature and achieve the widest regulative excellences of which each is capable. (529, emphasis added)

It is no accident that these three sentences are close to the universalistic efforts of classical liberal theory. Otherwise, the Rawlsian project is one in which statements of substantive issues tend to be qualified by cautious provisos that leave the original claim in a sort of vacuum. Thus we have, as a paradigmatic example, the categorical claim that justice is "uncompromising" (4) followed, one hundred pages later, by the qualification that we ought to support justice when it does not represent "too much cost" to us (115).

The fate of these three sentences is perhaps symptomatic of the historical root of systematic expositions of the liberal project. The historical root, I repeat, is a concern for order when combatants are too tired to keep fighting or when struggles have waned or have shown their uselessness.

Rawlsian justice is no exception. In his essays after *A Theory of Justice*, Rawls makes it clear that his principles are derived from the shared intuitive ideas of democratic societies and that his version of justice applies only to those societies. So the eternity of justice as fairness lasted a few years; it collapsed under the historical traits of a human society. In another essay he claimed that it is not philosophy's business to settle questions of truth; rather, those questions ought to be avoided in the name of order and cooperation.[13] So the heroic and uncompromising nature of truth has been abandoned in the name of a philosophical method that seeks to avoid conflicts. Rawlsian justice is the most famous contemporary version of a philosophical and political project that began talking about human beings in the salons and streets of eighteenth-century Europe and ended up as a defense of the tax-paying duties of American citizens.

In the Dewey Lectures and in *Political Liberalism*, Rawls seems to suggest that justice still expresses a person's best nature in the public realm, not in the private arena,[14] and this view, of the three mentioned above, is the only one that has withstood the onslaught of caution and qualifications that define the Rawlsian language. Nothing is new under the liberal sun: provisos and qualifications are also what defines Mill's arguments in *On Liberty*.[15] His radical statement ("over his own body and mind, the individual is sovereign") starts to be qualified as soon as Mill recovers his temper in the second and later chapters. At the end of the book, there are so many loopholes in Mill's reasoning that the original claim has become an empty outburst.

Moralizing the State

What is the goal I seek in describing some possible differences between classical liberal theory and contemporary liberal versions of liberal reasoning? It is to show that since the contractarian view supporting contemporary liberalism is not an invigorating philosophy, but an effort at accommodation between tired enemies, the enervating tendencies of liberal theory have finally taken their toll and exacted their due. For all of contemporary liberalism's suspicion of traditions and claims that its principles stand for a radically new vision of individuality, current expressions of the liberal-communitarian debate may prove that contemporary liberal theory is an attempt to defend the status quo. Or to put it differently, liberalism is now a conservative philosophy that, in these times when the end of history has been decreed and the universal validity of liberal principles has been proclaimed, seeks to buttress failing institutions in the name of justice and neutrality.

Contemporary liberal philosophy is deeply conservative in its attempt to bolster and expand the legitimacy of the present order. In Rawlsian justice, for instance, a company's owner may fire workers to enhance productivity or to expel, covertly, a militant union. In the liberal understanding of justice, there is no place to address that practice, and there is no opportunity to discuss the dominant understanding of productivity and efficiency.

What liberal theory does is to engage in an operation of displacements. The practice of firing people is not questioned since it is part of the right of property, but then the locus moves away from civil society to the state. The state, which ought to derive its policies from neutral reasons, will provide unemployment benefits or training programs. The values of productivity and efficiency are not at stake. The power of the state to design programs that favor a particular organization of work and certain visions of the human good associated with that organization is not an issue either. Liberal theory avoids or shuns the critique of certain practices of civil society by offering a state-regulated remedy. And since this remedy ought to be based on neutral reasons, there is no opportunity to challenge the conceptions of human flourishing which inform, say, the practice of productivity, which, in turn, gave way to the need for a state remedy in the first place. Those conceptions will remain intact.

The outcome is that liberalism ends up as a statist theory that requires a powerful state to regulate the inequalities that civil society produces. That is, liberal theory assumes the legitimacy of the current practices of civil society and then calls in the state to remedy what the theory may regard as unjust outcomes of those practices. Let's hear John Rawls:

> The sense in which persons are exploited by market imperfections is a highly special one: namely, the precept of contribution is violated, and this happens because the price system is no longer efficient. But . . . this precept is but one among many secondary norms, and what really counts is the workings of the whole system *and whether these defects are compensated for elsewhere.* (309, emphasis added)

The injustices brought about by civil societies are the "defects" that ought to be "compensated for elsewhere." "Elsewhere" is the Rawlsian state, which ought to provide remedies based on neutral grounds, which is another way of leaving intact those practices that justified the government intervention in the first place, and another way of saying that present practices of liberal civil society are the best for which we can hope.

As already indicated, one important problem is that liberal remedies have a tendency to address outcomes rather than the practices that made them possible. A polluting company may be fined, but the principles of efficiency and productivity which may be the causes of pollution are deemed valid. Thus liberal theory deters us from criticizing civil society and encourages us to go to the courts to seek a neutrally grounded remedy. The liberal order is supposed to get remedied, and we are expected to express those remedies in liberal terms enacted by liberal institutions. We may criticize liberal civil society because it is inefficient or because it violates our rights. That is, we all need to engage in the liberal game and play by liberal rules. It is the end of history.

Better still, in Rawlsian justice it is through a powerful and centralized state that people are connected to one another. Individuals pay taxes, and the state uses that money to provide social services to those in need. In justice as fairness, Tocqueville's worse fears become reality: a network of centralized agencies uniting individuals who become more and more dependent on centers of powers beyond their reach.

If there are conflicts, say, between people who defend the environment and people who defend the creation of jobs, a version of liberal theory will address it by looking at the cost involved in both alternatives. Here there is another displacement—one from a discussion of the human good expressed in an environmental policy to an assessment of the financial costs that each side may represent to society. And since numbers are presumably neutral, the lower the cost, the higher the chances of being adopted as a state policy. In this case, accounting substitutes a political or philosophical deliberation about visions of the human good.

If for example the disagreement is between a woman who wants to be faithful to her religion and believes that God will save her baby and the state concern that, without a cesarean operation, the baby will die, liberal theory will avoid a discussion of the conception of the good represented by a religious perspective, reduce the conflict to a legal problem, and address it with the vocabulary of rights. But rights are not meant to deal with the content of conceptions of the human good, but to regulate those conceptions without assessing their content.

There are thus three displacements: from civil society to the state (this displacement prevents a critique of liberal practices by providing a state remedy justified with allegedly neutral reasons); from the content of conceptions of the human good to the costs those conceptions may represent (this displacement avoids a critique of any conception of the human good by offering the objectivity of costs); from the content of any conception of the good to the courts and the vocabulary of rights (this third displacement avoids a discussion of the good expressed in ways of life by providing the impartiality of universal rights).

However, it is not only that contemporary liberal theory embodies a conservative project. It is that, in relation to the classical articulations of liberal theory, contemporary liberal theory represents an important shift. It does not seek to accommodate enemies any more; it seeks to colonize them. It attempts to move or to force them to adopt the liberal version of selfhood, justice, citizenship. In a nutshell, it seeks to force them to adopt a liberal vocabulary to frame their moral and political conflicts. This means that liberal diversity is diversity within the boundaries of the liberal marketplace, the liberal understanding of justice, and the liberal state. Contemporary liberal theory has defined the public realm as a liberal place. It is, consequently, off limits. It is free of nonliberal views or practices. If nonliberal conceptions of the human good enter the public realm, they have to wear the garb of the liberal vocabulary. Nazis can march; their doing so is covered by the right of free speech and thus becomes a legitimation of the liberal order.

It is necessary to emphasize the conservative character of contemporary liberal theory to avoid the theoretical traps implicit in accepting the liberal terms in the confrontation with communitarians. It is not a question of choosing between the "diversity" liberalism offers versus the alleged "uniformity" communitarians advocate. It is that the liberal order is characterized by a pervasive uniformity of acquisitive shoppers which liberal theory is unable to explain. And it is not a question between having the opportunity to choose one's conception of the human good versus having a communal or state imposition of the human good. Liberal theory carries with it a conception of the human good disguised as a framework of neutral principles and institutions.

Perhaps more importantly, the issue is not the authority of past traditions that communitarians are charged with defending in opposition to the rational scrutiny of those traditions that, allegedly, liberalism stands for. For all its rejection of entrenched traditions and received opinions, liberalism presupposes the authority of a past embodied in a legal tradition. That past is so authoritative that it allows Rawls to consider the issue of rights as "settled." If there is a feature of liberal order worth discussing as a political problem, it is the tendency to call on reason to scrutinize critically its opponents' claims while putting the core of its own principles beyond rational scrutiny. An outstanding trait of Rawlsian theorizing is to flee from contingency, to agree on principles of justice, and then to treat those principles as established once and for all.

Neither justice nor individual rights are subject to critical scrutiny. Neither the harmonious personality of Rawlsian selves nor Dworkinian selves whose lives are diminished if they live in an unjust society are open to reexamination. So liberalism places its core principles beyond rational scrutiny while claiming that its opponents' claims be subject to a permanent critical evaluation. Thus MacIntyre's claim that liberals always engage in a critical evaluation of positions is inaccurate.[16] The liberal argument seems to suggest that, since its principles were articulated and arrived at through a rational process, they do not need to be subject to any further rational evaluation. Rawlsian justice is meant for a society conceived in perpetuity.

The Liberal Self, Prozac, and Postmodernity

There is a mystery that seems to be inscribed in the liberal constitution of selfhood. In nonliberal societies, when the social order collapses and radical protests ensue—or, better, when radical protests break out before the collapse of the social order—those protests tend to end up in front of the police or the party headquarters or the parliament building. Masses that constitute themselves as citizens arrive at the centers of power. In what amounts to an intriguing contrast, in liberal societies, radical protests of right-bearers turned rioters invariably end up in shopping malls with hordes of marauders grabbing whatever their hands can get hold on. An unrestrained shopping spree seems to realize the wildest dreams of the liberal self.

Ronald Beiner has rightly emphasized the bogus diversity of liberal societies.[17] Most liberal creatures work from nine to five, pay a mortgage for thirty years, have a car loan every four or five years, choose among the "variety" of movies offered by Hollywood, eat the same junk food, and probably die of the same illnesses. It is obvious that there is a gap between the value of diversity which liberal theory stands for and the practices of liberal societies. And any possible reply suggesting the pristine and unsullied character of liberal principles will not do. Liberal theory is implicated in the actual practices of liberal societies; it bears responsibility for the individuals who carry its imprints and who have been socialized by its vocabulary. The market, after all, is a liberal institution, and present democracies inhabit a liberal universe.

It is thus intriguing that a theory that began exalting rational selves now presides not over Kantian or Nietzschean or Emersonian individuals, who are the exceptions and in any case (Kantians excluded) are not liberal, but over a world constituted by private herds of shoppers. If conflicts arise among different herds or different individuals, they can settle their disputes by meeting at the fifth locus of liberal communality: the courts. The first four are shopping malls, fast-food restaurants, theaters, and subways.

MacIntyre has suggested that lawyers are the priests of liberal modernity. But since lawyers, despite Dworkin's best efforts, are not precisely the brightest representatives of the liberal predicament, liberals are right in seeing MacIntyre's assertion as a demeaning statement of the liberal world. Without objecting entirely to MacIntyre's description, another character may serve as an emblem of the liberal culture: a citizen who dutifully pays his or her taxes and is on Prozac. By paying their taxes, such citizens reveal, if we believe Rawls, the maturity of their moral sense and show the Rawlsian "love of mankind." A mature moral sense entails a duty to principles which evinces, in justice as fairness, our willingness to help people who are strangers. By taking Prozac, they may be able to alleviate their angst, which might be a disruptive force to the liberal order. Their uncontrolled angst, depending on their sympathies, may lead them to bomb one of those places where Planned Parenthood performs its surgical procedures, or they may well follow in the footsteps of Thelma and Louise.

Liberal theory is nowadays haunted by a new specter, which is no longer utilitarianism, but postmodernity. Some versions of postmodernity challenge cherished notions of the liberal core such as reason, truth, and selfhood. Against the universalistic tendencies of the liberal discourse stands a postmodern perspective that seems to derive pleasure from saying, repeating, and nailing down on liberal throats the claims that our values are just historical and linguistic creations; that morality is a matter of we-intentions; that there is no truth, but opinion; that all we have are incommensurable language games played out in a public realm where consensus is not possible; that our moral principles have no more foundation than the preferences and temporary agreements of a gathering of human beings; that grand narratives, liberal ones included, died a quiet death some time ago, and that theorists who still cling to notions of truth, reason, dignity, etc. are like guards at a mausoleum guarding a corpse or, worse, watching over the wax statue of long-dead concepts.[18]

Richard Rorty stands out as an embodiment of pragmatist-postmodern arguments, which is why he has become a thorn in the side of liberal theory and why liberals could barely repress their dismay when Rorty announced that he was, after all, one of them: a liberal thinker trying to create, in the best liberal tradition, his own identity through a new liberal utopia of irony. And when Rorty's irony seems to be fading and the one who always gives the impression that he is laughing at the rest of us settles down and announces that we ought to have and honor a national identity, there comes another thorn represented by William Connolly's politics of paradox which apparently seeks to unsettle the liberal predicament by proclaiming, in good postmodern fashion, that *nothing* is settled under the sun of the liberal universe. Nothing is settled, not even rights, which ought to be a dangerous claim for theorists whose main goal is to purify reality from its contingent attributes and to arrive at beyond-contingency rights.[19]

Postmodernity should not be a scandal for liberal principles, though; for on closer examination postmodernity is not entirely foreign to liberal reasoning. Actually, some aspects of the postmodern perspective have been part and parcel of the liberal argument all along. There is, for one, Hobbes, the first modern who intimated a postmodern propensity by insisting on the linguistic and, for instance, historical nature of human truths.[20] And there are, as other examples, the Kantian[21] and Millian[22] claim that happiness is an individual pursuit—an argument that opposes a paternalistic state and stands for a culture of diversity and different experiments of living. It is true that both Kant's understanding of happiness and Mill's idea of diversity were linked to a comprehensive doctrine of morality (Kant) or autonomy (Mill). But the metaphysical views underlying the philosophies of Kant and Mill are unable to come clean with regard to postmodernity. If you wish, postmodernity is Kantian happiness floating adrift, disconnected from the larger metaphysical doctrine that was meant to give it meaning or a Millian autonomy that ran amok, equally dissociated from the bigger picture represented by Mill's philosophy of life.

Liberalism has paved the way for a world that can invigorate markets with new products, new fashions, and even new political slogans. But the liberal world has carved out a culture in which exhaustion is a fashion. Liberalism has witnessed and assisted the dawning of a radically "new" phenomenon in human civilization. It is not the first time that the end of history has been declared. Christianity and other utopias announced it, but they claimed that the culmination of history inaugurated a new way of understanding and looking at reality. To the best of my knowledge, liberal theory is the first in human civilization to proclaim the end of history and inaugurate the continuation of the same. Now, if this is not the exhaustion of the liberal order, what else can be? When a version of postmodernity (Baudrillard) decrees the end of all things and then portrays a future ruled by the same things that were allegedly gone, it is easier to understand why the postmodern is part of the liberal genealogical tree.

Back to *A Theory of Justice*

My investigation grew out of disappointment with the dominant articulations of contemporary liberal theory, the political project they embody, and its opponents in the communitarian camp. It is not only that those articulations promise what they cannot deliver[23] but also, and more importantly, that liberal theory, as all triumphant political doctrines, seeks to create the world in its own image, while, in contrast to all victorious paradigms, it takes pains to claim that that is not its project.

The Rawlsian paradigm holds that its theory is only concerned with the basic structure of society, namely, the political institutions regulating the distribution of goods and protecting the social order. But it ends up proposing a vision of the human condition in which justice (i.e., Rawlsian justice) must be the paramount virtue of our life because without it we disfigure our humanity or fail to exercise "full autonomy."

The Rawlsian view claims that we ought to acknowledge and respect the fact of pluralism in liberal modernity, the fact that people affirm incommensurable conceptions of the human good. But, despite that acknowledgment of diversity, we are *all* supposed to be fully cooperating members of the liberal order over a complete life. Rawls's philosophy emphasizes the plural character of contemporary liberal societies and then seeks to stand back from that pluralism and oversee it through a model of justice which somehow acquires the authority to regulate all conceptions of the human good.[24] Rawls's arguments insist on their neutrality with regard to different versions of human flourishing, and yet they propose a vision of moral personality anchored in an internal harmony and in a sharp separation of the private and public domains, which determines the *form* and *place* of human flourishing. Whatever his vision of the human good, the Rawlsian individual is supposed to have harmonious ends that are part of his rational good; and whatever his conception of the human good might be, it is supposed to flourish in the private realms of individuals rather than in the public sphere of citizens who are guided, not by their comprehensive doctrines, but by their agreement on Rawlsian justice.

It is perhaps a testimony to the force of liberal views that all of these tensions are either unacknowledged or completely erased from the liberal philosophical discourse. In Rawls's case, there is always a cautious and protective language that is at pains to show its differences with comprehensive doctrines—which are, allegedly, the only ones that despise the political neutrality that Rawls attempts to demonstrate so earnestly.

I pointed out that contemporary liberal theory attempts to colonize its adversaries. The colonizing aspects are nowhere more evident than in the universalistic efforts of the liberal order. If Larmore wants Romantics to be liberal,[25] liberal theory wants all individuals to adhere to and comply with liberal assumptions. Rawls wants cooperation over a complete life, and a typical liberal response to Alasdair MacIntyre's project of small communities pursuing their own conception of the good life is that it is irrelevant.[26] It is irrelevant because MacIntyre's communities are *outside* the liberal framework and resist the liberal attempt to colonize and turn them into groups confirming the liberal principle of pluralism or enriching the liberal political process. MacIntyre's claim that the good life "is the life spent in seeking for the good life for man"[27] is seen as a "liberal concession."[28] Similarly, a standard liberal response to Michael Sandel's claim that a communal identity may be open to reevaluation is that such a formulation is undistinguishable from the liberal principle of autonomy.[29] So liberal universality is always ready to identify the "liberal" principles underlying their interlocutors or opponents. History has ended, and the contours of that culmination are unmistakenly liberal.

This is not to say that communitarian arguments are more satisfying. They are, in some important respects, more convincing, and it is by now clear that a communitarian ontology that sees the self as a historical, situated creature, and a communitarian epistemology that sees knowledge as a historical process, have won the day. A liberal self that is just an embodiment of rationality and constituted independently or prior to all of its ends is too much for common sense. And not even Rawls, who first proposed this prior self, was able (see Chapter 5) to come up with a persuasive justification of that view.

Will Kymlicka came to the rescue and attempted to provide an ingenious formulation of the alleged priority of the self over its ends. The self is prior, Kymlicka argues, in the sense that no end is beyond the individual's capacity to revise it.[30] The only problem with Kymlicka's claim is that it is false. Rawls explicitly says that his two principles of justice should not be in conflict "with those judgments that are *fixed points,* ones that we seem unwilling to revise under any foreseeable circumstances" (318, emphasis added). I assume that those judgments may refer to a person's ends in life. But, more importantly, Rawlsian justice is beyond revision. Rawlsian cooperation *over a complete life* is beyond reexamination. And the monopoly justice exercises in our identity, as the virtue that best expresses our nature, is beyond reevaluation. The priority of the self over its ends disappeared as soon as Rawls saw justice as fairness as the end result of citizens who construct an agreement in the light of the received intuitive ideas of their society.

Yet, although a communitarian ontology and epistemology have eroded the contingency-free selves of the Kantian liberal discourse, the communitarian political and moral projects are not necessarily more appealing. Michael Sandel, for one, suggests a vision of identity in which attachments are "found" or "acknowledged" and in which the possibility of constructing an identity in opposition to dominant paradigms seems to be ruled out altogether.[31] Alasdair MacIntyre, for another, stands for the creation of communities where the Aristotelian notion of the virtues ought to guide individuals in their quest for the good life.[32] Other communitarians (e.g., Taylor, Beiner, Barber, Wolin, and Arendt) conceive of the political as the fundamental place to construct communality and to show and develop our genuine identity. What is important, some communitarians claim, is to articulate a new vocabulary around the notions of the virtues, character formation, the good life, and public participation.

This book seeks to reformulate the liberal-communitarian conflict through a return to John Rawls's *A Theory of Justice*. Rawls himself has narrowed the conflict by situating his theory in the political culture of the United States and by accepting a greater scope for the idea of the good. The justification of choosing Rawls to shed some light on the liberal-communitarian conflict is on firmer ground if we take notice of the three dominant critiques of justice as fairness: the *ontological,* the *epistemological,* and the *political.* The ontological critique holds that the way Rawls conceives his creatures in the original position is not the way things are; that is, the Rawlsian model and being are not compatible. The epistemological critique asserts that the processes through which people acquire knowledge of their moral or cultural or ethnic identity and attachments as well as the way their conceptions of the good shape that identity and attachments are seriously hampered by the Rawlsian device of representation. The political critique argues that Rawls's account of politics is not faithful to the conflicting nature of modern societies and, furthermore, that he does not recognize the fluid and indeterminate character of the political realm.

Already in *Theory,* Rawls had good replies to the ontological and epistemological critiques, and his political version of justice has put to rest much of the force that was left in those critiques. Rawls is ready to admit that his creatures are representatives of democratic citizens and that citizens develop attachments to others which are important and possibly central to their identity at least in their private domain. Rawls further accepts, since *Theory,* that some political issues are indeterminate, although he now insists that at least the basic liberties are settled once and for all. (I address this last issue in my discussion of the political character of Rawlsianism in Chapter 6.)

There is still an ontological problem that Rawls has been unable to remove from his paradigm: he still thinks that justice is the central component of our moral identity. In his view, "full autonomy" is not possible without a Kantian allegiance to justice, which, as we will see, is a willingness to pay our taxes for their own sake.

I can summarize the remarks of the previous paragraph by saying that, of two possible approaches to assessing the Rawlsian paradigm, one has been, by far, the dominant one. One approach to the analysis of Rawlsian justice might work from the *outside* of justice as fairness by stipulating *another* way of conceiving the self or the good and then using it to evaluate Rawls's arguments. The three critiques mentioned above might be construed as part of the external approach. Another approach can work from the *inside* and proceed to examine whether Rawls's *own* assumptions are persuasive enough to warrant his belief that his system is the best option available for citizens bent on designing a well-ordered society conceived in perpetuity. The external approach has been the dominant one.

With few exceptions (H. L. A. Hart, Patrick Neal),[33] those who follow the second approach, that is, the internal one, are Rawlsian liberals or thinkers who are sympathetic with the Rawlsian project. They tend to look at Rawls's assumptions and to come back so convinced of their validity that they proceed to apply them to other realms of philosophical inquiry.

My book is indebted to important contributions of the external approach, but it develops along the principles suggested by the internal approach. I want to read Rawls's texts and to examine his assumptions in the light of his own expectations and arguments. And so, instead of asking whether his account of the self or his view of conceptions of the good is convincing in the light of a historically constituted vision of the self or visions of the good, the questions orienting my inquiry adopt a different form. For instance, what if Rawlsian justice is *not* a moral paradigm? What if the Rawlsian order is not exempt from utilitarian dangers? What if the principles of justice themselves are unable to command the universal support Rawls expects and counts on? What if, applying Rawls's own standards, justice as fairness turns out to be incoherent, and thus bidding farewell to Rawlsian justice is the best option for democratic citizens?

This book seeks to prove the thesis that Rawlsian justice requires not a sequence of amendments but a farewell that can be justified both theoretically and politically. Since this is rather a big proposition, which is compounded when we acknowledge the complexity of Rawls's arguments, I have divided the issues to be examined into several categories whose boundaries certainly overlap but can nevertheless be distinguished from one another: the founding (issues pertaining to the original position and the nature of the Rawlsian contract); the promises and their relation to public institutions; the morality of justice as fairness and its relation to utilitarian policies; the place of community; political liberalism; and stability and the question of coherence.

In Chapter 2 I articulate the Rawlsian project as expressed in different parts of *Theory*. Once this task is completed, I discuss the role nature plays in formulating the two principles of Rawlsian justice as well as the place of institutions within it.

In Chapter 3 the discussion turns to an evaluation of the Rawlsian promise to design a society for mutual advantages by assessing the status of well-being. Although Rawls's texts offer two different readings of this issue, the question of mutual advantages haunts the stability of the Rawlsian order. Rawlsian citizens, I submit, may not agree on a conception of justice which does not provide room for their own judgment on whether they are obtaining the mutual advantages promised in the original position. It turns out, however, that the public sphere is a network of administrative apparatus which determines whether society is delivering its promises, and, in the case of the most disadvantaged, whether they are receiving the greatest benefits stipulated by the difference principle.

This is Rawls's way of avoiding the political calculus he sees in the utilitarian argument. But the issue is far from settled. Rawls does say that the political process ought to decide whether the goals of the difference principle are accomplished. In this way, political calculus is part of the Rawlsian paradigm despite Rawls's explicit effort to exclude contingent elements from the design and operation of his two principles of justice. Chapter 3, then, examines a conflict between the formal and administrative character of justice as fairness, and the political process.

In Chapter 4 I explore a conflict that is potentially more ominous to the stability of a Rawlsian society: the conflict between the first and second principles of justice as fairness. My investigation seeks to show that the second principle, especially the difference principle, is the real foundation of the Rawlsian system, and yet it is not supported by moral reasons. The morality of Rawlsian justice is constituted by the reasonable, which is a set of conditions imposed from without.

In Chapters 2, 3, and 4 I discuss problems that are internal to the structure of Rawls's arguments. In Chapter 5 I explore Rawls's communitarianism and how his view of moral personality questions—or at least offers a far more complex view of—the alleged priority of the right over the good. Chapter 6 fleshes out the metamorphoses of Rawls's conception of justice as they appear in his political liberalism.

In Chapters 7 and 8 I present problems not covered in the previous chapters and recapitulate the major shortcomings of Rawlsianism. Although the reader may refer to these two chapters for the major conclusions of my investigation, my arguments are incomplete if they are separated from the issues analyzed in the other chapters.

2

Rawls's Project

Conceptions of justice must be justified by the conditions of
our life as we know it or not at all.

We want to define the original position so that we get the de-
sired solution.

— John Rawls, *A Theory of Justice*

The tortuous development of Rawlsian justice is the story of a metaphysical
doctrine that became political; of a comprehensive doctrine that remains comprehensive; of a prudential arrangement that somehow convinced itself of possessing moral credentials but is still prudential; and of a "primitive theory
[Rawls] sketched" (504)[1] which somehow managed to present its tenets as the
blueprint for a well-ordered society conceived in perpetuity. This book explores
these developments by addressing some problems suggested by *A Theory of Justice* and examining its proposed solutions. I begin by presenting Rawls's argument before specifying its contours.

The Argument

I.

    A. Moral persons have two higher-order interests in developing the two
       central moral powers defining their personality, which are a capacity for

a sense of justice and a capacity to develop, revise, and to pursue rationally a conception of the good.

B. To reach this goal, they need to create a society and agree on the regulating principles of its public structure.

C. This agreement needs to be the outcome of a fair procedure within fair conditions.

D.

1. Fairness is conceived as the knowledge of the two highest interests and as the exclusion of historical traits such as gender, social status, religious orientation, conceptions of the good, etc.

2. Fairness is understood as a pure procedure in opposition to a perfect procedure.

E.

1. The parties' deliberations are rational and reasonable. The *rational* refers to "each participant's rational advantage, what, as individuals, they are trying to advance." The *reasonable* refers to fair terms of cooperation which "articulate an idea of reciprocity and mutuality: all who cooperate must benefit, or share in common burdens, in some appropriate fashion as judged by a suitable benchmark of comparison."[2]

2. "In justice as fairness, the Reasonable frames the Rational and is derived from a conception of moral persons as free and equal."[3]

F. People agree on two principles of justice. The latest version of these principles reads as follows:

1. "Each person has an equal right to a fully adequate scheme of equal basic liberties which is compatible with a similar scheme of liberties for all."

2. "Social and economic inequalities are to satisfy two conditions. First, they must be attached to offices and positions open to all under conditions of fair equality of opportunity; and second, they must be to the greatest benefit of the least advantaged members of society."[4]

The first principle has priority over the second. Fair equality of opportunity has priority over the difference principle, which holds that social and economic inequalities are justified when they provide the greatest benefit to the most disadvantaged.

G. The lexical ordering of justice as fairness is possible only when material conditions allow it. The lexical ordering of the two principles can be altered depending on existing circumstances. This is the principle of maturity (152, 542, 543).

H. Justice as fairness seeks stability for society, cooperation among all members of society, and the greatest benefits for the most disadvantaged.

I. Since justice requires a distributive arrangement, it is necessary to define what gets distributed. Justice as fairness distributes primary goods.

J. Primary goods are understood as basic liberties, freedom of movement, and choice of occupation, "powers and prerogatives of offices and positions of responsibility"; income and wealth; and "the social bases of self-respect."[5] All citizens "have the same equal basic liberties and enjoy fair equality of opportunity." The "only permissible difference among citizens is their share of the primary goods" referring to powers and prerogatives, income and wealth, and the social bases of self-respect.[6]

K. Since the second part of the second principle of justice refers to the most disadvantaged members of society, it is necessary to define this group. The most disadvantaged "are defined as those who have the lowest index of primary goods, when their prospects are viewed over a complete life."[7]

L. The most disadvantaged will receive primary goods, and they are responsible for the administration of those resources.

II.

A. The principles of justice are part of a political project that seeks to create a well-ordered society within a context of plural and incommensurable conceptions of the good. This project displays a method of avoidance in which controversial philosophical issues as well as political conflicts that might impair the stability of the political order are avoided as far as possible.[8]

B. The political project proceeds by looking at the funds of beliefs found in the political culture of democratic societies and then articulating those beliefs in a coherent argument.[9]

C. The political culture of democracy provides two foundations for justice in the form of two intuitive ideas: 1) the idea of society as a fair system of cooperation; and 2) the idea of persons as free and equal.

D. These intuitive ideas are *political,* which means that they are independent of any comprehensive doctrine, either partially or totally comprehensive.[10]

E. Citizens ought to make a distinction between their public identity and their private identity. Their public identity is defined by the principles of justice; their private identity is defined by their conceptions of the good, which ought to be compatible with the principles of justice.

III.

A. Justice as fairness is sustained by an overlapping consensus between reasonable doctrines. The goal of this consensus is accommodation of a reasonable pluralism, not truth.

B. Justice as fairness is not a modus vivendi but a moral agreement.[11]

The Rawlsian Good Society

This theory of justice is silent about Rawls's view of the good society and the human good. Yet, it is disconcerting that his understanding of a good society has not attracted the attention usually accorded to other parts of his theory. The majority of commentators seem to accept the Rawlsian claim that a well-ordered society is one regulated by the two principles of justice without implying a broad conception of the human good. To be sure, the central cause of this neglect is Rawls himself, who is always at pains to present his system as a matter of fair procedures and principles without reference to a substantive vision of the human good. In his version of political liberalism, he is explicit and emphatic in his claim that conceptions of the human good should be excluded from public deliberations on justice.

Yet, Rawlsian justice stands for a rather broad understanding of the good polis which is thicker and certainly more robust than the minimalist vision of the good he acknowledges as underlying his philosophical enterprise. I think that his vision of the good society is intertwined with a vision of the human good, which is more than a devotion to principles of right. In *Theory,* one might find scattered shards of the Rawlsian good society which, when pieced together, offer a substantive idea of what Rawls has in mind when describing an ideal order. It is a disservice to Rawlsian justice to confine it to a system of procedures, but it is a self-inflicted wound given Rawls's own arguments.

When looking at the Rawlsian good society, one is struck by the remarkable faith Rawls places on the operation of his two principles. He believes they will create harmony and cooperation, will socialize citizens into a new culture of rights and self-esteem, and will abolish or control the possible inclinations human beings may have to do injustice (245). One is also struck by the large shadow of the Rawlsian state, by its pervasive presence in the distribution of the social product, and by the absence of actual persons. People show solidarity toward one another (the love of mankind) through the state; they show respect to their fellow citizens through administrative bodies. The lingering power of the state shows its scope in the economic sphere regulated by pure procedural justice.[12] "The allotment of the items produced takes place in accordance with the public system of rules, and *this system determines what is produced, how much is produced, and by what means*" (88, emphasis added). How this encompassing Rawlsian state is compatible with the avowed goal of autonomy, which he stipulated in *Theory* and later abandoned, is hard to fathom, particularly in the economic realm.

What is the Rawlsian good society? It is an order of harmony and cooperation which is expressed through both institutions and personal relations among citizens sharing a commitment for justice. It is a space where people express their individuality through meaningful labor, and, more importantly, it is a society where disparities in the distribution of wealth are always seen with suspicion and leveled through state policies. Rawls stands for "a democratic regime in which land and capital are widely though not presumably equally held. Society is not so divided that one fairly small sector controls the preponderance of productive resources" (280).

Throughout *Theory*, the Kantian strategy of reforms pervades justice as fairness, and Rawls insists that the distribution of wealth must be corrected "gradually and continually . . . to prevent concentrations of power detrimental to the fair value of political liberty and fair equality of opportunity" (277).[13] Property and wealth should be "widely distributed by the appropriate forms of taxation, or whatever" (87; see also 225). Although inequalities remain, they are arranged in a way that contributes to the public good. "The function of unequal distributive shares is to cover the costs of training and education, to attract individuals to places and associations *where they are most needed from a social point of view*, and so on" (315, emphasis added). Rawls stands for the "principle of free association and individual choice of occupation" (310), but this choice is socially constituted; that is, each person is expected "to do those things that best accord with his aims" (315), but this decision takes place within a system that offers certain premiums to some activities in the search for the common good.

The Rawlsian order sees contingency not only as a threat, but also, when properly regulated, as a potential ally in the service of cooperation. This helps us understand why significant inequalities in the life prospects of citizens are, in Rawlsian justice, inevitable "or else necessary or highly advantageous in maintaining effective social cooperation. Presumably there are various reasons for this, among which the need for incentives is but one."[14] Since incentives can use inequalities for "effective social cooperation," Rawls's theory attempts to regulate inequalities that arise, in his view, from three sources: social starting points, natural advantages, and historical contingencies.[15]

The Rawlsian state is the watchdog of contingency. It does not seek to abolish inequalities, but to regulate them through a balancing act in which all parties ought to have "fair bargaining power." "Excess market power," he writes, "must be prevented and fair bargaining power should obtain between employers and employees."[16] This principle of fair bargaining power applies to citizens under a different form: they ought to have a "fair degree of influence" in the elaboration of public policy.

The reader should note that Rawls's idea of legitimate inequalities turns on his view of fairness, but it is not clear what he means by *fair bargaining power* or *fair degree of influence.* It is evident, however, that a fair bargaining power does not mean that your position as a worker will carry the day. Your employer may still be able to impose a salary cap, for example. But Rawlsian fairness entails the opportunity to present your case, to challenge your employer in court, to call your legislator, namely, to use public institutions that will restrain the employer's power. Your employer might still be able to impose his position but not to the same degree that he wanted. Rawlsian fairness is constrained power,[17] which is an idea of a Federalist provenance.

Power, as Madison argues in Federalist no. 10, has an encroaching and overreaching nature; it always seeks to overstep its boundaries, hence the need of counterpowers to balance the inherent instability of power whose roots are the passions ruling the human heart. Similarly, in Rawlsian justice, power, particularly the one stemming from private wealth, is a danger to just arrangements and to the stability of a well-ordered society. It is for this reason that it must be regulated, not through individuals who are themselves creatures of contingency, but through legal institutions that are anchors of regularity and stability in the midst of the uncertainties afflicting the human condition and its environment.

The power of employers is counterbalanced by the fair bargaining power of workers; the power of private wealth is constrained by the fair degree of influence of citizens; the power of natural advantages and historical contingencies is bridled by background justice and fair equality of opportunity for all members of society. In "Justice as Fairness," Rawls writes, "men agree to share one another's fate. In designing institutions they undertake to avail themselves of the accidents of nature and social circumstance only when doing so is for the common benefit" (102).

The state is the watchdog of contingency. It is there in permanent vigilance against the erosion of background justice, something that may come about even when individuals act fairly:

> the tendency is rather for background justice to be eroded even when individuals act fairly: the overall result of separate and independent transactions is away from and not towards background justice. . . . Therefore, we require special institutions to preserve background justice, and a special conception of justice to define how these institutions are to be set up.[18]

The key aspects of a Rawlsian good society thus appear as the intersection of social goals and a vision of the human good expressed in cooperation through just institutions; an ordering of inequalities aimed at promoting the public good; an environment that provides people with opportunities to engage in meaningful work; and distributive policies aimed at controlling the dangerous power of wealth. Rawls's distrust of wealth and private interests is hardly a secret; both are seen as corrupting forces. Actually, wealth is conceived as a suspicious practice, a "meaningless distraction" threatening to attract individuals toward emptiness and to lead institutions into corruption:

> What men want is meaningful work in free association with others, these associations regulating their relations to one another within a framework of just basic institutions. To achieve this state of things great wealth is not necessary. In fact, beyond some point it is more likely to be a positive hindrance, a meaningless distraction at best if not a temptation to indulgence and emptiness. (290)

There seems to be a tinge of Machiavelli's republicanism in Rawls's view of wealth. For his uneasiness about wealth refers to *private* wealth, which reminds us of Machiavelli's argument that in an ideal republic the state is rich, but its citizens are not. For Machiavelli, wealth is also a threat to the stability of society and the civic virtues of republican citizens.

It is worth noticing that Rawls's suspicion of private wealth goes together with his defense of meaningful work, an issue he takes up again in his discussion of social union, offering a vision that is similar to Marx's argument in the introduction to *The German Ideology*.[19] "To be sure," Rawls writes, "the worst aspects of [the division of labor] can be surmounted: no one need be servilely dependent on others and made to choose between monotonous and routine occupations which are deadening to human thought and sensibility. Each can be offered a variety of tasks so that the different elements of his nature find a suitable expression" (529).

Rawls's idea of a good society ought to be seen as an order where a "reasonable social minimum" is guaranteed to its most disadvantaged members (87); individuals realize themselves through others (525, 526) and engage in "willing and meaningful work within a just social union of social unions in which all can freely participate as they so incline" (529). It is also an attempt to preserve the gains of past generations in the struggle for a culture of rights and a more egalitarian democratic society. He says explicitly that we ought to preserve "the gains of culture and civilization" (285).

Crucially important, though neglected, the Rawlsian well-ordered society gives its members the *opportunity* to take an active part in public deliberations: "the constitution must take steps to enhance the value of the equal rights of participation for all members of society" (224). All citizens should be able to participate in the public realm; "they should have a fair chance to add alternative proposals to the agenda for political discussion" (225). To be sure, Rawls is not advocating a community in which all citizens ought to engage in active participation in the quest for the public good. His society hints at some Rousseauian traces, but Rawls is not a republican thinker. He is closer to the Federalist view of politics, not the anti-Federalist ideal of participatory communities pursuing and displaying civic virtue. Participation is an individual option, not a communal ideal.

Yet, at one point, at least, he links education and participation to self-esteem, which is the most important good in his society. Education, he claims, enables "a person to enjoy the culture of his society and to take part in its affairs, and in this way to provide for each individual a secure sense of his own worth" (101). Along similar lines, he emphasizes that public institutions ought to protect the fair value of the equal political liberties (225) and that the public good is the standard to measure public policies. Although he does not define what he means by *fair value*, he argues that the control of public discussion by those who possess greater private means undermines the liberties protecting the principle of participation (225). This explains his contention that political parties ought to be "autonomous with respect to private demands," and those demands are understood as "demands not expressed in the public forum and argued for openly *by reference to a conception of the public good*" (226, emphasis added; see also 222).

In other words, political parties are not supposed to represent a corporate or factional interest. As in Rousseau's community where the general will reigns supreme, a private interest must be measured by the standard of the public good. This suggests a sharp dichotomy between the political domain and the Rawlsian civil society. Private or public associations are communities of shared interests, and persons' latent powers come to fruition through and in them, but those associations are not meant to express separate interests in the political realm. If they join together to form a political party, or if they go to the political sphere as private associations, they have to redefine or abandon the private interests they might represent. The political realm is for the articulation of the public good regulated by a public conception of justice. It is not a realm for corporate or private agendas.

It might be possible to argue that this view entails the depoliticization of civil society; namely, that civil associations are apolitical in the sense that their interests are not necessarily defined with the public good in mind, and therefore they fall outside the scope of the state. This view, I think, is misguided. It assumes a statist vision of politics which denies the political character of any activity beyond the reach of governmental bodies. A private corporation organizing the private and public spaces where people live is not necessarily part of a state program but is a political body. A private school making decisions about what to teach and how to teach it engages in political decisions. Rawls's politics of the public good does not entail the depoliticization of civil society; what it implies is a politics without the state at the level of associations, and a state without the conflictual character of democratic politics, particularly in the area of public justice.[20]

To sum up: Rawls wants a society where wealth is distributed widely, people engage in meaningful work, citizens have the opportunity to participate in the political process, and political parties advance a vision of the public good (222, 226). He wants a society where inequalities are not explained away as natural but are justified to the least-favored members. "An inequality in the basic structure must always be justified to those in the disadvantaged position" (231). This justification is not primarily an argumentative justification; it requires liberties and material means that ought to maximize the long-term expectations of the disadvantaged.

This view of a good society is anchored in a philosophical and political project whose major contours were defended in *Theory* and redefined in his subsequent works. Let us turn to Rawls's initial project before examining its redefinitions.

The Rawlsian Project

As expressed in *Theory,* the Rawlsian project was metaphysical in its characterization of justice and the self, conservative in its idea of visions of the human good, and political in its understanding of theorizing.

The metaphysical character was so obvious that Rawls's turnaround in his essay "Justice as Fairness: Political Not Metaphysical" came as a striking effort to deny his own views. In *Theory,* justice was the central and most important virtue in the constitution of a person's character; it was presented as regulative of all other aims (574). The sense of justice, Rawls claimed, was not to be understood "as but one desire to be weighed against others. For this sentiment reveals *what a person is,* and to compromise it is not to achieve for the self free reign but to give way to the contingencies and accidents of the world" (575, emphasis added). Our nature as free and equal rational beings was fulfilled *only* by accepting the principles of justice (574; see also 255, 256, 528). In a well-ordered society, Rawls argued, individuals want to act justly "more than anything" (569).

The principles of justice, furthermore, led to the centrality of autonomy, a view he has since abandoned. "Following the Kantian interpretation of justice as fairness," he wrote, "we can say that by acting from these principles persons are acting autonomously: they are acting from principles that they would acknowledge under conditions that best express their nature as free and equal rational beings" (515). Autonomy was seen as "fitting for human beings; the notion suited to superior or inferior natures is most likely different." Therefore, "moral education is education for autonomy" (516).

Although autonomy was fitting for human beings—Rawls's version of Kantian justice was the defining trait of our nature, and he insisted on presenting it as embodying freedom from accidents—visions of the good underpinning his *actual* society were predicated upon a conservative view of harmony. In *Theory,* conceptions of the good are not expected to be far off from existing views and values. Quite the contrary, those conceptions are chosen from an existing array of possibilities handed down and simplified by past generations. "The many associations of varying sizes and aims, being adjusted to one another by the public conception of justice, simplify decision by offering definite ideals and forms of life that have been developed and tested by innumerable individuals, sometimes for generations" (563).

A person's autonomy, then, takes place within the parameters of existing ideals. Visions of the human good (i.e., "ideals and forms of life") are not chosen or constructed by isolated agents; those visions are offered by associations.[21] A well-ordered society makes sure that visions of the good are not going to be disruptive of the existing order. Those visions have been "tested" by "innumerable individuals," thus assuring their fitness for serving as appendixes to the essential core of choice, which defines his creatures.

The metaphysical character of justice and the conservative view of visions of the good form the background for Rawls's central philosophical and political project that was, and still is, to legitimize inequalities by using state policies to reform present practices. Here is his own description:

> In this complex of institutions, which we think of as establishing social justice in the modern state, the advantages of the better situated improve the condition of the least favored. Or when they do not, they can be adjusted to do so, for example, by setting the social minimum at the appropriate level. As these institutions presently exist they are riddled with grave injustices. But there presumably are ways of running them compatible with their basic design and intention so that the difference principle is satisfied consistent with the demands of liberty and fair equality of opportunity. It is this fact which underlies our assurance that these arrangements can be made just. (87)

The reader may note that this statement along with others of a similar persuasion in *Theory* buttress Rawls's claim that his notion of justice was rooted in the political culture of the modern state. In addition, Rawls's assumption is not only that the design and intention of present-state institutions are compatible with his version of justice, but also, and more importantly, that the basic intention of the modern state was to create a more egalitarian society. In this sense his is a Lincolnian reading of the American state and its founding traditions. He sees in the traditions and institutions of the American democracy the ideals of justice he puts forward just as Lincoln saw in the Declaration of Independence and the Constitution the promise of political equality for all human beings. This political character was already present in *Theory*.

It is worth noticing, then, that although the elaboration of the principles of justice takes place in a situation that is free of social accident and contingencies, the underlying assumption of his project is fully embedded in the historicity of the social world. The parties are not going to found a new society; they are going to reform an existing one. The leading premise, one that reflects the social accidents of the American society, is that the design and intention of the American constitutional democracy can be made compatible with the Rawlsian view of distributive justice. This is not presented as an opinion, but as a "fact" that underlies Rawls's "assurance that these arrangements can be made just."[22] This is his project.

If there is an area of justice as fairness which shows the Rawlsian project it is Rawls's discussion of social union in Section 79 of *Theory*. This section is crucial not only in portraying the Rawlsian project in all of its metaphysical ramifications, but also in defining its political character as Rawls has come to define it. The idea of social union brings to the fore what seems to be the central goal of justice as fairness: the flourishing of human personality through the collective activities of individuals who are regulated by a public conception of justice. For Rawls, justice is not only a natural trait of the human species in its struggle to survive (503). More importantly, it is a virtue that helps to realize the development of a person's excellence within a social context of mutual enjoyment and self-esteem.

"We need one another," he wrote, "as partners in ways of life that are engaged in for their own sake, and the successes and enjoyments of others are necessary for and complimentary [*sic*] to our own good" (523; see also 565, 571). So a well-ordered society is one where individuals pursue harmonious ends and engage in activities that complement one another's nature. The incommensurability of private endeavors and visions of the human good which is now the trademark of political liberalism was not present in *Theory*. There, the emphasis was on a strong community that, suddenly and without notice, parachuted into the Rawlsian arguments of reciprocity, costs, and interests.

After five hundred pages of disinterested parties striving for the best calculation and pitched, with annoying frequency, against their utilitarian counterparts to confirm what they, given Rawls's assumptions, already knew—that utilitarian sympathy did not work and that they were better off under justice as fairness—we are informed that a Rawlsian society is one of strong bonds of solidarity among its members. "So the members of a well-ordered society have the common aim of cooperating together to realize their own and another's nature in ways allowed by the principles of justice" (527). This common aim of realizing their own and another's nature presupposes a harmony among all members which not even the most passionate ruminations of communitarians have ever proposed. Neither Michael Walzer nor Alasdair MacIntyre nor Michael Sandel has ever proposed something approaching the Rawlsian utopia of cozy harmony. "There must be an agreed scheme of conduct in which the excellences and enjoyments of each are complementary to the good of all. Each can then take pleasure in the actions of the others as they jointly execute a plan acceptable to everyone" (526). I offer a detailed discussion of Rawls's communitarianism in Chapter 5.

In other words: the first version of Rawlsian justice relied on a metaphysical vision of human personality based on Kantian principles and the claim that justice represented our essential nature. For this reason, the Rawlsian language in *Theory* was prone to display universalistic overtones, the same ones Rawls has been avoiding ever since. He claimed, for instance, that "human beings [a universal category] have a desire to express their nature as free and equal moral persons, and this they do most adequately by acting from the principles that they would acknowledge in the original position." When they succeed in complying with Rawlsian justice, "their nature as moral persons is most fully realized, and with it their individual and collective good" (528). Hence his conclusion: "It follows that the collective activity of justice is the preeminent form of human flourishing" (529). He went so far as to claim that "everyone's more private life is so to speak a plan within a plan, this superordinate plan being realized in the public institutions of society" (528; see also 575).[23]

Now, Rawls has abandoned these views. He no longer talks about human beings but about democratic citizens, and his emphasis on incommensurable visions of the human good suggests that many people will not accept the claim that their nature is enriched by the activities of other people just because those other citizens happen to comply with Rawlsian justice. The latter may also engage in practices that the former consider repugnant and a threat to their own nature (see Chapter 6). In the latest version, private plans inhabit a separate sphere: they still must comply with Rawlsian justice, but they are no longer part of a harmonious larger whole. Private plans might express the inclinations of their bearers without thereby implying that their private actions are realizing other people's nature.[24]

I mention these features of Rawlsian justice to show the metaphysical character of justice as fairness and the lengths to which Rawls went to defend his version of Kantian personality.[25] It is thus disconcerting that a thinker who insisted again and again on the metaphysical centrality of justice in the constitution of moral selfhood brushed aside that centrality and claimed that any metaphysical trapping was an illusion read into justice as fairness by his critics.[26] Rawls is right in asserting that the metaphysical grounds of *Theory* are an illusion—though not invented by his critics but instead articulated by his own Kantian fervor.

When one looks at the Kantian confidence of *Theory*, one is in a better position to see the political rearticulation of justice as fairness as a bombshell thrown in the middle of a Kantian meeting (see Chapter 6), and one can empathize with the shock that Kantians might have felt when Rawls redefined his project. Just when the parties were ready to start their deliberations as Kantian ghosts deprived of contingent attributes, they were informed that they were representatives of democratic citizens. They had barely recovered from the intrusion of that contingent trait when they were summoned again and told that in their deliberations they would use the "intuitive ideas" that were part of a fund of shared agreements in the political culture of a democratic society. Their Kantian contours thus received a dose of historical (i.e., *American*) flesh. And when they—still crestfallen by the invasion of those contingent circumstances that put to rest their praised independence—prepared to resume their discussion, they received the fatal blow. The psychological "laws" underlying the moral development of Rawlsian creatures were no longer "true," but political, and the original position did not presuppose any long-lasting allegiance to Kantianism. Rather, the Kantian garb was much like the roles people adopt in a game like Monopoly.[27] They do not carry any weight outside their setting just as Monopoly players return to their real nature as, say, unemployed paupers, even if during the game they amassed a colossal fortune.

Even if Rawls's discussion of the notion of social union brings to the surface his metaphysical view of justice, it is here that he comes closest to the political character his theory now has. In the political traces he offers in *Theory*, Rawls sees himself as a citizen whose choices have the weight of the past, a thinker who is carrying on a task started by his predecessors. "Our predecessors in achieving certain things leave it up to us to pursue them further; their accomplishments affect our choice of endeavors and define a wider background against which our aims can be understood" (524–25). Rawls is not here the noumenal self of the Kantian argument; rather, he is enmeshed in the accidents and contingencies of the world, which "affect our choice of endeavors and define a wider background against which our aims can be understood." His project, accordingly, rests upon the cooperation of other generations and societies, and such "cooperation is guided at any moment by an understanding of what has been done in the past as it is interpreted by social tradition" (525). In *Theory*, he even argued that the principles of justice do not require theological or metaphysical doctrines to support them (454).[28]

I think these are the ideas Rawls has in mind when he suggests that the political character of his project was embryonic but not developed in *Theory*.[29] He is right. Still, this political character must be seen against the background of the evident metaphysical representation of justice. It is thus unfortunate that Michael Sandel's critique completely passes over these aspects of Rawls's paradigm and insists on an unencumbered self even in areas (like the Rawlsian version of community) in which Rawls explicitly denies it. In this regard, Sandel's critique, despite all its brilliance, partakes of an inflexible character that he applies to all areas of Rawlsian justice. Sandel seems to have found rather quickly the unencumbered self and proceeded to use it as the fulcrum to assess Rawlsian justice without allowing any place for alternative readings suggested by Rawls's text. Hence emerges the one-sided character of his arguments; from beginning to end he hammers at the idea that the Rawlsian project is an onto-logical impossibility, a convincing case that Rawls has circumvented in impor-tant ways by redefining his paradigm and placing it within the political culture of democratic societies. But even in *Theory,* I contend, there was a good dose of history, social tradition, predecessors, and associates to at least raise a flag against Sandel's reading.

The tack I follow here is different. Although I am aware of the important contribution of the Sandelian critique, my purpose is not to challenge the ontological character of Rawlsian justice, but to question its internal coher-ence and its political relevance in the light of its own premises, particularly its claim that it is the blueprint for a well-ordered society. My goal is not to see the limits of justice, but to bid farewell to *both* versions of the Rawlsian para-digm: the Kantian version of *Theory* and the political one of his subsequent works. If my arguments are correct they may spur a new way of thinking and approaching the idea of justice beyond the stalemate of liberal and communi-tarian arguments in the context of welfarist societies.

The Founding and the Monopoly of Justice

The Rawlsian project is not only an agreement on a social contract. Although inexplicably neglected, it is also a founding of human nature. It is thus an important departure from the classical versions of the social contract (Hobbes, Locke, Rousseau, and Kant). In Locke, Rousseau, and Kant, the contracting parties already possess a moral sense and a particular human nature.[30] They exercise their moral sense (Kant, Rousseau) and transform their nature (Rous-seau), or they construct a hospitable space for its unfolding (Hobbes) or real-ize it (Kant). In Rawls, by contrast, the parties possess neither a moral sense nor a particular nature. They are two abstract capacities (three, if we include the centrality Rawls ascribes to the alleged Kantian capacity to make choices) (255, 256). The original position is thus not merely a device to arrive at a con-tract on justice. It is a creation of morality and human nature, the counterpart of Eden, and Rawls presents himself as the creator of our moral character and nature.

To understand this argument we need to examine Rawls's understanding of the nature of the parties, his idea of natural duties, the monopoly justice exercises over its litigants, and his view of institutions. Let me address these issues in turn.

What is the nature of the Rawlsian parties? In *Theory,* they are presented as noumenal selves, that is, totally independent from contingent circumstances.

> My suggestion is that we think of the original position as the point of view from which noumenal selves see the world. The parties qua noumenal selves have complete freedom to choose whatever principles they wish. . . . They must decide, then, which principles . . . most fully reveal their independence from natural contingencies and social accident. (255; see also 256)

In an important sense, Rawls's paradigm thus represents a genuine creation *ex nihilo*. When the parties enter the original position they do not possess natural rights, nor do they possess a sense of morality; the only attributes they have are the two abstract capacities and, as we will see, a natural duty of justice. This is why the morality of Rawlsian selves comes from what Rawls calls a "potentiality," which seems to be a departure from the Kantian argument. For Kant, individuals have the capacity to discern and follow the moral law as social and situated creatures. The moral law is within them, which means that they are fully constituted moral agents. He recognizes that they are subject to temptations and that experience may lead them away from reason, but still they know that they ought to follow the commands of duty. Kant places the moral law in society and is willing to take the risks that social habits and entrenched practices may pose to reason.

Rawls, however, seeks to overcome contingency in a way that endangers the coherence of his project and cuts off the umbilical cord tying it to its Kantian roots. Kantian noumenal selves, for instance, are *moral* agents, whereas Rawlsian parties are not. We must examine Rawls's argument when explaining to whom justice is owed to see why this is so. Justice is owed to "moral persons," who are "distinguished by two features." First, they have a capacity for a conception of their good which is expressed in a rational plan of life. Second, they have a capacity for a sense of justice, which is defined as "a normally effective desire to apply and to act upon the principles of justice, at least to a certain minimum degree" (505). On closer examination, though, these moral persons are not really moral; they embody a "potentiality," and the two capacities are considered the minimum for moral personality: "moral personality is here defined as a *potentiality* that is ordinarily realized in *due course*" (505, emphasis added). This potentiality—that is, capacity—is enough to receive equal justice: "the *capacity* for moral personality is a sufficient condition for being entitled to equal justice. Nothing beyond the essential minimum is required.

Whether moral personality is also a necessary condition I shall leave aside" (505–6, emphasis added).[31]

In other words, the parties to the original position embody the capacity for moral personality, a capacity that is realized through, and by, the principles of Rawlsian justice. Or, as Rawls, says, "the two powers of moral persons are represented in a purely formal way." Since the principles of Rawlsian justice "are not yet agreed to, the parties' sense of justice lacks content."[32] Before arriving at the two principles, then, the parties are not moral agents. They do not possess natural rights. Their inherent worth is "undefined" (586). They do not deserve anything since desert may depend on natural abilities that are morally arbitrary. They do not even have interests. Nor do they have character. In the original position, Rawls claims, "our interests and character are still to be formed."[33] They are two abstract capacities waiting for their realization under Rawls's watchful eye. It is in the original position where the parties give themselves their morality and even their human nature by choosing the two principles of justice.[34] This is what I call the monopoly Rawlsian justice exercises in the constitution of a person's moral character.

In the original position, a moral reason is defined by the principles of justice (348), which means that prior to the agreement on the principles of justice there are no moral reasons. The principles of right define the moral virtues (192), which means that prior to those principles, there are no moral virtues. Moral facts "are determined by the principles which would be chosen in the original position" (45), which means that in the absence of those principles there are no moral facts. Moral attitudes, which "are part of our humanity," "appeal to sound principles of right and justice [i.e., Rawlsian principles] in their explanation" (489–90), which means that moral attitudes are not possible without the principles of Rawlsian justice which are the standards to explain them.

The idea of moral goodness (404), the concept of moral worth (438), the good of the moral virtues (398), and the virtues of integrity (519–20) all depend on the principles of Rawlsian justice. The same principles determine autonomy and objectivity (516, 518). "Thus acting autonomously is acting from principles that we would consent to as free and equal rational beings, and that we are to understand in this way. Also, these principles are objective" (516; see also 518).

The principles of justice determine the appropriateness of our moral sentiments.[35] Our judgment about whether the just or the benevolent person is morally good requires the principles of right.[36] Civil disobedience "rests solely upon a conception of justice" (384). Even "natural duties and obligations arise only in virtue of ethical principles," namely, "those that would be chosen in the original position" (348). The monopoly of Rawlsian justice is so encompassing that not even the notion of human dignity or respect is independent of Rawlsian principles. These two ideas, Rawls claims, are "not a suitable basis for arriving at these principles" (586), which have to be in place before the idea of respect or the inherent worth of a human being can be deemed relevant. Rawlsian justice claims to provide "a more definite meaning" to both notions. Or to put it differently, we need the principles of Rawlsian justice to define respect and human dignity.

Rawlsian justice, in short, is the virtue that "best" expresses our nature (529).[37] It is also "the preeminent form of human flourishing" (529), whereby it follows that "the desire to express our nature as a free and equal rational being can be fulfilled only by acting on the principles of right and justice as having first priority" (574).[38]

This monopoly of justice makes it clear that there is no room for morality, and better still, there is no space for a moral deliberation before the two principles are agreed upon. The parties' self-creation is so encompassing that they even choose the psychological processes underlying the acquisition of their moral sense. The choice of one's own psychological processes is intriguing, but this is what Rawls's text depicts. Rawls concedes that "we sometimes doubt the soundness of our moral attitudes when we reflect on their psychological origins" (514). How could we respond to a person who may regard his sense of justice as a neurotic compulsion? We can say to him that "his moral education . . . has been regulated by the principles of right and justice to which he would consent in an initial situation" of fairness; that the moral conception adopted in that initial situation is independent of contingencies; "and therefore the psychological processes by which his moral sense has been acquired conform to principles that he himself would choose under conditions that he would concede are fair and undistorted by fortune and happenstance" (514–15). In other words, by choosing the principles of justice, a person is selecting the standards that are going to guide his moral education and to regulate the psychological processes underlying the development of the sense of justice.

Hence my hypothesis: the Rawlsian contract is predicated upon a twofold founding, a founding of a social contract and, more importantly, a founding of human nature. Justice and the very nature of Rawlsian individuals are artificial creations: they are the end result of an agreement.[39] There are some lingering problems, though. There is a sense of uneasiness in the original position arising from the reasonable suspicion that these nonmoral entities will probably fail in their attempt to agree on principles of justice. For example, how and why do nonmoral entities decide to give themselves moral agency and even their (presumably full-fledged) human nature? How could entities so conceived be able to arrive at principles of justice? The answer lies in nature. The natural sense of justice and the natural duty Rawls ascribes to his creatures come to the rescue of a project mired in a moral vacuum.

Rawls conceives of justice as a built-in mechanism in our nature,[40] a safety device to ensure the survival of the human race,[41] and the basis of equality in the original position is given by a natural capacity for justice (508).[42] Natural abilities, however, are "contingencies that are arbitrary from a moral point of view" (511), a claim that keeps the Rawlsian project aground and returns it to its beginning, namely, to its attempt to escape contingency. The reason for this stranding of the Rawlsian venture is evident: since natural attributes are arbitrary and morally irrelevant, the natural capacity for justice can be seen as a contingent attribute that is morally irrelevant too. And so it is. This natural capacity is the only contingency that is decisive in the original position: "The only contingency which is decisive is that of having or not having the capacity for a sense of justice. By giving justice to those who can give justice in return, the principle of reciprocity is fulfilled at the highest level" (511).

Since Rawlsian justice is an artificial attribute, and this artificiality is compounded by its dependence on a contingency that is decisive, the deliberations in the original position do not seem to be very auspicious. The uncertainty of this situation calls for a remedy, particularly from a philosopher who is not prone to take chances—hence the "natural duty" of justice. Before the calculative parties start their deliberations in the original position, Rawls reminds us that they possess some natural duties among which the duty of justice is preeminent. "This duty requires us to support and to comply with just institutions that exist and apply to us. It also constrains us to further just arrangements not yet established, at least when this can be done without too much cost to ourselves" (115).

The duty to support just institutions is "unconditional." It is valid regardless of whether a person has consented to it (115, 116). Natural duties "apply to us without regard to our voluntary acts." They "have no necessary connection with institutions or social practices" (114). They "hold between persons irrespective of their institutional relationships; they obtain between all as equal moral persons" (115). In a word, natural duties are *preinstitutional* characteristics that do not require consent and which are owed to all persons. Despite their preinstitutional character, Rawls makes it clear that natural duties are derived from the institution of the social contract: "though the principles of natural duty are derived from a contractarian point of view, they do not presuppose an act of consent, express or tacit, or indeed any voluntary act, in order to apply" (15).[43] How this derivation occurs is something I have not been able to decipher.

We may understand the central place natural duties have in justice as fairness when we recall that Rawlsian parties are not moral persons, but two abstract capacities. And since those capacities do not necessarily lead to justice, and creatures so understood are not necessarily committed to furthering that virtue, the whole philosophical project might unravel.

In showing *why* the parties must agree on justice, Rawls writes, "The thing to observe here is that there are several ways in which one may be bound to political institutions. For the most part the natural duty of justice is the *more fundamental*, since it binds citizens generally and requires no voluntary acts in order to apply" (116, emphasis added). In this way, Rawls secures what, in his own account, is a precarious foundation since a natural trait may be weakened by other traits of a person's character (e.g., vindictiveness). The duty to establish just institutions, accordingly, should not be subject to the uncertainties of voluntary consent. The individual's consent to support the natural duty of justice is too risky to meet Rawls's quest for a safe haven where his principles can be chosen. Rawls does not take chances.

> The bearing of these remarks [on the assurance problem] is that basing our political ties upon a principle of obligation would complicate the assurance problem. Citizens would not be bound to even a just constitution unless they have accepted and intend to continue to accept its benefits. Moreover this acceptance must be in some appropriate sense voluntary. But what is this sense? It is difficult to find a plausible account in the case of the political system into which we are born and begin our lives. And even if such an account could be given, citizens might still wonder about one another whether they were bound, or so regarded themselves. The public conviction that all are tied to just arrangements would be *less firm, and a greater reliance on the coercive powers of the sovereign might be necessary to achieve stability.* But there is no reason to run these risks. Therefore the parties in the original position do best when they acknowledge the natural duty of justice. . . . I assume, then, that the natural duty of justice would be agreed to rather than a principle of utility, and that from the standpoint of the theory of justice, it is the *fundamental requirement for individuals.*"[44] (337, emphasis added)

It is worth noting the two different formulations Rawls uses when describing the natural duty of justice. First, he says that natural duties are natural (114–17). Then he argues that the principles of natural duty and obligation "would be *chosen* in the original position" (333, emphasis added) or "agreed to" by the parties (337). The choice of something natural is intriguing, but it fits into Rawls's departure from the social contract tradition. As already indicated, the Rawlsian founding is one of society as well as a founding of moral personality and human nature. Political theorizing thus collapses into a metaphysical endeavor, which is why the Rawlsian retreat into politics and his constant insistence that his theory is devoid of metaphysical assumptions are more than justified.[45] The natural duty of justice is not only the foundation of Rawlsian justice. It is also the ground of our allegiance to the Constitution, an issue I will discuss in Chapter 7.

To sum up, individual rights are contingent and artificial creations that Rawls needs to secure by assuming the natural duty of justice and making the contract a perpetual one, a pact that settles questions of justice once and for all. This is why the natural duty of justice is placed beyond the sphere of deliberation, which is one of the trademarks of Rawls's philosophy. Whenever there is the prospect of uncertainty, Rawls proceeds to remove his principles and his creatures from any arena open to uncertain results and to place them beyond risks and chance.

This is why the agreement on justice arises, not from the parties' *willingness* to be just or to support just institutions, but from a natural duty that is assumed in advance. Although Rawls defends the centrality of choice in the constitution of a person's moral personality, the parties *do not choose* to be just; they are informed that they possess the natural duty of justice, a duty that does not depend on their consent or voluntary acts. Further, since the parties may forget their possession of this precious trait, they have the Rawlsian agreement as a constant reminder of their "nature."

The Priority of Institutions

How do the choice of Rawlsian principles and the founding of human nature occur? This question leads us to the place of *institutions* within justice as fairness. The Rawlsian founding of human nature takes place through institutions. Individual rights and moral character are given by public institutions. Institutions inform individuals as to what is right and provide them with the means of pursuing their individual life plans. Instead of being given a law directly, individuals create the institutional framework that will govern them in their public and private domains. This explains why the principles for the basic structure are argued first, followed by the principles for individuals (110).

That principles for institutions are chosen first show the social nature of the virtue of justice, its intimate connection with social practices so often noted by idealists. When Bradley says that the individual is a bare abstraction, he can be interpreted to say, without too much distortion, that a person's obligations and duties *presuppose* a moral conception of institutions and therefore that the content of just institutions must be defined *before* the requirements for individuals can be set out. And this is to say that, in most cases, the principles for obligations and duties should be settled upon after those for the basic structure. (110, emphasis added)

This is what I call the priority of institutions over individuals, the equivalent of the priority of the right over the good. Individuals are expected to do their part "as defined by the rules of an institution" (111). They are supposed to do their fair share, and the *fair share* is defined by the two principles of justice (112), which in turn are defined by public institutions. And "the content of obligation is always defined by an institution or practice the rules of which specify what it is that one is required to do" (113). Rawlsian parties, in short, are publicly institutionalized creatures, and justice as fairness appears as a statist theory.

This statism, where just institutions are defined first, and then principles for individuals are offered, suggests that institutions, *not* individuals, constitute the central concern of Rawlsian justice.[46] Thus the Rawlsian claim that the right has priority over the good is understandable if we understand institutions as embodiments of the right, and individuals as expressions of visions of the good. In effect, in the Rawlsian paradigm institutions embody, *primarily* rights, which they *grant* to individuals; and individuals embody, primarily, contingent attributes, which are present in their conceptions of the good. This is why the task of constructing or arriving at principles of justice is either an impossibility or an unsafe enterprise until individuals are stripped of anything resembling a contingent trait and reduced to the bare necessities of Rawlsian justice, namely, the two capacities.

Rawlsian institutions, I submit, have a moral priority over individuals, and the priority of the right over the good should be reformulated as the priority of institutions over persons.[47] Rawlsian justice refers, primarily, to institutions; the principle of participation refers to institutions (227); even saving seeks to sustain, primarily, just institutions.[48] Rawls sees institutions as firm anchors of morality guiding individuals in their relations with the state and one another and keeping at bay any threat arising from the contingent character of the human condition (102). The Kantian moral law, which is an expression of the individual's will, becomes, in Rawls's view, an institutionalized statute, which is certainly in line with the Kantian idea of public reason. This moral priority of institutions over individuals will be embodied in the public system of administration defining the Rawlsian order. An examination of the status of well-being within justice as fairness will show why.

3

Well-being and
Political Calculus

In justice as fairness there are no philosophical experts. Heaven
forbid!

   —John Rawls, "Reply to Habermas"

The problem of well-being represents a conflict that is at the root of the Rawlsian paradigm; namely, a conflict between the first and second principles of justice, the principle of morality and the principle of prudential calculations. The
first principle is universal and expresses a freedom from contingency; the second embodies a deep awareness of contingent factors that may place individuals in the ranks of the most disadvantaged. The first principle is unconcerned
with the actual achievement of well-being; the second *seems* to be concerned
with people's well-being to the extent that it advocates policies clearly aimed
at maximizing it.[1] The first principle is Kantian; the second is exposed to utilitarian dangers.

Justice and Well-being: Different Scenarios

It is odd that a theory that attacks inequalities so vehemently and defends the
freedom and moral equality of persons seems to be indifferent to the actual

well-being of individuals. It is as though all of the arguments about moral freedom and equality refer to two abstract capacities—a sense of justice and a conception of the good—without reference to bodily needs or psychological satisfactions. Yet, at first sight, this is what justice as fairness clearly suggests. Rawlsian justice seems to stand for bare individuals defined as these two abstract capacities and for a rather strong state defined by constitutional principles and welfarist policies aimed at improving the lot of the most disadvantaged. This characterization seems to validate the criticism that sees choice as the central value of the Rawlsian order.[2]

Is this really the case? Is it really true that the paramount value of Rawlsian justice is choice regardless of the content of those choices? I attempt to address these questions by exploring the following hypothesis: Rawlsian justice is deontology with a utilitarian bent which is present in the maximizing traits that—Rawls's claims to the contrary notwithstanding—are inherent in his paradigm of justice.

There are different and not necessarily compatible versions of the utilitarian goal of maximizing satisfaction. The utilitarian bent I see in justice as fairness refers to ends that may or may not be related to a conception of the good, that may or may not be construed as objective needs, but that are part of a person's rational plan and the satisfaction derived from it.[3] A violation of these ends is a violation of a person's integrity. Those ends, however, might be sacrificed under Rawlsian justice, a claim that Rawls does not necessarily deny if those ends happen to be incompatible with his version of justice. My hypothesis is that there are ends that are not supposed to be incompatible with Rawlsian justice and may nevertheless be sacrificed. The utilitarian bent weakens the avowed goals of legitimacy and stability which Rawlsianism purports to offer, a claim that Rawls disputes.

The deontological basis of justice as fairness is represented by a situation of fairness from which fair results ought to follow. This situation of fairness is supposed to respect the distinctiveness of persons even though that distinctiveness melts away in front of the theorist's reasoning; what was supposed to be a plural deliberation ends up as ventriloquism. The goal, still, is to represent a plurality of individuals and to take seriously their uniqueness. The utilitarian bent is evident in one of the main objectives that Rawlsian justice pursues: to maximize the well-being of all members of society.

This claim is certainly controversial given all the emphasis Rawls places on the differences between justice as fairness—a nonmaximizing theory, according to Rawls's views (509)—and utilitarianism—a maximizing theory. Since Rawls attempts to dissociate his system from the utilitarian molding, which seeks to maximize the well-being of the greatest number, it is incumbent upon me to present the evidence that substantiates my claim. I propose to examine the status of well-being in justice as fairness by looking at two different Rawlsian answers: first, that justice as fairness has nothing to do with well-being; and second, that the justification of justice hinges upon whether people choose conceptions of the good which are worthy of human endeavor.

According to the first answer, justice is interested not in the well-being of individuals, but in the well-being of society through well-ordered public institutions. As Rawls says when discussing the role of primary goods within justice as fairness, "Thus, the share of primary goods that citizens receive is not intended as a measure of their psychological well-being. In relying on primary goods, justice as fairness rejects the idea of comparing and maximizing satisfaction in questions of justice. Nor does it try to estimate the extent to which individuals succeed in advancing their ends, or to evaluate the merits of these ends (so long as they are compatible with the principles of justice)."[4] Individual well-being is thus a private and personal issue, not a public and social one.[5] And yet, it is odd to conceive of a well-ordered and just society composed of unhappy and disgruntled individuals whose ends in life have been truncated. Actually, the whole purpose of having a just society is to provide individuals with the spaces and opportunities to choose their ends in life; the working assumption is that by choosing those ends individuals are able to live a flourishing life, thereby obtaining well-being.

This is the working assumption, but it is not made explicit in *Theory*. In that book the core of the Rawlsian project seems to be the creation of just institutions aimed at allowing individuals to choose their rational plans in agreement with justice. But having liberties and means to choose a rational plan is not the same as actually choosing one. Similarly, having the liberties and means to lead a rewarding life is not the same as actually choosing and leading one. A Rawlsian society may create opportunities for well-being, but it does not force people to take advantage of those opportunities.

On this reading, then, Rawlsian justice should not be measured either by how many individuals are able to fulfill their goals or by their happiness or accomplishments: "The aim of justice is not to maximize the fulfillment of rational plans" (450–51). Logically, then, a Rawlsian society may well be one of disgruntled subjects whose aims in life are not achieved and who lead depressing and even diminished lives. As long as society offers them the resources to choose and lead a rewarding life, their failure to do so is a problem of personal judgment rather than public justice.

Yet, the fact that justice is not measured by personal well-being does not mean that justice is indifferent to it. The assumption is that a just society, not an unjust one (or more than an unjust society), allows individuals to choose and lead a rewarding life. Well-being is important for justice as fairness, but in contrast to utilitarianism, it is not willing to sacrifice the well-being of some individuals to maximize the well-being of the majority. Or so it claims.

The best test case to prove the assertion that Rawlsian justice is not indifferent to personal well-being might be represented by a society in which individuals lead rewarding lives but where the social product is distributed unjustly. A possible liberal argument is that if those rewarding lives are not chosen, but imposed by traditions, then those individuals are mistaken in their beliefs that their lives are rewarding.[6] But this reply begs the issue by introducing a sort of metaphysics of choice. This metaphysics presents choice as a universal value that all individuals ought to accept and as the central standard to define whether a life is rewarding or diminished. This metaphysics places choice beyond choice to the extent that it is not chosen, but given in advance by the theory.[7] Another possible argument is that a life that is not open to revision is not or cannot be rewarding. This is the metaphysics of revision. It, like choice, is given in advance and is posed beyond the individual judgment.

If, in our example, individuals living in an unjust society claim and prove that their lives have been chosen and are open to revision, I do not know what arguments are available to the liberal theorist to justify to those people the need for justice. The theorist may claim that justice is necessary for its own sake, but this argument goes nowhere. It is not even presented to liberal citizens. Or the theorist may claim that by having justice individuals will have more opportunities to exercise choice and revision, a strategy that would prove that choice and revision are both the antecedent grounds of justice and its central goals. In the Kantian tradition underlying Rawlsian justice, however, neither choice nor revision is a deontological value. They are not justified in themselves nor for their own sake. Actually, in Kant's view, deontology is incompatible with both of them, for the moral law is not chosen, but given by reason. And the moral law is not subject to any revision because it is neither empirical nor contingent.[8]

In Rawlsian justice, I preliminarily submit, choice and revision are important, not for their own sake, but for the opportunities they provide to individuals to construct and lead rewarding lives. So justice is not sought for its own sake, but for the goal it contributes to make possible rewarding lives based on choice and revision. A rewarding life is not necessarily the same as well-being, but is not incompatible with it either. To those people living in an unjust society and nevertheless leading a rewarding life that they are able to choose and revise, a Rawlsian theorist may still argue that justice represents a more stable foundation for a long-lasting cooperation. But if justice implies that those people's lives will no longer be rewarding even if justice opens or expands the possibility of choice and revision, I do not see a convincing Rawlsian argument free of metaphysical assumptions. In this example, these people are tied to a religious doctrine that glorifies an unjust distribution of the social product in the light of liberal values, but it is a distribution they accept on the basis of their religious beliefs and culture.

Rawlsian justice can argue, on the one hand, that those people are mistaken in their religious beliefs and that, even if they are right, those beliefs are contingent attributes they should eliminate for the sake of a genuine understanding of fairness and justice.[9] On the other hand, Rawlsian justice can apply the maturity principle, namely, that such a society is not yet ready for justice. What the Rawlsian paradigm cannot argue is that justice is valid regardless of whether the individual's life is rewarding or diminished. Nor can it claim that justice is uncompromising. If these are nevertheless the arguments a Rawlsian theorist invokes to defend justice, then it is clear that the Rawlsian paradigm relies on a metaphysical doctrine according to which deontological justice is the essential trait of our essential moral identity, and, consequently, it must be accepted for its own sake.

This argument, however, is not at the disposal of the Rawlsian system. For, despite any appearance to the contrary, Rawlsian justice is *not* uncompromising. Rawls, to be sure, holds that it is, but this claim appears at the very beginning of *Theory*, and the reader discovers rather quickly that the uncompromising character of justice as fairness is intriguing. Rawlsian justice is a matter of reciprocal advantages, and it is something that we ought to support when it does not represent a high cost to us (115, 334). In Rawls's arguments, then, justice is not a deontological value, which is justified in and by itself. Quite the contrary, justice as fairness pursues several external goals: mutual advantages, cooperation, and stability.

I suggest that Rawlsian justice seeks to create conditions in which individuals can enjoy well-being by leading rewarding lives. To clarify: well-being as a psychological state related or unrelated to the fulfillment of rational plans is distinct from well-being as the real possibility of pursuing a life plan on the basis of opportunities and material means. Rawls opposes the first while intimating support for the second.[10]

This distinction justifies the view that Rawlsian justice seeks to maximize the well-being of society by promoting stability and cooperation through justice and the well-being of its members by giving them liberties, opportunities, and all-purpose means to pursue their life plans. In other words, Rawls is not interested only in choice and revision or in a just society composed of depressed and unfulfilled individuals; rather, he wants to create a well-ordered society where people can realize their two moral powers by attaining the good of self-esteem through associations, developing their talents in and through the activity of many others, and expressing their nature through justice. If they so choose.

The assumption seemingly is that Rawlsian justice allows individuals to act and choose autonomously, and by so acting and choosing they can fulfill their ends in life. This view brings to the surface the minimalist conception of the human good underlying Rawlsian justice, which is to allow people to develop and exercise their two moral powers by designing a system of justice that recognizes and protects their freedom and allows them to design their rational plans.

Well-being and Rawlsian Trade-offs

In keeping with the second understanding of well-being (i.e., well-being as the real possibility of pursuing a life plan), it is possible to say that justice as fairness seeks to maximize the well-being of all members of society, not by satisfying their preferences and desires (as in utilitarianism), but by maximizing their share of primary goods that are considered central to the development and exercise of persons' two moral powers. To put it differently, Rawlsian justice does not seek to maximize internal satisfaction stemming from preferences, but rather external means that individuals are free to use as they see fit compatible with the Rawlsian system of public justice.

The two moral powers of Rawlsian personality are considered "the essential features of human beings,"[11] and, seemingly, the Rawlsian project is to actualize these moral powers. The capacity for a sense of justice is actualized through the process of choosing the principles of justice, and the capacity for a conception of the good is actualized through the pursuit of ways of life which ought to be "worthy of human endeavour."

I can now address the second answer Rawls's texts suggest when dealing with the question of well-being. According to this answer, justice is not justified in itself, and well-being must be part of the Rawlsian argument since justice depends on the conceptions of the good people pursue. In "Social Unity," Rawls writes, "On the other hand, just institutions would have no point unless citizens had conceptions of the good they strove to realise and these conceptions defined ways of life fully worthy of human endeavour."[12] However, this claim brings up three problems that challenge the internal coherence of Rawls's own system. First, the above citation questions the Rawlsian claim that the right (justice) is derived and justified independently of the good. Justice is not justified until people choose rightly; that is, until people choose conceptions of the good "fully worthy" of human endeavors. The implication is that worthy conceptions of the good are the final grounds determining whether justice is worthwhile; in which case, the original position is not enough to arrive at eternal principles of justice.

This leads to the second problem: the principles of justice should be assessed on the basis of the conceptions of the good which people's rational plans embody. Yet, in justice as fairness, there is no institutional mechanism to reexamine justice. The principles of justice are agreed upon in the original position, and they are meant to be perpetual.

The third problem is that Rawlsian justice is not concerned with the ends people choose as long as those ends are compatible with justice. But since justice as fairness is indifferent to people's ends, why does it claim that those ends should be "worthy of human endeavour?"

These problems may represent important paradoxes of the Rawlsian argument. But despite them, we can say, very cautiously, that by developing and exercising their "essential features," Rawlsian justice suggests that people are able to choose conceptions of the human good "fully worthy" of human endeavors which allow them to lead flourishing lives.[13] Now, by leading a flourishing life a person's well-being is achieved; and by maximizing their share of primary goods, which Rawls sees as necessary conditions of any conception of the good, the person's well-being is also maximized.

I am referring now to the determinate notion of well-being, as the satisfaction of bodily and psychological inclinations. By pursuing worthy conceptions of the good, people may lead rewarding lives, and by leading rewarding lives, they may enjoy psychological well-being. This view supports the second answer that can be found in Rawls's argument, namely, that justice as fairness is not indifferent to well-being understood as the satisfaction of bodily needs or psychological inclinations. The idea of primary goods seems to be concerned explicitly with those needs and inclinations.

If we take into account the understanding of well-being as the possibility of realizing the two moral powers, it is possible to claim that justice as fairness seeks to maximize the well-being of *all* members of society by maximizing the primary goods and stipulating that inequalities are justified when they accrue to the greatest benefit for the least advantaged members of society. "For when society follows these principles," Rawls argues, "*everyone's good* is included in a scheme of mutual benefit and this public affirmation in institutions of each man's endeavors supports men's self-esteem" (179, emphasis added).

In his discussion of primary goods, Rawls writes: "While an index of primary goods serves some of the purposes of a utility function, the basic idea is different: primary goods are social background conditions and all-purpose means generally necessary for forming and rationally pursuing a conception of the good. The principles of justice are to ensure *to all citizens* the equal protection of and access to these conditions, and to provide each with a fair share of the requisite all-purpose means."[14] One important difference is that utilitarianism seeks to maximize the preferences that people have or even a notion of well-being publicly stipulated,[15] whereas Rawlsian justice rejects any public definition of personal well-being[16] when well-being is understood as the satisfaction of bodily or psychological inclinations. However, the well-being of all members of society seems to be achieved through a system of taxation and social programs intending to provide primary goods to all members and to improve the lot of the worse-off.

The following reply deserves consideration: even though justice as fairness seeks to maximize the well-being of all members, it cannot maximize the well-being of the better-off. Actually, through the tax system, justice as fairness could sacrifice the interests of the better-off to provide the greatest benefits to the most disadvantaged. This argument is sound, but it needs to be seen against the background of the Rawlsian view of inequalities.

In Rawlsian justice, the better-off are what they are *only* because there are inequalities in the distribution of economic, social, and political power; those inequalities, from a Rawlsian standpoint, are illegitimate. The only way to make inequalities legitimate is by using them to benefit, to the greatest extent possible, the most disadvantaged. The better-off, then, have a choice: either to preserve their illegitimate inequalities and place themselves outside the legal framework and the bounds of cooperation or to pay a price for the inequalities they are enjoying. (See chapter 4.)

The second principle of justice as fairness is thus a kind of political bribe. The better-off ought to understand that inequalities should benefit the worse-off; and if this condition is not met, Rawlsian justice seems to demand a strong egalitarianism that, according to Rawls, is the main characteristic of justice as fairness. As he says when explaining the difference principle: "the difference principle is a strongly egalitarian conception in the sense that unless there is a distribution that makes both persons better off (limiting ourselves to the two-person case for simplicity), *an equal distribution is to be preferred*" (76, emphasis added).

We must recall here that the only standard to determine whether a person is better or worse off is his or her share of primary goods. In the context of actual liberal societies, however, it is not clear whether this Rawlsian egalitarianism is a moral goal or a prudential threat against the better-off. At first sight, it could be either. As a moral goal, Rawlsian justice may be claiming that a strict egalitarian society is the best order. As a prudential threat, Rawlsian justice seems to depend on something quite different. It seems to say to the better-off: "Look at what would happen if you are not willing to provide the greatest benefits to the most disadvantagd of society."

There are three possible arguments that incline us to see Rawls's egalitarianism either as not feasible in the light of his own assumptions or as prudential. First, Rawls's egalitarianism requires altruistic individuals, and Rawls says explicitly that justice as fairness does not depend upon altruism (188).

Second, seen against the background of the political culture of liberal societies, the goal of egalitarianism is on precarious footing. Recall here that in his work after *Theory*, Rawls has insisted that his principles are derived from the political culture of democratic societies. Consequently, it would be difficult to find intuitive ideas defending a strict egalitarianism and capable of commanding the type of universal consensus Rawlsian justice requires. From the intuitive ideas of society as a system of cooperation and the person as a moral agent, it is not evident that a strict egalitarianism follows.

Third, if egalitarianism is the main moral goal, it is not clear why society must compromise it by accepting the second principle of Rawlsian justice, which provides the condition required to justify inequalities: the greatest benefits to the worse-off. If egalitarianism is moral, we should not accept inequalities at all. Or at least the Kantian tradition would require us to reason in that way. These three arguments may suggest that Rawls's egalitarianism is less a moral goal than a prudential threat against the better-off to force them to comply with the second principle of justice, thereby justifying the inequalities they enjoy.

We need not go too far to find Rawls's own reexamination of the egalitarian tendencies of justice as fairness, a reexamination that was already present in his major work. In *Theory*, he argues that even though the parties start with an equal distribution of income and wealth,

> there is no reason why this acknowledgment should be final. If there are inequalities in the basic structure that work to make everyone better off in comparison with the benchmark of initial equality, why not permit them? The immediate gain which a greater equality[17] might allow can be regarded as intelligently invested in view of its future return. If, for example, these inequalities set up various incentives which succeed in eliciting more productive efforts, a

person in the original position may look upon them as necessary to cover the costs of training and to encourage effective performance. One might think that ideally individuals should want to serve one another. But since the parties are assumed not to take an interest in one another's interests, their acceptance of these inequalities is only the acceptance of the relations in which men stand in the circumstances of justice. (151)

Furthermore, in explaining his distinction between liberty and the worth of liberty, Rawls writes:

> Freedom as equal liberty is the same for all; the question of compensating for a lesser than equal liberty does not arise. But the worth of liberty is not the same for everyone. Some have greater authority and wealth, and therefore greater means to achieve their aims. The lesser worth of liberty is, however, compensated for, since the capacity of the less fortunate members of society to achieve their aims would be even less were they not to accept the existing inequalities whenever the difference principle is satisfied.[18] (204)

Here is the evolution of Rawls's egalitarianism. In *Theory* he presents two different, but compatible, versions of equality. The first one was presented above: an equal distribution is preferable in the absence of an unequal distribution that can make people better off (76).[19] The second version, however, partakes of a Hobbesian make-up. It holds that without the inequalities allowed by the second principle, people's capacity to achieve their ends would be even less. In "Social Unity," a strict equality is not considered rational. In *Political Liberalism*, Rawls stresses, once again, the Hobbesian view of the lesser evil already defended in *Theory*.

For Hobbes, an authoritarian sovereign may bring some "inconveniences," but its absence would bring about something worse—the calamities of the state of nature. As Hobbes writes: "And though of so unlimited a Power, men may fancy many evil consequences, yet the consequences of the want of it, which is perpetual war of every man against his neighbour, are much worse."[20] In a similar vein, for Rawls the large inequalities that may coexist with his well-ordered society might be considered as unacceptable, but those inequalities would be far larger in the absence of his two principles of justice. He writes: "the all-purpose means available to the least advantaged members of society to achieve their ends would be even less were social and economic inequalities, as measured by the index of primary goods, different from what they are. The basic structure of society is arranged so that it maximizes the primary goods available to the least advantaged to make use of the equal basic liberties enjoyed by everyone. This defines one of the central aims of political and social justice."[21]

The Rawlsian paradigm thus appears to be a dead-end situation. On the one hand, the parties would not agree to a more egalitarian distribution of primary goods because it would run counter to their rational interests. On the other hand, they would not oppose Rawlsian justice either because they would risk losing even the limited benefits they might obtain under justice as fairness. Rawlsian justice is a philosophy of the possible, and the possible depends on the dominant moral agreements of a constitutional democracy.

The second principle, then, represents a trade-off: inequalities are exchanged for the greatest benefits they will bring to the most disadvantaged. Since the inequalities the better-off enjoy are maintained, the well-being of the better-off is guaranteed, but the well-being of the worse-off is also taken into account. And the bases of social cooperation are guaranteed. As Rawls says: "we depend upon the cooperative endeavors of others not only for the means of well-being but to bring to fruition our latent powers" (571). The outcome is that, theoretically at least, the well-being of all members of society is maximized. The well-being of the better-off is assured by legitimizing their inequalities and by establishing the benefits of social cooperation.[22] Otherwise, their situation would resemble the rich of Rousseau's *Second Discourse* whose lives are in danger and whose property is uncertain. The well-being of the worse-off is assured because they will receive the greatest benefits.

As Rawls says:

> Consider any two representative men A and B, and let B be the one who is less favored. . . . Now B can accept A's [*sic*] being better off since A's advantages have been gained in ways that improve B's prospects. If A were not allowed his better position, B would be even worse off than he is. The difficulty is to show that A has no grounds for complaint. Perhaps he is required to have less than he might since his having more would result in some loss to B. Now what can be said to the more favored man? To begin with, *it is clear that the well-being of each depends on a scheme of social cooperation without which no one could have a satisfactory life.* Secondly, we can ask for the willing cooperation of everyone only if the terms of the scheme are reasonable. The difference principle, then, seems to be a fair basis on which those better endowed, or more fortunate in their social circumstances, could expect others to collaborate with them when some workable arrangement is a necessary condition of the good of all." (103, emphasis added)

So far, then, my initial hypothesis seems to be valid: justice as fairness is not indifferent to well-being but rather seeks to maximize the well-being of all members of society by making inequalities dependent on social cooperation "without which no one could have a satisfactory life." The difference principle is thus the foundation of cooperation—without which the well-being of each would not be possible—and a fair basis for a workable arrangement, which is a necessary condition of the good of all.

By demanding higher taxes from the better-off Rawlsian justice might seem to decrease their well-being, but the outcome is to benefit the worse-off, thereby strengthening the bonds of cooperation. The well-being of the better-off may be on a stronger footing (or they may feel that way) if they are left alone and not required to pay more taxes, but then they cannot expect any cooperation from the most disadvantaged.

The Difference Principle and the Priority of Administrative Procedures

Let us explore further the difference principle in the light of the notion of the greatest benefits for the most disadvantaged. Specifically, what constitutes the greatest benefits for the worse-off? And, more importantly, who or what determines them? The *greatest benefits* can be defined in several ways: 1) those that a society is *able* to provide; 2) those that the better-off are *willing* to give; 3) those that the better-off are *able* to offer; 4) those that public institutions determine; 5) those that the worse-off want as an expression of their preferences; or 6) those that the worse-off *need* as an expression of their objective interests. Rawls's texts do not reveal clear answers about the first three definitions, but, as we will see, they offer clear indications about definitions 4, 5, and 6.

Are the greatest benefits determined by society through its public institutions (definition 4)? Or are they determined by the worse-off (definition 5)? At first sight, utilitarianism appears to haunt the Rawlsian project. If, on the one hand, the greatest benefits are determined by public institutions, those institutions may use uniform criteria that may put at risk, if not altogether ignore, the distinctiveness of persons, in which case justice as fairness would not be substantially different from utilitarianism. Both would have an aggregative character, the same trait Rawls finds repugnant in utilitarianism. Some people may want sport facilities to strengthen their health and do sports; others may want decent housing. If the economic resources are scarce, a choice in either direction may have negative effects on those whose preferences are rejected. The difference between utilitarianism and Rawlsian justice is that utilitarianism would include in its aggregative calculus *all* members of society, whereas Rawlsian justice would include in its determination only the worse-off. This is a difference of degree rather than substance.

If, on the other hand, the greatest benefits are determined by the least advantaged members, the diversity of interests and preferences may be so incommensurable that a reasonable agreement on the distribution of resources may be out of reach. But the worse-off do not determine what amounts to their greatest benefit; the public structure does. This is, precisely, Rawls's contention: justice as fairness provides an index of primary goods which includes liberties, fair equality of opportunities, and all-purpose means in the form of income. This index of primary goods, coupled with the difference principle, constitutes the greatest benefits the most disadvantaged can hope for. Rawlsian justice presents itself as a combination of resources administered by the state (like education) and resources given to individuals (like income).

Of course, this view suggests, as William Connolly has rightfully argued, that society will always have enough resources to provide opportunities and financial assistance to its most disadvantaged members.[23] In a situation of scarce resources, Rawlsian justice might be inadequate, although it may redefine its understanding of the greatest benefits by lowering the amount of income the needy will receive.

The important issue here, however, is that in the public determination of the greatest benefits, justice as fairness is not exposed to any utilitarian danger since it treats persons as completely separated from their desires, inclinations, or life plans. In an argument that appears to be central to the design of the Rawlsian project, Rawls envisions individuals as agents whose essence ("what we are or can be") is defined exclusively by their liberty to choose rather than by the specific forms that essential trait may take (256). Those specific forms are seen as contingent attributes that add nothing to the core capacity for choice, a view that lends credence to the critique that sees justice as fairness as relying on choice as the central foundation of the human good while claiming to be neutral with respect to those values that define a person's idea of the good. Rawls himself provides grounds for that critique in his discussion of the Kantian interpretation of justice as fairness: "Properly understood, then," he points out, "the desire to act justly derives in part from the desire to express most fully *what we are or can be, namely, free and equal rational beings with a liberty to choose*" (256, emphasis added).

What justice as fairness does, then, is to abstract from persons' distinctive traits to arrive at a universal and essential feature: a capacity for choice which the public structure of a Rawlsian society is committed to maximizing. By abstracting from people's specific preferences and life plans, Rawlsian justice does not violate the distinctiveness of persons; it erases it.[24]

Martha Nussbaum has argued that, in some cases, more is not necessarily better.[25] The problem I want to pose now is similar though not identical to this view. Suppose that Rawlsian justice provides policies of fair equality of opportunity and income to the worse-off to enable them to pursue their life plans. But since the worse-off are responsible for the money they receive from the state, they may spend it on luxuries or gambling activities, leaving them in the same condition in which they found themselves before the redistribution of the social product according to the second principle. In other words, fair equality of opportunities (like education and health services) and welfare benefits (like unemployment benefits) do not necessarily lead to the greatest benefits.

This is not Rawls's view, though. The greatest benefits are predetermined by the public structure, and they are there regardless of how the most disadvantaged use or assess them. Rawlsian justice is concerned with an index of primary goods, which are the background conditions for the pursuit of any life plan. It is not concerned with outcomes or with how those primary goods are used by the most disadvantaged. The primary goods are not a public investment given to the most disadvantaged so that they are responsible for obtaining the greatest benefits according to their own judgment. Actually, the individual's judgment is irrelevant, a sign that bodes ill for the autonomy of Rawlsian citizens; for they—autonomous creatures living in a well-ordered society—are not allowed to decide whether the benefits they receive are, in fact, the greatest benefits. This is an administrative decision, not a personal or political one.

Hence the centrality of administrative procedures ties in with the priority of institutions over persons, as identified in Chapter 2. The Rawlsian state designs an administrative interpretation of the greatest benefits in the form of an index of primary goods and declares that if the worse-off are employed, educated, and safe, they will be getting the greatest benefits regardless of how they assess their own situation. This administrative conception of the greatest benefits suggests that while the first principle respects the distinctiveness of persons by protecting their capacity for choice, the second principle abolishes it. The first principle separates individuals as right bearers, and the second principle lumps the worse-off together as recipients of public benefits and determines what they need to obtain the greatest benefits that Rawlsian justice calls for.

Justice as fairness is, then, strictly formal. It provides resources to individuals. How people fare and whether they are able to fulfill their plans or to have the greatest benefits on the basis of their own assessment of that category or to enjoy well-being defined as a bodily or psychological state seems to be entirely beyond its scope.[26] My previous conclusion—that justice as fairness was not merely concerned with choice and revision—was short lived indeed.

Rawlsian justice stands for three abstract capacities[27] that Rawls mistakes for personhood. It stands for a strong welfarist state that he sees as an indispensable condition of a well-ordered society. Persons are central during the foundational moment of the social contract, and then they disappear once justice becomes an administrative apparatus that allocates resources. But Rawls has two possible replies.

First, following his arguments in *Theory,* Rawls might say that regardless of how people feel, if they comply with the principles of justice, they have reached the highest level of morality, and they are, accordingly, realizing their essential nature. He might add, following his arguments in the "Dewey Lectures," that their public identity as citizens ought to recognize and enjoy the benefits of living in a well-ordered society without regard for the inclinations of their private identities. Although neither happiness nor satisfaction is a concern of justice as fairness, Rawls might conclude by saying that people should be satisfied citizens even if they are unsatisfied private individuals.

Second, Rawls might claim that persons remain central, but their centrality is demonstrated when their choices are respected. They are, essentially, "rational beings with a liberty to choose" (256). This possible answer brings to the fore whether choice is, in fact, the underlying value of Rawlsian justice. On this view, all members of justice as fairness may fail in fulfilling their plans and in obtaining well-being, and their failure does not say anything about justice. They have, after all, the liberties and the means to make their own choices. On this reading, Rawlsian justice is firmly secured, and a contingent attribute (like well-being) should not be used to evaluate the fairness or the moral character of justice. The first principle of justice, the principle that protects choice, prevails.

The Difference Principle and the Political Realm

The principle that protects choice does not prevail for long. Although the formal character of justice as fairness seems to insulate it from the contingencies associated with people's ability to fulfill their plans and to obtain well-being, there is a contingent ground from which Rawlsian justice has no escape: the idea of mutual advantages. Rawlsian justice may claim that its purpose is not to maximize personal well-being, but it still must address this question: How could well-being be excluded from the assessment of Rawlsian justice when the goal of justice—a goal that antecedes the deliberation in the original position—is to form a society for mutual advantages, a society where they can advance their own interests and ends (19, 119). How could mutual advantages and the persons' interests be achieved without personal well-being?

If people do not accept the goal Rawls ascribes to them (they have, as rational persons, to maximize their ends) and if they do accept that they are not going to judge justice in the light of the well-being they achieve, at least they ought to assess justice in the light of the mutual advantages they are getting. Mutual advantages were given explicitly as one of the central goals of justice as fairness. If people—as they ought to on the basis of Rawlsian criteria—use mutual advantages to judge the performance of justice, then there is an overt contradiction between the formal character of justice (to provide and maximize the primary goods regardless of how people's lives fare and regardless of whether they fulfill their life plans) and the goal of mutual advantages which justice is meant to make possible. The formal character of Rawlsian justice requires it to be judged by its adherence to the rules and principles of justice independently of its outcomes, whereas the standard of mutual advantages requires justice to be evaluated by its outcomes, by how many mutual advantages people are receiving. And those advantages, reasonably, may include whether people's rational plans are fulfilled.

The conflict at the root of Rawlsian justice—namely, the conflict between the first and the second principles—returns, and this time, the second principle ought to prevail. People must examine the primary goods that the second principle offers and determine whether their society is, in fact, a venture for reciprocal advantages. It is thus clear that although justice as fairness is, directly, indifferent to well-being defined as a bodily or psychological state, it cannot be indifferent to the idea of mutual advantages which, in turn, might need the satisfaction of bodily and psychological needs.

There is another problem related to this issue of mutual advantages. Justice as fairness is a philosophy of the possible, and we can now add that "the possible" is measured by the resources society possesses and by people's understanding of mutual advantages in the light of settled convictions and an interpretive political culture. If this formulation is correct, it brings up another problem: people may agree on 1) the settled political convictions capable of bringing about an agreement on justice, and 2) the Rawlsian principles of justice which are based on those convictions. But they may not necessarily agree on 3) what constitutes a universally acceptable level of mutual advantages. The level of mutual advantages may have to be determined by the political process, something that denies the Rawlsian project and its effort to insulate justice from contingency. Using the political process to determine what is an acceptable level of mutual advantages and, for instance, whether society is just, would inject a controversial and highly uncertain feature into the whole paradigm. And the same contingent feature Rawls wishes to avoid—the will of the people—would exact its due. With revenge. The outcome would be that justice cannot be decided a priori in the original position but a posteriori in the actual political process of democratic societies. The political calculus that might underlie the question of mutual advantages thus threatens the stability of Rawlsian justice.

I do not see a way out of this problem without violating the avowed goal of fairness. Rawls might say that mutual advantages are determined not by the political process but by the index of primary goods which the public structure, presumably through its administrators, establishes. However, it is doubtful that the parties in the original position would agree on a system of justice in which the citizens they represent will not be allowed to pass judgment on the issue of mutual advantages, an issue that along with cooperation and stability, constitutes the main goal of Rawlsian justice.

Rawls might say that reciprocal advantages were already decided in the original position; namely, public administrators will implement the principles of justice, and *whatever* results from that implementation will constitute the acceptable level of mutual advantages. But what kind of autonomy is there in imposing a public definition of mutual advantages and excluding the people's judgment on that issue? How could justice as fairness treat persons as free and equal while denying them access to a political process to settle the issue of mutual advantages and the most important question of whether they are advancing their interests and ends? It is worth noticing that even though justice as fairness no longer promotes the ideal of autonomy as a philosophical project encompassing a person's life, autonomy is still presented as a political value that is one of the foundations of an agreement on justice. It seems, however, that persons are autonomous to agree on Rawls's principles, but their autonomy does not extend to an assessment of the consequences of those principles.

This is, exactly, the case. "Let us suppose," Rawls writes, "that the above account of the background institutions is sufficient for our purposes, and that the two principles of justice lead to a definite system of government activities and legal definitions of property together with a schedule of taxes. In this case the total of public expenditures and the necessary sources of revenue is well-defined, and the distribution of income and wealth that results is just *whatever it is*" (282, emphasis added). Better still, "the idea of justice as fairness is to use the notion of pure procedural justice to handle the contingencies of particular situations. The social system is to be designed so that *the resulting distribution is just however things turn out*" (275, emphasis added).

In other words, when public institutions follow the two principles of justice, the outcome will be just, whatever it is; and citizens, accordingly, have no ground to express, for example, their dissatisfaction with the advantages they are receiving. One begins to have a better understanding of why Rawls places such a great emphasis on the issue of commitment and on the avoidance of voluntary acts (335). In the original position "[a] person is choosing once and for all the standards which are to govern his life prospects. Moreover, when we enter an agreement we must be able to honor it *even should the worst possibilities prove to be the case.*[28] Otherwise we have not acted in good faith. Thus the parties must weigh with care whether they will be able to stick by their commitment in *all circumstances*" (176, emphasis added). Rawlsian citizens are expected to support Rawlsian justice in all circumstances and "even should the worst possibilities prove to be the case" because they may well discover that their mutual advantages are rather innocuous when they are already chained to a perpetual contract, and "there is no . . . second chance" (176).

Rawls might accept this conflict between the formal character of his idea of justice and the people's reasonable interest in judging whether justice is able to deliver its promise of mutual advantages as an unavoidable paradox of justice as fairness and ask us to live with it. But then the original method of *Theory* shows its marks: in *Theory* Rawls argues that it is necessary to work behind common-sense notions, whereas in *Political Liberalism* he seems to depend on those very notions. (For a discussion of this, see Chapter 6.) But if Rawls accepts my argument as an unavoidable paradox, it shows that he is still working behind people's view of common sense and that he is not deriving his understanding of justice from the political culture he identifies as his hermeneutic ground. A public definition of mutual advantages without the citizens' participation could certainly be justified on the basis of the political culture (a tradition of legal interpretation might serve as a ground), but that justification would not be based on a settled conviction. Democratic citizens may have a reasonable interest in determining whether the mutual advantages they are receiving are acceptable.

Rawls himself seems to support this view. In Section 36 of *Theory* he discusses a democratic regime and writes: "All citizens should have the means to be informed about political issues. They should be in a position to assess how proposals affect their well-being and which policies advance their conception of the public good" (225). Along similar lines, he also argues that the parties must evaluate the principles of justice in the light of their consequences (138) and examine the possible effects of justice (454).

If well-being is a reasonable ground when evaluating public policies, why should it be excluded from the assessment of justice? We need here to call attention to the fact that the parties have now been defined as representatives of democratic citizens. If citizens have a legitimate concern in assessing how public policies affect their well-being in the political realm, why should well-being be excluded from the evaluation of justice? If the effects brought about by justice are legitimate concerns in the original position, why are they excluded from an actual society?

We should recall that one of the guiding assumptions of justice as fairness is that the parties prefer a larger to a lesser share of primary goods (126), and accordingly they might be dissatisfied with the advantages as well as with their share of primary goods received from society. Rawls's argument is that well-being is a very elusive category that might require political calculus and jeopardize the priority of the principle of equal liberties. However, my investigation suggests an interesting shift in the Rawlsian argument. The liberties protected by the first principle of Rawlsian justice are not subject to political calculus as long as social circumstances allow the lexical order to obtain; but the difference principle,[29] by contrast, is exposed to the political process, a development that might support my claim that citizens could go to the political realm to settle their possible disagreements about the mutual advantages delivered by the Rawlsian order. Rawls states:

> Infractions of the difference principle are more difficult to ascertain. There is usually a wide range of conflicting yet rational opinion as to whether this principle is satisfied. The reason for this is that it applies primarily to economic and social institutions and policies. A choice among these depends upon theoretical and speculative beliefs as well as upon a wealth of statistical information, all of this seasoned with shrewd judgment and plain hunch. . . . The resolution of these issues *is best left to the political process* provided that the requisite equal liberties are secure. In this case a reasonable compromise can presumably be reached.[30] (371–73, emphasis added)

The liberties enshrined in the first principle are then removed from the political process and protected by their status as constitutional essentials that are settled once and for all.[31] The difference principle, by contrast, *seems* to inhabit the realm of contingency, and citizens can assess it armed with "theoretical and speculative beliefs," statistical information, "shrewd judgment and plain hunch." Does this mean, then, that citizens can challenge the greatest benefits and the definition of mutual advantages put forward by the public structure? Does this mean that Rawlsian justice is not, after all, a conception embodying pure procedures? Rawls's statements in the context of his discussion of civil disobedience suggest an affirmative answer, but his overall argument, particularly his insistence on pure procedures and his claim that justice is whatever it is, denies it.

Citizens, I propose, may have an interest in reexamining justice in the light of their well-being and in going to the political arena to see whether the mutual advantages and the greatest benefits are acceptable *unless* (and the following clause is becoming more and more ubiquitous in trying to come to terms with Rawlsian justice), they are so concerned with a stable public order that they are willing to surrender their judgment to the public structure and its servants, to the formulas they may use to define mutual advantages, and to the "shrewd judgment and plain hunch" they may employ to satisfy the difference principle. But if order is the ultimate ground of Rawlsian justice, then it may be necessary to reconsider its moral character. In the name of order, people may be willing to accept large inequalities and to acquiesce with a public definition of mutual advantages. It remains to be seen why order is so important that it demands acceptance of practices that run counter to our understanding of morality and common sense.[32]

In the Rawlsian paradigm, then, we may arrive at a situation in which regardless of the distribution of resources, as long as that distribution complies with the two principles of justice and achieves stability, there will be justice. People may get meager benefits. They may not be able to fulfill their rational plans. They may lead a depressing existence. But as long as the public structure adheres to the procedures of Rawlsian justice, society is well-ordered. Rawls's claim that in a democratic society "each citizen is responsible for his interpretation of the principles of justice and for his conduct in the light of them" (390) remains an unfulfilled promise.

The index of primary goods, the greatest benefits for the most disadvantaged, and even whether society is just are determined by the public system of rules. The citizen's interpretation of Rawlsian justice is irrelevant. Justice as fairness is concerned with the *possibility* of realizing the three abstract capacities defining Rawlsian personhood. People will get resources. And in addition to their civil rights, that will be enough to certify society as just and well-ordered. Whether people are fed, clothed, sheltered, and healthy is something quite different.[33] Rawlsian justice will not tamper with their liberty to make choices. The principle of liberty has priority over the principle of distribution.

Scarce Resources and Utilitarianism

Let us now imagine a situation in which Connolly's arguments become reality; instead of abundance, the public structure must cope with scarce resources. I propose the following hypothesis: In a situation of scarcity, Rawlsian justice becomes utilitarian.

Suppose a community of mainly retirees and senior citizens attracts an influx of uneducated and untrained newcomers. The newcomers are now the worse-off and present social and political pressures on the local government. Rawlsian justice requires that inequalities ought to accrue to the greatest benefits of the most disadvantaged. But if the state raises taxes to provide education and training programs, the retirees and senior citizens, most of whom depend on a fixed income always exposed to the ravages of inflation, will suffer. They, for example, may not be able to pay higher property taxes and may be forced to sell their houses and settle for a smaller place or a nursing home. If this is the outcome, it is clear that Rawlsian justice is sacrificing the liberties and life plans of some members of society to comply with the second principle, that is, to create conditions for the maximization of the well-being of some members of society (the most disadvantaged).[34]

This example also suggests a tension between the goal of stability and the goal of mutual advantages. In this community, senior citizens are having less of the primary goods (their income and their worth of liberty), but perhaps that is the price to pay for stability.[35]

In the light of my previous discussion, I am prepared to return to the initial hypothesis—perhaps already forgotten by the reader—that Rawlsian justice is deontology with a utilitarian bent. Justice as fairness appears to be a mixture of Kantian principles (the two moral capacities plus the first principle of justice) and the maximizing traits that, more often than not, are associated with the utilitarian doctrine. What is maximized in Rawlsian justice? The benefits for the most disadvantaged (these benefits ought to be the greatest); their long-term expectations (151); primary goods; the worth of liberty (205); stability (over generations); the individual's cooperation (over a complete life). In addition to these maximizing traits, Rawlsian justice explicitly seeks mutual advantages for individuals and conceives of the person's rational plan as one that maximizes his or her ends. Thus, justice as fairness places within a Kantian straitjacket maximizing traits that are usually associated with utilitarianism.[36]

Finally, the stability of Rawlsian justice seems to require a kind of passivity on the part of citizens. Citizens are supposed to pay their taxes, which will allow the state to design programs for the greatest benefits of the most disadvantaged members of society. But if those programs fail, citizens should not refrain from paying their fair share. This civic obligation should be unwavering: "unless tax laws . . . are clearly designed to attack or to abridge a basic equal liberty, they should not normally be protested by civil disobedience" (372). Citizens could protest or suggest alternatives, but they should not challenge the monopoly the public structure has in the administration of the second principle.

Yet, even though the main weapon of radical resistance in a Rawlsian society, a tax revolt, is off limits, both citizens and public officials might have a legitimate interest in seeing to it that social programs are genuinely improving the lot of the disadvantaged. Public officials may thus design certain criteria that the worse-off must meet to be entitled to the greatest benefits of Rawlsian justice. Welfare recipients have to go to training programs, dropouts have to return to school and do well, drug users have to go to detox clinics, immature parents have to take courses in parenting, and so on. The state may need a swarm of agencies and public servants to oversee and guide the least advantaged members of society.

This is, however, a therapeutic society, a feature that seems to be part of the Rawlsian project as it is a feature of the welfare state. The worse-off may need state guidance to steer them away from habits that undermine their self-esteem and limit their possibilities as citizens. Rawlsian justice thus implies an administrative notion of the greatest benefits and an administrative therapy. This might suggest that it may well need what Kant feared the most: a paternalistic state.[37]

The problems of paternalism and dependence lurking behind Rawlsian justice are compounded as soon as we take notice of one of the central goals of justice as fairness: to turn individuals into self-sufficient citizens and fully cooperating members of society over a complete life. If society is unable to provide the grounds for self-sufficiency in the economic realm, full cooperation may adopt the form of passivity in the political realm. Full cooperation, after all, means that revolutions within the Rawlsian liberal order are over. Rawlsian liberalism and the end of history go hand in hand.

Let me recapitulate the following issues:

1. On one reading, justice as fairness is completely indifferent to the actual achievement of well-being or the actual fulfillment of people's life plans. It is not even concerned, in contrast to Amartya Sen's views, with a person's body. On another reading, Rawlsian justice maximizes the well-being of all members of society by maximizing their primary goods and

the benefits the most disadvantaged will receive, thus promoting social cooperation, which is the precondition of well-being. This suggests that justice as fairness maximizes well-being indirectly by maximizing the preconditions—primary goods and cooperation—which make well-being possible. These two readings contradict one another. Yet, it is worth noticing that the first one seems to be dominant in the Rawlsian discourse. Justice as fairness is explicitly reluctant to use notions of well-being to judge the status of justice. It explicitly postulates the priority of liberty— a priority that allows people to make choices. And this suggests that, despite my efforts to provide an alternative reading of Rawls's arguments, the criticism that sees choice as the ultimate good of Rawlsian justice is not entirely inaccurate even though it excludes the alternative interpretation that Rawls's own texts suggest.

2. The difference principle is an insurance for the better-off and a kind of political bribe for the most disadvantaged aimed at guaranteeing social cooperation.

3. The deontological status of Rawlsian justice is in jeopardy if, as Rawls says, justice has no point unless citizens pursue conceptions of the good "worthy of human endeavour." This claim implies that justice must be reexamined in an actual well-ordered society by looking at the ends people pursue to see whether Rawlsian principles are justified. And this is something that Rawls explicitly opposes.

4. Even if Rawlsian justice should not be judged on the basis of people's fulfillment of their rational plans, it should be evaluated in the light of the mutual advantages they are receiving under just institutions. But this requires going to the political process, an option that overtly contradicts the Rawlsian goal of avoiding contingent factors (e.g., the will of the people) in any deliberation about justice.

5. Points 3 and 4 show that justice cannot be decided a priori in the original position. It has to be decided a posteriori in an actual society by looking at the forms of life people choose and the mutual advantages they are receiving.

6. If mutual advantages and the greatest benefits are determined by the public structure and whatever public institutions decide accounts for the mutual advantages and the greatest benefits people ought to accept, then the scope of judgment of Rawlsian citizens is constrained. They are supposed to be autonomous in the original position, but in an actual

society they are subordinated to the government. The state will tell them whether their mutual advantages are acceptable and whether the most disadvantaged are receiving the greatest benefits.

7. If point 6 is correct, Rawlsian justice is a statist theory that might not be able to use statism as a settled conviction of the political culture of a democratic society and to command the universal support it wants in public deliberations.

8. The subordination identified in point 6 can be justified if order and stability become the paramount values of the Rawlsian paradigm.

If order and stability are the dominant values of justice as fairness it remains to be seen whether they arise from a moral sense or from the prudential calculations of people who want to advance their own interests. An examination of what I consider the cornerstone of Rawlsian justice, the difference principle, will place us in a better position to answer this question.

4

Conflicts of the Heart

The First versus the Second Principle
of Rawlsian Justice

Whether a spy or assassin is a good person is a separate question altogether; to answer it we should have to judge the cause for which he works and his motives for doing so.

—John Rawls, *A Theory of Justice*

The status of well-being within justice as fairness proposes a conflict between the first and the second principles of Rawls's system. Let us take a closer look at the difference principle as a way of exploring the role of prudential calculations in the design of Rawlsian justice. This task provides an opportunity to establish some connections between the reasoning informing the Rawlsian parties and the arguments Rousseau ascribes to the rich in the transition from the state of nature to civil society. It also enables me to conclude my case about the utilitarian aspects of justice as fairness.

The Difference Principle:
The Real Foundation of Rawlsian Justice

Justice as fairness includes two central paradoxes. The first is that its most important principle of justice, the difference principle, has a subordinate status. The second paradox is that the difference principle is based, primarily, upon prudential reasons even though Rawls insists on the moral character of the whole theory.[1]

That the difference principle has a subordinate status does not need argumentation. It is ancillary to the first principle of justice and to the first clause of the second principle. In Rawls's most recent formulation it is not even part of what he calls "constitutional essentials," although it still occupies a central place in the whole system. But my assertions that the difference principle is, in fact, the central aspect of Rawlsian justice and that it relies on prudential reasons need to be proved. Let me address these two issues in turn.

The priority of liberties is a well-known argument of the Kantian tradition, which serves as the theoretical soil nourishing Rawlsian justice. This priority is also part of the American political culture as expressed in the Bill of Rights, which is an attempt to place some fundamental rights beyond the contingencies of the political process. The principle of fair equality of opportunities has been part of the liberal argument for quite some time. The difference principle, however, is neither a Kantian development nor a principle found in the American political culture. It is a genuine Rawlsian contribution.

Rawls envisions his theory as an elaboration and application of Kantian principles to the problem of justice, and he understands his principles as a faithful rendering of the Kantian goal of treating individuals as ends in themselves rather than means. He says, "The two principles of justice give a stronger and more characteristic interpretation to Kant's idea. They rule out even the tendency to regard men as means to one another's welfare. In the design of the social system, we must treat persons solely as ends and not in any way as means" (183).

This central goal of both Kantian and Rawlsian justice cannot be achieved by the first principle of justice alone. Granting universal rights says nothing about the way society ought to be organized or about the principles that should govern individuals' character in their relationships with one another. My right to property neither forbids nor prevents me from using other fellow creatures as my means. If they have the same right I have but lack the property I own, they can become my tools despite all of my Kantian assurances that since I respect their formal rights, I am treating them as ends in themselves.

It is the weaving together of the first and second principles which allows people to treat one another as ends in the Rawlsian argument. By arranging inequalities to the benefit of the most disadvantaged, society recognizes their moral agency and treats them as ends. It is not accidental that when Rawls explains how his conception of justice realizes the Kantian ideal of treating individuals as ends in themselves, he reverses the lexical ordering of his principles and presents the difference principle, rather than that of equal and universal liberties, as the main foundation that allows society to treat its members as ends. "To regard persons as ends in themselves in the basic design of society," he writes, "is to agree to forgo those gains which do not contribute to their representative expectations. By contrast, to regard persons as means is to be prepared to impose upon them lower prospects of life for the sake of the higher expectations of others. Thus we see that the difference principle, which at first appears rather extreme, has a reasonable interpretation" (180).

The difference principle is also the one that contributes the most to achieving two central goals of Rawlsian justice: cooperation and self-esteem. Rawls writes that "men's self-esteem hinges on how they regard one another. If the parties accept the utility criterion, they will lack the support to their self-respect provided by the public commitment of others to arrange inequalities to everyone's advantage and to guarantee an equal liberty for all" (181). Notice again the reversal of the lexical ordering.

The difference principle, in short, provides the foundation for cooperation by providing the greatest benefits to the most disadvantaged. It also leads to self-esteem and fulfills the Kantian ideal of treating persons as ends. Still, a stronger justification of the difference principle is suggested, but never made explicit, by Rawls's own arguments: the difference principle discourages people from succumbing to the temptation of sacrificing liberty to welfare, of accepting a lesser liberty for, say, greater economic benefits.

Now it is evident that some people may find it both rational and reasonable to surrender some or all of their liberties, temporarily or permanently, if they believe that the end result of their decision will be an increase of their welfare. People who are starving may trade off their right of expression for food. In justice as fairness these trade-offs are not necessary since the public structure guarantees mutual benefits for everyone, and inequalities ought to provide the greatest benefits for the most disadvantaged. In other words, people need not surrender their liberties because they all will receive primary goods, and the least advantaged will receive the greatest benefits. Rawlsian justice thus partly realizes the Rousseauian ideal of a society in which no one is so rich as to be able to buy another, and no one is so poor as to be forced to sell himself. In a Rawlsian society there might be rich people with the capacity to buy others, but Rawlsian poor are not for sale. They are protected by the second principle and its promise of the greatest benefits.

The Rawlsian arrangement suggests a puzzling discovery: despite Rawls's lexical ordering, the difference principle turns out to be the real foundation of the first principle, which cannot stand on its own. The first principle promotes neither cooperation nor stability. It does not contribute to the individual's self-esteem. Left alone, the first principle of Rawlsian justice may lead to another version of the Hobbesian state of nature: a society torn apart by permanent conflicts arising from universal rights. Liberties have priority because the difference principle discourages people from renouncing them. Were the difference principle absent, the first principle would be neither justified nor preserved.

Another feature sheds a completely new light on the difference principle: it contributes to the ideal of fraternity. The difference principle, Rawls claims, "does seem to correspond to a natural meaning of fraternity: namely, to the idea of not wanting to have greater advantages unless this is to the benefit of others who are less well off" (105). It is possible to say, then, that the difference principle guarantees cooperation, promotes stability, leads to self-esteem, fulfills the Kantian ideal of treating people as ends, preserves the first principle of Rawlsian justice, specifies a conception of equality, and provides an idea of fraternity. It is, in this sense, the consummation of the French Revolution. This is enough to justify my assertion that the difference principle is the cornerstone of justice as fairness. That it is a subordinate principle justifies my claim that its status represents the primary paradox of Rawlsian justice.

Rawls disagrees. In explaining the priority of liberty, he writes: "By the priority of liberty I mean the precedence of the principle of equal liberty over the second principle of justice. The two principles are in lexical order, and therefore the claims of liberty are to be satisfied first. Until this is achieved no other principle comes into play" (244). My discussion suggests that the priority of liberty is not always possible, and accordingly, the Rawlsian demand to satisfy the claims of liberty first cannot be met.

My right to property, despite all of its importance, is irrelevant if I do not have the means to exercise it, and those means are provided by the primary goods that the difference principle makes available to all citizens. My right to freedom of expression is central to my liberty, but if I lack the means to exercise that freedom, I will be unable to communicate my ideas to the larger public who, in my judgment, ought to know them. I need material means (money, more often than not) to publish my ideas and to make my freedom of expression meaningful.

In these two examples, the claims of liberty cannot be satisfied first unless that satisfaction refers to a formal recognition of rights. But a formal recognition of rights is perfectly compatible with the actual impossibility of making those rights meaningful to my circumstances. My right to go to Jupiter does not mean that I will ever be able to do so, and similarly, my right to property does not mean that I will ever be able to own something. Consequently and contrary to Rawls's claim, I need the second principle to satisfy the principle of equal liberty. Rawls's assertion that "no other principle comes into play" until the first principle is satisfied is thus inaccurate. Without the second principle, the priority of liberty cannot stand on its own. It is a formal recognition that intimates a promise perhaps destined never to be fulfilled.

In addition to providing the foundation for the first principle, the difference principle allows justice as fairness to claim that it is a more stable conception of justice. In rejecting the principle of utility, Rawls argues that it lowers the life prospects of some individuals for the sake of others, thereby undermining the possibility of stability and cooperation. "In fact," Rawls writes,

> when society is conceived as a system of cooperation designed to advance the good of its members, it seems quite incredible that some citizens should be expected, on the basis of political principles, to accept lower prospects of life for the sake of others. It is evident then why utilitarians should stress the role of sympathy in moral learning and the central place of benevolence among the moral virtues. Their conception of justice is threatened with instability unless sympathy and benevolence can be widely and intensely cultivated. Looking at the question from the standpoint of the original position, the parties recognize that it would be highly unwise if not irrational to choose principles which may have consequences so extreme that they could not accept them in practice. They would reject the principle of utility and adopt the more realistic idea of designing the social order on a principle of reciprocal advantage. (178)

Rawls's argument, then, holds that the difference principle is necessary to the extent that "society is conceived as a system of cooperation," and cooperation need not be based on such stringent requirements as sympathy and benevolence. Benevolence is "so strong a condition" (149), and sympathy is not realistic. Cooperation is on a stronger footing when it is based on the "more realistic . . . principle of reciprocal advantage." Now, the only Rawlsian principle that provides reciprocal advantage is the difference principle. Without it, Rawlsian justice would never be able to achieve the goals of cooperation, stability, and order, not to mention the goal of a "genuine reconciliation of interests" for which it stands (142).

Finally, in "A Well-ordered Society," Rawls offers another ground to justify the view proposed here: the difference principle is the real foundation of Rawlsian justice. He writes:

> The first problem of justice is to determine the principles to regulate inequalities and to adjust the profound and long-lasting effects of social, natural, and

historical contingencies, particularly since these contingencies combined with inequalities generate tendencies that, when left to themselves, are sharply at odds with the freedom and equality appropriate for a well-ordered society. (10)

It is evident that the "first problem of justice" is addressed, primarily, by the second principle of the Rawlsian system, particularly the difference principle.

The Original Position and Prudence

In Chapter 2 I showed that in the light of Rawls's own arguments there is no place for morality before the agreement on the principles of Rawlsian justice. In this section I want to explore how and why the only reasons the parties have to support Rawls's principles are entirely prudential; namely, they are concerned with the person's own good, and that good is devoid of any moral attribute.

It has been said that the parties in the original position display a sense of sympathy to the extent that they imagine themselves as members of the most disadvantaged. "In order to make the principle regulating inequalities determinate," Rawls writes, "one looks at the system from the standpoint of the least advantaged representative man. Inequalities are permissible when they maximize, or at least all contribute to, the long-term expectations of the least fortunate group in society" (151; see also 285). By placing themselves in this position, the Rawlsian parties have the capacity to understand the plight of the worse-off and the grounds the worse-off may have for supporting an agreement on justice which promises to give them the greatest benefits.[2] This view claims that Rawlsian justice arises from a "strong empathy,"[3] a feature that seems to suggest some Rousseauian overtones in justice as fairness. Just as Rousseauian individuals see in the suffering of others their potential suffering and feel compassion toward those in pain, so also do the Rawlsian parties see the miseries of the worse-off as their potential misery and feel sympathy toward those who happen to be part of the most disadvantaged members of society.

An alternative reading seems more persuasive. I suggest a Hobbesian element which, to the best of my knowledge, has not been addressed in the literature on Rawlsianism. This Hobbesian element is fear. The parties to the original position are committed to advancing their own good and fear the prospect of finding themselves in a situation devoid of the means to attain their goal. In their calculations[4] they know that the worst-case scenario is to be part of the most disadvantaged. But if that is their lot, it is better to make that situation more palatable through the greatest benefits of the difference principle. "Not only do the parties protect their basic rights but they insure themselves against the worst eventualities" (176). This argument suggests that the willingness to give the greatest benefits to the most disadvantaged arises less from mutual sympathy than from people's fear of being part of that group as well as their prudential interest in having a safety net, a kind of insurance against bad luck, should the "worst eventualities" happen, and they find themselves in the company of the worse-off.

In Rousseau's state of nature, there is a genuine bond cemented by the feeling of compassion between the individual and the other, between the stranger and the sufferer. There is no compassion in the Rawlsian original position. When the Rawlsian parties look at the most disadvantaged they do not see others; they see themselves, and they try to ameliorate their potential predicament as far as possible. It could not be otherwise since, in the original position, they are choosing principles of justice in a situation of "great uncertainty" (175); they are trying "to acknowledge principles which advance their system of ends as far as possible" (144); and they are "allowed only enough knowledge to make a rational choice to protect their interest" (378).

In other words, the parties are committed to advancing their interests, but since they do not know the specific content of those interests, they are unable to assess their moral character. They know that they have a capacity for a conception of the good, but since they lack knowledge of that conception, they are unable to judge the moral character or lack of it which their ideas of the good may have. They possess general knowledge of the facts of life, but they do not know their psychological propensities, so they are unable to determine whether they will care, and in what degree, about moral ends. They do not even know whether they care for primary goods. They may turn to ascetic habits, in which case primary goods are not central. The parties know that they might even end up as means to other people in a hierarchical society, if the removal of that condition worsened their situation.[5] The only thing they know for certain is that they may become members of the most disadvantaged, and through a mixture of prudential calculations and fear, they arrive at Rawlsian justice.

Interestingly, even though the centrality of compassion which Rousseau presents in the *Second Discourse* is unfit for the original position, his view of mutuality in the constitution of the general will serves as an apt characterization of the motives guiding Rawlsian selves. "Why is it," Rousseau writes,

> that the general will is always upright, and that all continually will the happiness of each one, unless it is because there is not a man who does not think of

"each" as meaning him, and consider himself in voting for all. This proves that equality of rights and the idea of justice which such equality creates originate in the preference each man gives to himself, and accordingly in the very nature of man. (204)

The "preference each man gives to himself" is also the justification for the second principle of Rawlsian justice.[6]

The difference principle, then, does not rely on an identification with the interests of others expressed in sympathy or benevolence. Neither does it depend on altruism. It hinges upon reciprocal advantages. "The principle of utility," Rawls says, "seems to require a greater identification with the interests of others than the two principles of justice. Thus the latter will be a more stable conception to the extent that this identification is difficult to achieve" (177).[7]

Rawls argues, however, that in the original position the parties are forced to take into account the good of others (148). But one is hard pressed to find how could this be the case. "When the two principles are satisfied," Rawls argues, "each person's liberties are secured and there is a sense defined by the difference principle in which everyone is benefited by social cooperation. Therefore we can explain the acceptance of the social system and the principles it satisfies by the psychological law that persons tend to love, cherish, and support whatever affirms their own good" (177).

This argument makes it clear that the benefits arising from social cooperation are predicated not upon the first principle, but upon the difference principle (i.e., "a sense defined by the difference principle"). It also makes clear that the parties do not support Rawlsian justice out of sympathy for the interests of others, concern for their good, or out of altruism. In the original position, sympathy is an impossibility: the parties "are mutually disinterested rather than sympathetic" (187). They do not display concern for the good of others since they lack knowledge of both their own conception of the good (which may lead them in an actual society to misanthropic attitudes) and of other people's conceptions of the good. And they do not act out of altruism because "the theory of justice assumes a definite limit on the strength of social and altruistic motivation. It supposes that individuals and groups put forward competing claims, and while they are willing to act justly, they are not prepared to abandon their interests" (281; see also 189).

To sum up: in the original position, there is no place for sympathy; no need for benevolence; no role for altruism; and, Rawls's claim to the contrary notwithstanding, there is no space for a concern for others. The parties are trying "to advance their conception of the good as best they can," and "in attempting to do this they are not bound by prior moral ties to each other" (128). Nor are they bound by "extensive ties of natural sentiments," something that a conception of justice "should not presuppose" (129). The principles of justice are supported because each party is concerned with his own good and wants to advance his own interests (19, 184),[8] and those interests are bereft of any moral content. The parties, after all, are rational creatures whose "reasonableness," as we will see, is imposed from without.

I stress the prudential character of Rawlsian justice to counter Rawls's efforts to present his theory as the moral blueprint for a well-ordered society, an effort that has been prominent in his writings after *Theory*. However, Rawls himself recognized the prudential motives of his creatures, and so he wrote:

> This initial situation [the original position] combines the requisite clarity with the relevant ethical constraints. It is partly to preserve this clarity that I have avoided attributing to the parties any ethical motivation. They decide solely on the basis of what seems best calculated to further their interests so far as they can ascertain them. In this way, we can exploit the intuitive idea of rational prudential choice.[9] (584)

"Rational prudential choice" is the foundation of justice as fairness, and Kantianism offers a dignified semblance to people struggling (in an interesting lapse, Rawls calls them "litigants" [90]) to come out in the best and safest position possible.[10]

Since Rawls is ready to admit this, where does morality come from in justice as fairness? How could "rational prudential choice" bring about moral outcomes? The answer was intimated in *Theory* and articulated explicitly in Rawls's subsequent works. The morality of Rawlsian justice comes from without; it is given in advance by the constraints of the original position. Hence the rational and the reasonable—two concepts first developed in the "Dewey Lectures"—occupy a central place in Rawls's reasoning to prove the moral character of his theory.

Rawls envisions the rational and the reasonable as complementary ideas that are also distinct and independent. The *rational* refers to a person's private interests, which are in turn associated with that person's conception of the good.[11] The *reasonable* refers to a person's willingness to accept fair terms of cooperation as the guiding principles of society. The rational is, primarily, a private disposition; the reasonable is public.

Rational agents "lack . . . the particular form of moral sensibility that underlies the desire to engage in fair cooperation as such, and to do so on terms that others as equals might reasonably be expected to endorse."[12] Reasonable persons, by contrast, "are not moved by the general good as such but desire for its own sake a social world in which they, as free and equal, can cooperate with others on terms all can accept. They insist that reciprocity should hold within that world so that each benefits along with others."[13] The reasonable thus embodies a basic morality that is a precondition of social life. The rational constitutes a moral vacuum. The desire to engage in fair terms of cooperation is not part of its perspective.

In the face of what seems to be open opposition, how could these concepts complement each other? They do so to the extent that "merely reasonable agents would have no ends of their own," and "merely rational agents lack a sense of justice and fail to recognize the independent validity of the claims of others."[14] The presence of the rational in the original position is overwhelming. But where does the reasonable begin? Rawls argues that the reasonable, as the expression of public morality, is not derived from the rational; it is an external imposition. Rational parties—creatures seeking to advance the conception of the good of the persons they represent—arrive at the reasonable not because they intend to, but because the restrictions they face guarantee a reasonable outcome. "It seems likely that any plausible derivation [of the reasonable from the rational] must situate rational agents in circumstances in which they are subject to certain appropriate conditions *and these conditions will express the reasonable.*"[15] Rawls is more categorical: the "constraints of the reasonable are simply imposed from without."[16]

Since the parties are placed within a reasonable situation, the outcomes of their deliberations will also be reasonable. This is a major feature of Rawls's philosophy: his major conclusions are always anticipated and, better still, guaranteed by the way he frames his assumptions. The role of external assumptions acting as guarantors of the whole theory is so pervasive that one is tempted to see a subtle but consistent distrust of actual persons.

To illustrate: The parties are willing to agree on Rawls's principles of justice because they possess a natural duty of justice, which is given in advance. Those principles are moral because the external conditions surrounding their public articulation are moral, and that moral character is also given in advance. People (in one reading, at least) live in a society of mutual advantages because public institutions declare so. The most disadvantaged receive the greatest benefits because administrative bodies inform them that is the case. Everything comes from without in Rawlsian justice. Everything is guaranteed in advance by an institutional context. The only persons Rawls trusts are judges, preferably Supreme Court justices who are, in Rawls's political liberalism, the embodiments of public reason. The picture is more complex, though. The previous arguments support the thesis of distrust, and yet his understanding of society as a union of social unions denies it. Both aspects are witnesses to the complexities of Rawls's philosophy.

Rights and Interests: Rousseau and Rawls

If we acknowledge the prudential reasoning informing the parties in the original position, we can then look at the Rawlsian project as another response to the problem Rousseau sets out to solve in Book I of *The Social Contract*: how to reconcile right (justice) and interest taking men "as they are and laws as they might be." Rousseau's solution is the creation of a just society through the social contract; the individual's interest is best served by joining and preserving the contract. Still, the Rousseauian paradigm is always exposed to a potential conflict between the general will (justice) and the individual's interest, which explains why the former, if need be, must force the individual to be free and to recognize where his true interests lie.

Rawls addresses the same problem, but his solution is not to separate justice and interest and even less to impose the former over the latter. The alternative he puts forward is to derive justice from interest; that is, justice is the product of the three primary interests he ascribes to the individual: 1) his interest in maximizing his capacity for choice; 2) his interest in insuring his life against the possibility of being a member of the most disadvantaged (the "worst" eventuality); and 3) his interest in a stable political order. Rawlsian justice thus emerges from people's interest in advancing "their system of ends as far as possible" (144) through their compliance with a system of justice which requires little cost and promises mutual advantages.

Hence emerges the centrality of prudence, an aspect that now can be examined through the reasons that the most disadvantaged may have to receive the greatest benefits from the public structure and the motives of the better-off to pay for those benefits. In *Theory* Rawls's justification for the greatest benefits going to the least favored members is that since justice seeks to provide mutual advantages and cooperation, the most disadvantaged should not be left at the mercy of contingency; that is, they should not be deprived of the means that are preconditions for the fulfillment of their rational plans. The greatest benefits provide those means, thereby eliciting and ensuring their cooperation.[17] Cooperation is justified further on the ground that it is necessary for well-being (103).

It is clear that cooperation can be a moral goal and that people might perceive it either as a moral end in itself or as the foundation for the pursuit of other moral ends that may be part of their rational plans. From this understanding of cooperation the difference principle appears to be a moral aspect of Rawlsian justice. But the original position prevents us from taking that route. The profile of the parties in the original position shows that cooperation is devoid of any moral standing in the founding moment of the Rawlsian contract and that it is not possible to uncover moral reasons in the original position (see Chapter 2).

To the possible argument that in an actual society cooperation and stability are moral goals, I reply: neither cooperation nor stability, in itself, is a moral goal. Cooperation can be sought to extract material gains from others. It can also be the end result of ignorance or fear. The claim that stability is, by itself, a moral objective does not merit much consideration. Dictatorial governments are stable, but not moral. The motivational force of the Rawlsian parties is the promise of mutual advantages with as little cost as possible. And cooperation and stability appear to be the prudential grounds of those mutual advantages. In the original position, then, the most disadvantaged lack moral grounds to justify the greatest benefits they expect from public institutions. And, more importantly, in an actual society these benefits are not derived from the situation of the worse-off but from the predicament of the most fortunate members of society.

To clarify: The better-off benefit from inequalities, and, to justify those inequalities and still have social cooperation, they must provide the greatest benefits to the most disadvantaged. They have to buy the compliance of the least fortunate members of society by providing them with the greatest benefits. We have seen that Rawls explicitly rejects sympathy as a ground of justice, and he eschews altruism in favor of the "more realistic idea" of mutual advantages. If this is so, the willingness of the better-off to pay for the greatest benefits arises not from a sense of morality which leads them to identify with the interests of others, but from their own very real interest in gaining the collaboration of the most disadvantaged and preserving an unequal status from which they derive benefits. The difference principle, Rawls argues, "seems to be a fair basis on which those better endowed, or more fortunate in their social circumstances, could expect others to collaborate with them when some workable arrangement is a necessary condition of the good of all" (103).

Rawlsian justice is the legitimacy insurance that the better-off need. As Rawls himself argues, by adopting the two principles of justice the parties not only "protect their basic rights but they insure themselves against the worst eventualities" (176). This description certainly applies to all members but is definitely telling in the case of the better-off. For this group, the worst eventuality would be the loss of their status. The legitimacy of the inequalities from which the better-off benefit is guaranteed when they pay to society the necessary insurance in the form of taxes that are meant to provide the greatest benefits for the most disadvantaged.

The privileged status of the better-off is compounded by the Rawlsian requirement of universal improvement, which appears prominently in the first chapter of *Theory* and then seems to be replaced gradually by the long-term expectations of the most disadvantaged. "The general conception of justice," Rawls writes, "imposes no restrictions on what sort of inequalities are permissible; it only requires that everyone's position be improved (62; see also 64, 65). This formulation can be interpreted in two different ways: 1) The advantages the better-off already have will constitute the improvement they should expect from Rawlsian justice, or 2) the advantaged position they already hold should improve even further.

Rawls's argument is problematic on both counts but is particularly striking on the second. Members of the better-off might see the financial contributions Rawlsian justice demands as a denial of what they understand as improvement. The possible reply that improvement is defined by the public system of rules—by public functionaries—is hardly a consolation. The second interpretation might strike many citizens as unreasonable. If the better-off already have social and economic advantages, why must their situation be enhanced even further? Of course, it improves in the sense of obtaining legitimacy and the benefits of cooperation: this is what Rawls probably intends, but it is not what his text necessarily states.

Regarded in this way, the Rawlsian contract appears increasingly similar to the contract Rousseau describes in the *Second Discourse,* and the grounds the better-off may employ are similar to the justifications the rich use to move from a state of uncertainty to a legitimate social order.[18] In Rousseau's argument, the property title of the rich is not legitimate, thus they advocate the right of property for all persons. In this way, they succeed in legitimizing the property they already have, and the rest have a formal right to a property they do not possess.

One important difference between Rawlsian justice and Rousseau's description of the conspiracy of the rich is that the disadvantaged in the civil society Rousseau attacks do not receive any benefit beyond formal rights; Rawlsian citizens do. But in both cases—and this is the issue I want to emphasize—neither the rich (in Rousseau's case) nor the better-off (in Rawls's case) have moral grounds to justify their status and the inequalities from which they benefit.

Their status is the end result of contingency, which has produced inequalities that are morally unjustified. The crucial political problem of the Rawlsian paradigm is to justify those inequalities while preserving a stable cooperation among citizens. Rawls's solution is to justify inequalities by ascribing a moral character to them via state actions.

In other words, the Rawlsian state, which, as in Kant, embodies the right, moralizes the existing order. And it does so not by erasing inequalities but by reaching the least favored members through redistributive policies aimed at maximizing their expectations (285). The state plays a leveling role to the extent that it reduces the large inequalities of wealth.[19]

The individual's motives and personal sense of morality are irrelevant. Individuals might grudgingly pay taxes to support the most disadvantaged while disagreeing with the morality Rawls ascribes to the difference principle. But as long as they comply with their tax-paying duties and as long as society provides the greatest benefits to the most disadvantaged, society will be moral and well ordered. Recall that Rawlsian morality is an operation embedded in public institutions and existing external to individuals. In theory, then, we may have a moral society (one that practices Rawlsian justice) composed of individuals guided by prudential interests in their public relations with one another.[20] What determines the moral character of the Rawlsian order is the way the social product is administered and distributed, not the way people behave as long as they comply with the principles of justice, respect rights, and pay their taxes.[21]

In Rawlsian justice, the better-off may even pay nothing. If natural resources are plentiful and if those resources are controlled by the state, the public structure may provide the greatest benefits to the most disadvantaged without dipping into the pockets of the better-off. In this imaginary but plausible case, nature would make moral an inequality that is, in itself, immoral according to Rawls's theory. In short, Rawls tackles inequalities not by abolishing them, but by moralizing them through primary goods (opportunities and cash) via the state, which is why the analogy with Rousseau's analysis is relevant. The rich of the *Second Discourse,* too, attempt to legitimize and moralize their privileges, not by renouncing them, but by instituting a government that grants rights to all citizens in much the same way as the Rawlsian state provides rights plus primary goods to all members of society. But the fact remains: after the state bestows rights (in Rousseau's view) or rights plus primary goods (in Rawls's case), the original material inequalities remain. They are now more palatable, and the hope is that through policies of fair equality of opportunities large inequalities will not prevail.

The better-off, then, lack moral grounds to justify the inequalities that make them the most advantaged members of society. Nor do they have moral grounds to support their willingness to universalize rights (in Rousseau's argument) or to provide the greatest benefits to the most disadvantaged (in Rawls's case). The better-off are willing to live with the fact that the most disadvantaged will get the greatest benefits, not because they are committed to a society of autonomous citizens and the least advantaged need those benefits to achieve that goal, or because they want strong communitarian bonds, or because they feel morally obliged, in Thoreau's sense, to helping people who may be oppressed. The better-off support the idea of the greatest benefits because they want to preserve the inequalities that benefit them.

The better-off have no moral reason to support the greatest benefits to the most disadvantaged. Neither do the most disadvantaged have moral ground to demand the greatest benefits from the better-off. Those greatest benefits are the price tag they put on their acceptance of inequalities. It is also the price society pays through its public institutions to retain the cooperation and support of the least fortunate members, who are willing to accept that their worth of liberty is unequal and to accept their status as the most disadvantaged as long as society gives them the greatest benefits. Rawlsian justice becomes a prudential assessment of the costs required to maintain legitimacy for the better-off and stability for the social order. It is worth emphasizing, however, that the greatest benefits do not necessarily lift the worse-off up from their status, nor are they meant to.

The Difference Principle and Accountability

Although Rawlsian justice conceives of individuals as moral agents and constructs a model of justice in which they are able to choose their ends in life, the prudential character of the difference principle might encourage passive individuals. I assume that moral agency is expressed not only in a person's ability to chose his or her ends in life but also in a willingness to accept the consequences of those choices. From the standpoint of public institutions, however, those choices do not carry consequences in a Rawlsian society. If the individuals' free and informed choices land them in the ranks of the disadvantaged, justice is concerned with the outcome (they are now disadvantaged), not with the decisions or processes that brought about that outcome. More intriguing—and for some people, more disturbing—is that in the Rawlsian paradigm, individuals may well continue to indulge in the same choices, processes, or practices that made them disadvantaged in the first place. They know that as long as their activities are legal, they are in a no-lose situation.

If their choices make them successful, they have won. If their choices turn them into disadvantaged, they will still have won because they will receive the greatest benefits. This possible outcome challenges Rawls's claim that individuals "are always accountable for their deeds" (389). Public institutions have financial responsibilities toward the disadvantaged, who in turn have no financial responsibility toward those institutions. This trait leads to the collapse of the principle of reciprocity, one of the cornerstones of Rawlsian justice.

Rawlsian reciprocity has two components: *law abidingness* in the sense of respecting other people's rights, and *cooperation* in the sense of paying a fair share through taxes. Reciprocity exists since the components are meant to provide benefits for the law-abiding citizen and the taxpayer. Yet the second component of reciprocity—cooperation through a person's willingness to pay taxes—breaks down among the worse-off. They are expected to respect people's rights, but, logically, they are not expected to pay taxes since their status as the most disadvantaged may prevent them from doing so. Because Rawlsian justice is blind about the choices and actions of the worse-off and because they will always receive the greatest benefits, if they indulge in practices that keep them disadvantaged (I leave aside the Rawlsian big assumption about fully cooperating citizens), then the Rawlsian paradigm has turned them into passive recipients of benefits rather than active participants of a collective effort. Rawlsian justice may thus nourish passive subjects. It is worth mentioning here that, for Rawls, mutual respect is shown, among other things, "in our being prepared to give reasons for our actions whenever the interests of others are materially affected" (337). But it is not clear how the most disadvantaged can present reasons for actions that may represent a tax burden for other citizens or how the state can persuade or force them to offer those reasons.

The lack of accountability on the part of the most disadvantaged is compounded by the accountability Rawlsian justice expects from the most favored members of society, particularly in the area of economic gain. The most favored must justify their gains to the most disadvantaged, but the least advantaged need not explain their losses or any worsening of their condition, even when they are directly responsible for the situation. "Taking equality," Rawls writes, "as the basis of comparison, those who have gained more must do so on terms that are justifiable to those who have gained the least."[22] This justification, of course, is not a private operation, but a process that takes place in the public structure.

It is confusing to claim, as Rawls does, that "we have a right to our natural abilities and a right to whatever we become entitled to by taking part in a fair social process"[23] and then to claim that the most favored members must justify their "right to whatever [they] become entitled to" in a fair social process. In the Rawlsian system, rights seem to be settled and are not subject to further justification. But this is untrue of the right of the most advantaged members to enjoy their economic gains. Those gains must comply with terms that are "justifiable" to the most disadvantaged, and those terms are specified by the difference principle. As I mentioned in Chapter 2, Rawls distrusts wealth.

Justice as Fairness and the Status of Middle Sectors

The Rawlsian emphasis on the relationship between the better-off and the most disadvantaged shows that a Rawlsian society is basically a two-class order. It is, in this sense, similar to the Marxist reading of *The Communist Manifesto* in which the bourgeois order is composed of two opposing camps—the bourgeoisie and the proletariat—without room for middle sectors. Similarly, in the Rawlsian order, there is no space for the middle class, which is, presumably, part of the better-off. In theory then, a Rawlsian society might have the following arrangements: 1) a lower rate (or even a zero rate) of taxation for the upper ranks of the better-off, a sector that society may consider responsible for the creation of wealth[24]; 2) a middle class bearing the brunt of higher taxes; and 3) a group exempted from tax responsibilities given its status as the most disadvantaged.

If this arrangement provides the greatest benefits to the most disadvantaged, if the long-term expectations of this group are maximized (285), and if any change of such an arrangement worsened the status of the most disadvantaged, society is just, even if the middle class receives no benefit at all and even if its long-term expectations are worsened. This justifies my hypothesis that justice as fairness is deontology with a utilitarian bent in which the long-term expectations of some groups (in this case, the middle class) might be sacrificed to maximize the long-term expectations of another group (the most disadvantaged). Equally important, the worth of liberty of the middle class might be lowered without compensation. They may not have the liberty to retire with the level of economic security they want or to send their children to the school they like or to experience the quality of health care they prefer. Rawlsian justice is blind to the long-term expectations of some groups whose life plans might be unreasonably constrained by the demands of the Rawlsian order. Of course, society may possess the resources and the willingness to maximize the long-term expectations of *all* groups. But the first requirement—the material resources—needs an abundance that might not be found (this is Connolly's argument). And the second requirement—a willingness to maximize the long-term expectations of *all* groups—requires a level of communality and agreement which may be lacking and which, more importantly, Rawls seems to reject in advance.[25]

In his discussion of public funds for the arts, Rawls argues that

> a well-ordered society can devote a sizable fraction of its resources to expenditures of this kind. But while the claims of culture can be met in this way, the principles of justice do not permit subsidizing universities and institutes, or opera and the theater, on the grounds that these institutions are intrinsically valuable, and that those who engage in them are to be supported even at some significant expense to others who do not receive compensating benefits. (332)

Applying this concern to the difference principle, what are the compensating benefits that the middle class might receive in a Rawlsian society? Stability and cooperation? If these are indeed the reciprocal advantages Rawlsian justice might come to, they may be quite different from what many (if not most) people understand by *mutual advantage*. Rawlsian justice also claims that inequalities ought to be to everyone's advantage (150) and for the benefit of all (546). But this does not mean the same benefits or the same advantages for all; it means instead stability for some and material goods for others. That this outcome will engender a stable public allegiance to justice as fairness is not something that Rawls has proven convincingly.

The two-class order of Rawlsian justice brings into clear focus the conflictual nature of the two principles: the universality of the first and the particularity of the difference principle. The first principle provides equal liberties to all citizens. The difference principle refers to how one particular group, the most disadvantaged, fares. "Given certain assumptions, economic and social inequalities are to be judged in terms of the long-run expectations of the least advantaged social group" (44; see also 199, 277).

This is an odd feature of Rawlsian justice. The just character of a well-ordered society is assessed in the light of equal liberties granted to all citizens and the performance of a particular group in terms of the benefits it receives and its long-term expectations regardless of how the long-term expectations of other groups fare. To be sure, this is not a surprising or new trait of the Western canon, but it is one that is certainly out of place in the Kantian tradition. For Kant, justice is a question of complying with a reason that is universal; it is not a matter of the particular performance of one group of citizens.

The Rawlsian predilection for the disadvantaged is more akin to the Marxist discourse than to Kant's philosophy. For Kant, emancipation is neither a communal nor a social task, but the responsibility of an individual who, as a rational agent, has the capacity to legislate universal norms for all rational beings, God included.

Marx, however, stands for a conception of justice grounded in how the particular interests of the proletariat are satisfied under a particular regime.[26] Accordingly, he assesses the social order by studying the condition of the wealth producers and emancipating the working class, the group that incarnates all suffering and to whom is given the responsibility of liberating humankind. The workers must become political agents and seize political power to free themselves. In Rawlsian theory, by contrast, even though the just character of society is determined by the status of the most disadvantaged (whether their expectations are rising and whether they are receiving the greatest benefits), this group is not responsible for improving their own condition or changing it altogether. That is the exclusive task of the Rawlsian state. The Marxist paradigm seeks to abolish the status of the workers; the Rawlsian paradigm seeks to render more palatable the status of the most disadvantaged.

In this regard, the Rawlsian paradigm outmaneuvered Marxism by abolishing the class conflicts and social struggles rooted in the control of society's wealth by a few. The Marxist theoretical universe is no longer relevant. The sphere of needs and competition falls under the jurisdiction of the Rawlsian state, and Rawlsian citizens are beyond that sphere, which, in Marxism, is the place par excellence of conflicts. Rawlsian citizens find their needs met by the state, which insofar as justice is concerned, is the genuine autonomous entity in a Rawlsian society.[27]

Moreover, in Rawlsian justice, the crucial issue is not one of emancipation. Indeed, that is never a political issue since, in the original position, Rawlsian subjects are situated equally, and no one is oppressed. The crucial issue of the Rawlsian order is how the long-term expectations of the most disadvantaged fare within a context of formal liberties and without regard for how the long-term expectations of other groups are fulfilled.[28] To tie justice to the lot of one group while formally claiming to treat all individuals as ends is an important problem haunting the Rawlsian paradigm. It is also another reminder that Rawls cannot have it both ways. He cannot respect the distinctiveness of all persons and willingly sacrifice the interests of some on behalf of the interests of others. He cannot defend the universality of the first principle while weaving it to the particularity of the difference principle.

Rawls claims that sacrificing the interests of some is in done the name of justice. But this argument is hardly appealing to its victims, particularly the middle class, who thought Rawlsian society was committed to providing mutual advantages and who then discovered, rather late, that those mutual advantages were income for the worse-off and stability for the rest. This places my discussion, once again, on the utilitarian bent of a philosophical enterprise committed to deontological values and procedures.

The Utilitarian Bent: Back Again

In "Fairness to Goodness" (537), Rawls says that people's ideas of the good are irrelevant from a moral point of view. In *Political Liberalism* (79), he modifies this position and claims that these conceptions are irrelevant "politically speaking." Yet, politically speaking, people may want to see how justice impacts their ideas of the good in order to determine whether that justice is acceptable. In Rawlsian justice, this is impossible because the principles of justice are settled once and for all. Rawls is correct in his view that the consequence test annuls any possibility of ever arriving at a stable agreement on justice. If people demand, as a precondition of their acceptance of justice, that its effects should have no adverse consequences on their conceptions of the good, a public agreement would not be possible. This demand would not be reasonable given the diversity and incommensurability of conceptions of the good.

However, it is reasonable to argue, as many people would, that should justice affect adversely their conceptions of the good, they ought to have the opportunity in the political arena to persuade their fellow citizens to reexamine the agreement on justice. In Rawls's paradigm, this is not possible either. Citizens should not reexamine the status of justice on the basis of contingencies—their views of the human good—which are irrelevant, "politically speaking." The problem is that this political ground—the irrelevance of people's ideas of the good in any public deliberation searching for an agreement on justice—will not be accepted by all citizens, particularly those for whom their views of the good take precedence over justice.

Rawls might reply that justice cannot waver on this issue. In this case it is clear that Rawlsian justice sacrifices the interests of some on behalf of others but uses different justifications to support its actions. The sacrifice of some people's interests is justified not on the ground of its necessity in satisfying the preferences of the greatest number but on the ground that it is the outcome of principles that were decided in a situation of fairness. Therefore, so the Rawlsian reasoning goes, any outcome arising from principles accepted under conditions of fairness is fair. The original position appears, increasingly, not only as the founding moment of Rawlsian justice, but also as its shield against any possible criticism.

Rawls devises a Kantian procedure. He detaches his parties from all contingencies that, in his judgment, are morally irrelevant. He expurgates his creatures from any psychological propensity. And when he arrives at the core of Kantian selfhood—a capacity for choice—he declares that such a Kantian conception of personality is neutral among competing views of human personality and the human good, and even better, that such a Kantian standard is the ground to define fairness. Yet, the question is not only whether the Rawlsian parties are capable of exercising choice. It is also that, for many people, the original position is far from fair. When, in the name of principles that seek to protect a person's capacity for choice, a person's actual interests are sacrificed on the ground that those interests were morally irrelevant when the commitment for justice was made, it is clear that the zeal of the philosopher to legislate his rules and to represent all his fellow citizens has gone too far.

I suggest that the utilitarian elements of justice as fairness are already present in the original position, but they are hidden behind a veil of ignorance. In the original position, people may agree on principles that may ultimately sacrifice their projects and ends to maximize the primary goods, the greatest benefits, and the stability of society. But since the agreement on justice takes place behind a veil of ignorance and in a situation that, according to Rawls, is fair, and since, moreover, the principles of justice do not depend on any philosophical doctrine, Rawls might claim that there are no utilitarian aspects in his doctrine. Politically speaking, however, the original position is a fiction. And, in an actual society, Rawlsian justice is willing to legitimize utilitarian outcomes with a Kantian procedure.

Imagine the following scenario. After the veil of ignorance is lifted, some people find themselves as part of a minority group living in an area rich in diamonds. They discover that their religion reveres those diamonds, but that reverence is an obstacle to the goal of cooperation—a goal already settled in the original position. The religious belief is such an obstacle because the majority live in poverty, and their condition could be remedied by the sale of those diamonds to the members of neighboring communities who revere diamonds instead as commodities that give prestige to those who possess them.

What can justice as fairness do? 1) In the light of the first principle, it can leave the original group in control of the diamonds. 2) On the basis of the principle of order, it can claim that some people's liberties are limiting other people's liberties to pursue their life plans, and, therefore, it can expropriate the diamond mines to prevent the upheaval that the majority is plotting. 3) On the basis of the second principle, it can argue that a private idea of the good (in this case, a religious idea) is undermining the public structure and its capacity to provide an adequate share of primary goods so that all members of society are able to pursue their life plans. It can argue further that "justice as fairness is not at the mercy . . . of existing wants and interests" (261), and it can treat religious ideas as part of existing interests.[29]

However, neither the actual pursuit of life plans nor their actual fulfillment is an acceptable standard on which to base decisions on justice.[30] Better still, the idea of pure procedures envisions justice as arising from the operation of the two principles; in this case, the majority must accept the minority control of diamonds even if this means that their long-terms expectations will not be maximized. Rawlsian justice, after all, is compatible with large inequalities. In this scenario, society does not even face large economic inequalities; the minority that controls the diamonds also lives in poverty. The third option is thus unpersuasive in the light of justice as fairness. The second option is utilitarian; it accepts the demands and the preferences of the majority to avoid social instability. Only the first option seems to be consistent with justice as fairness. "The question of equal liberty of conscience," Rawls writes, "is settled. It is one of the fixed points of our considered judgments of justice" (206). Better still, "an individual recognizing religious and moral obligations regards them as binding absolutely in the sense that he cannot qualify his fulfillment of them for the sake of greater means for promoting his other interests" (207).[31]

Although the first option is the most consistent with justice as fairness, it is more likely that Rawlsian justice will select the second option on two grounds. First, the "liberty of conscience is limited . . . by the common interest in public order and security" (212).[32] Second, liberties can be restricted for the sake of liberty. Notice, however, that in the example under discussion the restriction of liberty is permanent. Further, if any group threatens the stability of society, the Rawlsian state is willing to invoke the preservation of liberty to limit or abolish altogether some persons' liberties. The possible Rawlsian claim that, in this example, the state is simply restricting liberty for the sake of liberty, is suspect. It is, in fact, restricting liberty for the sake of a particular group's understanding of liberty.

The centrality of order and stability informing Rawlsianism is more telling when we notice the links Rawls presupposes between order and the formal liberties protected by the first principle. Formal liberties are agreed on in the original position, and then Rawls assumes that any possible disruption of those formal liberties is an illegitimate threat to public order and security. This may explain why large inequalities are acceptable, and not even flagrant violations of the difference principle justify protests that might put in danger the order of Rawlsian institutions. Only the violation of the formal liberties defined by the first principle is "the more appropriate object of civil disobedience" (373), and Rawlsian civil disobedience is an exercise of orderly conduct aimed at strengthening public institutions.

The centrality of order and stability may lead to a state that protects formal liberties and oversees a system of large inequalities which citizens should accept for the sake of public security. This order certainly complies with Rawlsian justice but not with the considered judgments of many citizens. The marriage Rawls pronounces between liberty and order might be valid in the original position, namely, in a situation where people do not eat, do not get sick, have no need of shelter, and do not attend church. However, it does not hold up in an actual society in which, by Rawls's standards, people are authorized to protest violations of formal liberties but in which they have to put up with meager primary goods that might barely allow them to satisfy their basic needs and in which they must accept restrictions of their religious practices for the sake of an order that is antecedently justified.

Rawlsian policy makers might be inclined to explore another option: imposing a higher taxation rate on people whose lands possess exploitable natural resources. This higher rate would be applicable to all lands of the nation and therefore not discriminatory of any particular group on account of its religious beliefs. Yet suppose, as in the diamond mine example above, the only area possessing exploitable natural resources is that occupied by a religious community. Faced with this "neutral" policy, the religious group may decide either to exploit those resources to pay the new taxes or to negotiate with public officials. Thus, through this administrative and neutral process, justice as fairness would be salvaged. But this solution has a utilitarian bent: it would sacrifice the deepest religious beliefs of some individuals to maintain order and to maximize people's share of primary goods. It would forfeit religious beliefs in the name of neutral procedures aimed at promoting justice. There is, of course, another option represented by Rawls's principle of maturity: this society is not ready yet for justice.

It is, however, not necessary to resort to an assessment of the maturity principle. A different tack leads to the same conclusion, but with different justification. On the basis of Rawlsian justice, it might be argued that a contingent trait—in this case, a religious belief—should not override the goal of cooperation which was already agreed upon in a situation of fairness. The religious practice of revering diamonds can be treated as part of "the contingencies of social circumstance" (102), thereby lacking the moral precedence of principles arrived at in a situation of fairness. Better still, it could be treated as a desire or aspiration that should be discouraged by Rawlsian justice (261). The public structure, accordingly, ought to expropriate those diamonds, sell them to the neighboring communities, and distribute the social product according to the second principle of justice, thus promoting cooperation in the light of Rawlsian justice.[33]

If this is the outcome, then it is clear that the parties agreed on principles of justice whose consequences might partake of substantial utilitarian elements. In this case, the liberty of some people to practice their religious beliefs is limited in the name of cooperation or order (two goals that are declared fair in advance), which suggests that Rawls invests cooperation with a moral and fair character in the original position and then ascribes morality and fairness to all actions whose goal is cooperation. The fiction of the original position becomes a theoretical trick. The trick becomes even more loaded when we notice that, if this reading is correct, cooperation would be considered moral and fair, even before the agreement of the principles of justice, which is the basis of morality and fairness.

Thus in both utilitarianism and justice as fairness the liberties of some people to pursue their ends in life are constrained, and the integrity of their commitments is violated.[34] In utilitarianism, a utility function seeks to maximize people's satisfactions. In justice as fairness, the goal is to maximize not personal satisfactions such as those expressed in the utility function of the utilitarian paradigm, but rather institutional goods such as those expressed in mutual advantages, the greatest benefits for the most disadvantaged, their long-term expectations, primary goods, and the stability of the public order. These goods are institutional in the sense that they refer primarily to the public structure, which is the central web of institutions defining them. Note that utilitarianism seeks to maximize the interests of actual persons, whereas justice as fairness, according to Rawls, does not try to maximize the interests of anyone. Theoretically, then, utilitarianism envisions persons as possessing bodies and psychological inclinations that ought to be satisfied as far as possible. Justice as fairness sees them as possessing three abstract capacities, with justice as a means of actualizing those capacities without any regard to the satisfaction of bodily or psychological needs. By respecting those capacities, justice as fairness treats persons as autonomous individuals.

Let us return now to the claims advanced in the preceding chapter: that justice as fairness is deontology with a utilitarian bent; that it partakes of a utilitarian vocabulary that seeks to maximize institutional goods; and that this maximizing trait is placed within a Kantian straightjacket. However, if choice is the central goal of Rawlsian justice, then it is possible to see choice as a utility function, in which case the boundaries separating justice as fairness and utilitarianism are clearly porous. The former seeks to maximize not preferences but rather the conditions of those preferences: liberty and choice (the public utility function) by maximizing the means people need to exercise them: primary goods, stability, and cooperation.

Rawlsian Justice and Machiavelli's Dilemma

The utilitarian aspects of justice as fairness acquire a new dimension when they are seen against the backdrop of Rawls's views of wealth and property. Earlier I argued that Rawls moralizes inequalities via state actions hoping that large inequalities will not last in a well-ordered society.

In his discussion of the worth of political liberty, Rawls writes, "The liberties protected by the principle of participation lose much of their value whenever those who have greater private means are permitted to use their advantages to control the course of public debate. . . . Compensating steps must, then, be taken to preserve the fair value for all of the equal political liberties. . . . For example, in a society allowing private ownership of the means of production, property and wealth must be kept widely distributed and government monies provided on a regular basis to encourage free public discussion" (225). Along similar lines, when Rawls refers to the institutions responsible for policies of fair equality of opportunity, he says:

> It is these institutions that are put in jeopardy when inequalities of wealth exceed a certain limit; and political liberty likewise tends to lose its value, and representative government to become such in appearance only. The taxes and enactments of the distribution branch are to prevent this limit from being exceeded. Naturally, where this limit lies is a matter of political judgment guided by theory, good sense, and plain hunch, at least within a wide range. (278)

This is what I call the Machiavellian dilemma of Rawlsian justice. In his discussion of the causes that contributed to the preservation of the Roman republic, Machiavelli argues that social conflicts between the nobles and the people promoted the good laws and stability of the republican order.[35] But, Machiavelli warns, social conflicts are a salutary trait up to a point. If these conflicts evolve into factional struggles in which each side tries to impose its corporate interests, they are no longer the soil of virtue but the swamp of corruption.[36] The republic must keep a watchful eye on these conflicts to see when they cease contributing to the enactment of good laws and begin undermining order. This is an extremely difficult assessment to make. The boundaries separating conflicts that encourage the search for a common good and conflicts that fragment the political order into incommensurable interests are extremely precarious.

Something similar occurs in Rawls's analysis. His theory of justice requires the creation of wealth, without which there will be no way to satisfy the policies of fair equality of opportunity, not to mention the difference principle. But, as in Machiavelli's analysis, the creation of wealth in Rawlsian justice is salutary up to a limit, which, if transgressed, will bring havoc to a well-ordered society. In Rawls's views, wealth engenders inequalities that tend to erode the value of political liberty; thus arises the need for a state agency responsible for preventing the transgression of that limit (277).

How is this limit determined? As in Machiavelli's view, this very difficult assessment may require "theory, good sense, and plain hunch." The problem, however, lies not so much in the limit as in the challenge it represents to the first principle of Rawlsian justice. As far as I know, Rawls never explains how a policy that seeks to moderate inequalities through a governmental control of the level of wealth is compatible with the first principle of justice. Perhaps large economic inequalities threaten the fundamental goals of cooperation and order. This means that the priority of the first principle of justice must be seen in a light quite different from what Rawls's analysis suggests.

If my right to property makes me a mogul who may attract the envy or contempt of my fellow citizens or make them question the legitimacy of the institutions that allowed me to amass my fortune, the Rawlsian state should intervene and, presumably, reduce my fortune to a level that my fellow citizens or the Rawlsian state may find acceptable. But this necessitates that the priority of the first principle be subject to Rawls's understanding of a well-ordered society, one that accepts inequality, but not too much inequality; one that advocates my liberty to exercise my right of property, but not too much liberty.

This dilemma suggests an intriguing development. In Rawls's argument, justice is not to be assessed in the light of how individual plans fare. However, if my rational plan is too successful, if by following my life plan I become the mogul whose wealth threatens the stability of the political order, my success would cast a shadow on Rawlsian justice. The performance of my life plan is used to judge whether Rawlsian justice has met its own expectations of a well-ordered society. In other words, the psychological satisfactions people derive from the fulfillment of their life plan are irrelevant in the evaluation of Rawlsian justice; but the psychological dissatisfactions they may derive from the fulfillment of other people's successful life plans become major factors in the assessment of Rawlsian just institutions. People's dissatisfaction with my success may lead them to "withdraw into apathy and resentment" (226). The problem of envy, which is not present in the original position, is a nagging one in an actual Rawlsian society.

One could argue that the real problem is that the inequality of wealth gives power to people who might use it unjustly. In this case, a Rawlsian political order would have to wait until I use my wealth to buy a few candidates who happen to sit on the committee that oversees policies regulating my business. If Rawlsian justice waits until the power purchased by my excessive wealth becomes all too evident, it might be too late to salvage a well-ordered society.

This is, incidentally, another Machiavellian insight. When corruption has set in and become ingrained in the habits and practices of people and institutions, there is no turning back. The end of the political process is inexorable. If, on the contrary, knowing that my wealth is a potential danger to the political order, Rawlsian institutions act before my money saps the virtuous fiber of a just society, that preemptive Rawlsian action denies one of the assumptions of Rawls's psychological principles: that people deriving benefits from just institutions have a natural tendency to support those institutions; a "well-ordered society tends to eliminate or at least to control men's inclinations to injustice" (245). By acting against me, Rawlsian justice declares that, in my case, neither of those conditions obtains. The Rawlsian state would not take any risk with actual persons, finding itself comfortable only with abstract entities.

Rawlsian justice does not stand for after-the-fact actions, though. Rather, it stands for preemptive policies that prevent the accumulation of wealth, which explains the need of a distributive branch. "Its task is to preserve an approximate justice in distributive shares by means of taxation and the necessary adjustments in the rights of property. . . . [The distributive branch] imposes a number of inheritance and gift taxes, and sets restrictions on the rights of bequest. The purpose of these levies and regulations is not to raise revenue (release resources to government) but gradually and continually to correct the distribution of wealth and to prevent concentrations of power detrimental to the fair value of political liberty and fair equality of opportunity" (277).

In the same vein, "it may be better . . . to use progressive rates only when they are necessary to preserve the justice of the basic structure with respect to the first principle of justice and fair equality of opportunity, and so to forestall accumulations of property and power likely to undermine the corresponding institutions" (279). And, finally, "the aim of the branches of government is to establish a democratic regime in which land and capital are widely though not presumably equally held. Society is not so divided that one fairly small sector controls the preponderance of productive resources" (281).

The Machiavellian dilemma in Rawls's theory suggests that the value of community is stronger in justice as fairness than Rawls himself allows. Rawls writes:

> If society does not bear the costs of organization, and party funds need to be solicited from the more advantaged social and economic interests, the pleading of these groups are bound to receive excessive attention. And this is all the more likely when the less favored members of society, having been effectively prevented by their lack of means from exercising their fair degree of influence, withdraw into apathy and resentment. (226)

That is to say, economic disparities may be so large, and the corporate takeover of the political process by those who have economic power may be so overwhelming, that many people may be prevented from exercising their "fair degree of influence." The resentment that is not present in the original position may become a festering plague in an actual Rawlsian society.

Yet, the problem of alienation is completely unrelated to the first principle of Rawlsian justice. My right to vote is still there, and I am free to use it regardless of how wealthy some of my fellow citizens are. My liberty to influence the political process may be null, but then Rawlsian justice never promised a political structure whose outcomes would be neutral among citizens. Nor did Rawlsian justice promise that my fair degree of influence would give me the right to demand beneficial outcomes from the political process. Those outcomes, inevitably, are going to affect adversely some people more than others. And I am no longer a mogul, but an Emersonian or a socialist whose ideas, in any event, are found weird by the rest of mortals who share a chunk of time with me.

In a Rawlsian society, the worth of liberty, no doubt, is unequal, but Rawls's solution to this problem is economic compensation (204–5) and policies designed to maximize that worth. Rawlsian justice never promised that the value of liberty would be enhanced through a violation of the principle of equal liberties of other citizens. If, in order to maximize my worth of liberty or to overcome my sense of alienation, the Rawlsian state encroaches on the rights of some people to own property, then the priority of the first principle disappears. Rawls, however, excludes the right to own property from the first principle of justice, the principle of equal liberties. But then his system is unable to find support for that view in the common fund of beliefs he uses to buttress his conception of justice. This common fund treats the right of property as a central feature of a person's integrity.

I return to this issue in Chapter 6. Now it suffices to say that if large inequalities are to be avoided to prevent apathy and resentment and to maintain the bases of cooperation, we are again facing the problem already mentioned: people's psychological dissatisfactions with the success of others are playing a central role in the assessment of justice; but Rawls, explicitly, has excluded this ground from his system. If the Rawlsian state limits wealth to prevent my alienation and that of the other fifteen Emersonians who live on a Vermont mountain, it is not doing so for the sake of liberty, but for the sake of cooperation and order.

One may argue that cooperation is not independent of liberty. If liberty and cooperation are intertwined, then policies restricting liberty (as the liberty to revere diamonds or to amass a fortune) for the purpose of fostering cooperation are made for the sake of liberty. The same argument is then available to the utilitarian theorist, who can restrict the same liberties (to revere diamonds and to amass fortunes) on the ground that, by doing so, the utilitarian government preserves the bases of cooperation necessary for the satisfaction of the preferences of the greatest number. Thus those people who want to maintain their liberties even at the risk of lowering the satisfactions of the greatest number are threatening the stability of society as much as the mogul threatens the stability of the Rawlsian order.[37]

In the earlier example, the goal of cooperation may limit the religious freedom of people who revere diamonds. Elsewhere, the goal of equality might limit the right of property of wealthy individuals whose fortune may be found threatening by Rawlsian administrators. In both cases, the right is subordinated to a political conception of the good expressed in cooperation and equality[38] as the grounds of a strong community. Perhaps the Rawlsian argument is that the preservation of basic liberties requires a stronger sense of community, one free of resentment and one that large economic disparities would place in jeopardy. Yet, if the value of community through cooperation and equality is the central goal of Rawlsian justice, then the priority of right needs to be reformulated.[39] Community, and the value it embodies, would be the ground sustaining the first principle of justice. The right would not be prior to the good.

In a Rawlsian order, the person's right to property beyond a certain point is trampled. In the name of public order and cooperation, a person's liberty of conscience may fall victim to the political calculations of accidental majorities. Thus the lexical ordering of Rawlsian justice is not as accurate as Rawls wants it to be. The second principle is more important than the first principle; and cooperation—a goal that the second principle, more than anything else, makes possible—is more important than the right of property and a person's liberty of conscience.[40] In other words, a goal stemming from the second principle is more important than the first principle. The Machiavellian dilemma of Rawlsian theory leaves us only hunches as to which priority, after all, is still available for the principle of equal liberties.

5

Rawls's Communitarianism

> In each case, persons need one another, since it is only in active
> cooperation with others that any one's talents can be realized,
> and then in large part by the efforts of all. Only in the activities
> of social union can the individual be complete.
>
> —John Rawls, *Political Liberalism*

The discussion of the Machiavellian dilemma brought up the importance of
a strong community in a Rawlsian society. However, because most discussions
of Rawls's philosophy tend to neglect this strand of his theory, the debate between liberals and communitarians over Rawls's account of community has
been for the most part absent.[1] This chapter is an attempt to fill in that gap by
discussing the Rawlsian understanding of community as it was presented in
Theory and its possible implications for a pluralist society.[2] At the same time,
I want to take issue with one of the most influential critiques leveled against
Rawls's conception of the self, Michael Sandel's analysis of the "individuated
subject," which, in his view, underlies justice as fairness. Rawls's constructions,
so Sandel argues, rest on an unencumbered self that is individuated in advance
and whose identity is fixed once and for all.

Sandel's critique has largely gone unchallenged. Some liberals seem to accept
it (Galston 1989), others attempt to improve on Rawls's formulation (Kymlicka
1988), and still others simply ignore it (Gutmann 1985). Actually, the thrust of
liberal arguments against Sandel is consistent in avoiding a critical examina-

tion of Sandel's attack on the Rawlsian self, while confusing, in Charles Taylor's (1989) words, issues of ontology and issues of advocacy. Those arguments tend to concentrate on Sandel's vision of community, which is, in my view, the weakest part of his analysis. Here I argue that another reading of the Rawlsian self is possible. Following the hermeneutic principle that a text goes beyond its author's intentions, I attempt to reconstruct Rawls's argument along lines that, to the best of my knowledge, have been unexplored.

Rawlsian Associations; or, How the Priority of the Self Vanishes

Rawls's account of community is anchored in the goals of cooperation, stability, harmony, and transparency. *Cooperation* entails mutuality and reciprocity, which means that members of a Rawlsian community are going to share in the distribution of benefits (*Theory*, 3–6). *Stability* implies that the members' cooperation with one another is expected to extend over a complete life. *Harmony* and *transparency* mean that individual plans are complementary (563) and, more importantly, that the individual is transparent to himself to the extent that his ends cohere with each other[3]; he is transparent to others to the extent that his life plan is part of a larger social plan just as individuals, through their institutions, are part of "a social union of social unions" (527).[4]

These goals inform Rawls's vision of community which possesses what seems to be a neglected feature of Rawls's philosophy. His communitarianism does not depend upon the original position and its parties; it relies instead on his understanding of associations, institutions, and moral psychology. In all of these areas, justice is the principle that orders and regulates both the Rawlsian individual and the Rawlsian community.

Rawls conceives of associations as institutional settings that comply with the precepts of justice and provide a space for mutual recognition and appreciation of the person's abilities. Associations socialize individuals into the principles of trust and friendship, strengthen the individual's self-esteem, and provide a "secure basis" for the worth of their members (442). Associations thus are central in the Rawlsian universe since self-esteem, in Rawls's theory, is "the most important primary good" (440). To put it differently, since the good of self-esteem requires that our person and deeds be appreciated by others and since "associative ties" strengthen this aspect and "tend to reduce the likelihood of failure and to provide support against the sense of self-doubt when mishaps occur" (441), the individual's membership in associations is not an attribute but a substantial trait of his/her character.

What is important is that in his descriptions of associative ties, not only does Rawls present a picture of moral personality which is far from the unencumbered self so often ascribed to his theory, but also—and more importantly—his reasoning undermines the priority of the self over its ends (560), which seems to be one of the core elements of his conception of justice. In Rawls's account, there are three principles that I will call the principle of *mutual recognition,* the principle of *external confirmation,* and the principle of *dependence.* *Mutual recognition* means that the conviction of the worthiness of the individual's endeavors is placed, not in an unencumbered subject of possession, but in a historical individual who is guided by social standards of judgment. "Unless our endeavors are appreciated by our associates," he says, "it is impossible for us to maintain the conviction that they are worthwhile" (441). *External confirmation* means that the person's endeavors need to be confirmed by his or her associates in a community of shared interests: "what is necessary is that there should be for each person at least one community of shared interests to which he belongs and where he finds his endeavors confirmed by his associates" (442).

It is the principle of *dependence,* however, which is central to understanding the implications of Rawls's communitarianism. In Rawls's view of associative ties, the individual must obey the norms regulating his or her group. If the individual acts wrongly, Rawls argues, "he has failed to achieve the good of self-command, and he has been found unworthy of his associates upon whom he depends to confirm his sense of his own worth" (445).[5]

I suggest that these principles deny the priority of the self over its ends. First, if our endeavors—and for instance the ends they pursue and the identity they shape—must be appreciated by others, and if it is this social appreciation that determines the worth of our endeavors and ends, we are no longer prior to our ends in any meaningful sense. Those ends are determined in important ways by social (principles accepted by society) and communal (principles recognized by a "community of shared interests") standards of worthiness. Second, if the standards to confirm the individual's endeavors are provided by a community of shared interests (a claim that Rawlsian liberals tend to neglect)[6] and if the individual's confirmation of self-worth is derived from norms and criteria accepted by his or her associates, then again, the Rawlsian self is not prior to its ends. The ends I choose are determined by the approval of others.[7]

Rawls's view of associative ties thus suggests that the Rawlsian individual is not the autonomous self who, in Dworkin's description, lives life from the inside[8] and who, in Kateb's account, may be suspicious of social standards.[9] The very capacity for judgment in Rawls's individual may be compromised by membership in a community of shared interests. The individual may be unwilling to revise personal ends to maintain his associates' approval and the self-esteem that depends on it.[10] "He is apprehensive lest they reject him and find him contemptible, an object of ridicule" (445). This conception of the self shows how misleading are the fixed boundaries that are often found in liberal arguments against communitarian discourses. In open contrast to those arguments, the Rawlsian individual appears as one who needs a community that provides standards of worthiness and preservation of self-esteem; associations and communities supply "a secure basis for the sense of worth of their members" (442).

It may be argued, however, that even though Rawls's communitarianism emphasizes mutual recognition and communal standards of worthiness, he still provides enough room for the individual's judgment by insisting that, "for the purposes of justice," citizens are to "avoid any assessment of the relative value of one another's way of life" (442). But this argument is unconvincing, and Rawls's contention is short lived. He contradicts it to the extent that the individual "regards the virtues, or some of them anyway, as properties that his associates want in him and that he wants in himself" (444). If no one assesses "the relative value" of ways of life, why should we care about virtues or properties that our associates want in us? If they want certain properties as traits of our character, they are making judgments on the value of our way of life.

Thus, in the associations that Rawls describes the individual is no longer prior to his ends. Quite the contrary, those associations have their ends already and possess a clear understanding of the virtues required by them. The individual may be prior to his ends before entering an association. But once he enters it, that priority is blurred because it is the membership that strengthens self-esteem, not the other way around. If the individual is shaped by the values and attachments of the association, he has never been prior to them. They have formed his character.[11]

Psychology, Reciprocity, and
the Sense of Justice

We may have a better assessment of Rawls's view of associations by examining it against the backdrop of his principles of moral psychology. In stating those principles, Rawls abandons his original position altogether. "The acquisition of the sense of justice takes place in stages connected with the growth of knowledge and understanding. One must develop a conception of the social world and of what is just and unjust if the sentiment of justice is to be acquired" (495). In the sequence of moral development, Rawls's model assumes three stages that stress "the forming of attachments as final ends" (495).[12] These stages are: the morality of *authority*, the morality of *association*, and the morality of *principles* (462–79).

In the first stage, the child develops a relationship of love and trust with his parents, but this relationship is based on authority; hence the primitive character of the morality of authority as one in which the child does not comprehend the principles of right and justice which justify the rules to be followed. "The child does not have his own standards of criticism, since he is not in a position to reject precepts on rational grounds" (464). Parental norms, in this sense, embody a "superior knowledge and power" (465). However, even though the child may perceive the parental prohibitions as arbitrary, if he yields to temptation and fails to comply with those norms, "he will be inclined to confess his transgression and to seek reconciliation" (465). The child will experience the feeling of authority guilt.

In the second stage, the morality of association, individuals develop bonds and relationships through their membership in groups that are characterized by forms of cooperation requiring trust. In associations, individuals "are bound by ties of friendship and mutual trust" (470). Individuals acquire attachments to one another, and if one person fails to do his part, he "tends to experience feelings of (association) guilt" (470). He may be inclined to admit that what he has done is unfair and "to apologize for it" (470).

The third stage, the morality of principle, assumes that individuals develop allegiance to the principles of justice regulating their society and become attached to the highest order principles expressed in a public conception of justice (473). The morality of principles holds that if "we and those for whom we care are the beneficiaries" of just institutions, those institutions and the benefits we derive from them will "engender in us the corresponding sense of justice" (474). Accordingly, "we want to do our part in maintaining these arrangements" (474). If we betray our sense of justice, we are likely to experience "feelings of guilt by reference to the principles of justice" (474). Once we arrive at this stage, the "complete moral development has now taken place" (474).

In Rawls's view, the morality of principles is the final and highest stage in the individual's moral development. The morality of principles depends not upon our relationship with our parents or upon ties of friendship and mutual trust but upon allegiance to the principles of right. If we violate these principles, we will feel guilty not because we have harmed our parents or friends, but because we have harmed people whom we do not even know. The sense of justice, as Rawls says, "is continuous with the love of mankind" (476).

The principles of moral psychology are "reciprocity principles" (453), and justice itself is anchored in reciprocity. Justice is the capacity to answer in kind, which means that it depends on everyone's willingness to do his share. In an important way justice requires the activities of other selves to be preserved. If others do not do their fair share, their attitude may weaken our commitment to justice.[13]

Even though the principle of reciprocity is central to the acquisition of a sense of justice, it finally swallows up the Rawlsian self, which is supposed to be the only source of aims and ends (the self is prior to its ends). But the Rawlsian self develops sentiments and attachments based on the influence it experiences in its dealing with other selves. The "three laws" of moral psychology governing the development of the Rawlsian self "assert that the active sentiments of love and friendship, and even the sense of justice, arise from the manifest intention of other persons to act for our good. Because we recognize that they wish us well, we care for their well-being in return. . . . The basic idea is one of reciprocity, a tendency to answer in kind" (494). So justice does not rely on altruistic feelings, but on our expectations of a response in kind, whereby the agency of the self—a self that is supposed to be prior to its ends—becomes reactive to "the actions of others" (494). The self needs both institutions and "the actions of others" to develop a mature sense of justice.[14] How, then, can the self be prior to its ends when its sense of justice, the sense that allows it to be prior, is not prior (it follows from the actions of others)?[15]

I suggest two additional problems that are related to Rawls's notion of the priority of the self over its ends and his claim that the "essential unity of the self is already provided by the conception of right" (563). First, if a developed sense of justice requires the presence of others, the self may find that in the process of acquiring this sense of justice it also acquires other ends without ever having the priority Rawls ascribes to it. Second, if this is so, the self is not going to follow a sequence in which, first, it develops its sense of justice, and then justice provides unity to its ends. The self may be open to several overlaps in which the ends it may acquire in the process of developing its sense of justice may significantly affect the nature of that sense.

Seen from another perspective, it is possible that even assuming that the unity of the self depends upon the principles of right, those principles rely on the presence of others, and that presence—along with the associative ties that the good of self-esteem requires—may constitute a part of the individual's conception of the good. If this is so, the unity of the self, in Rawls's own terms, cannot be given by the principles of right alone. The individual's good may play an important role in defining that unity. Stated differently, the principles of right are acquired through social interactions that may become part of the self's conception of the good and which may contribute to shape its unity.[16]

To sum up: the self cannot be prior to its ends since a developed sense of justice requires the actions of others; and in order for us to value those actions we need a "common perspective" (517), which assumes communal standards of worthiness to judge our endeavors and ends. Accordingly, our sense of justice and our ends overlap in the community of shared interests where individuals confirm their worth and feel recognition. If this argument is valid, it suggests that the priority of the self over its ends either vanishes or ought to be viewed in a more complex relationship.

The Monopoly of Justice, the Human Condition, and the "Love of Mankind"

What is important, for our purposes, is that the principle of reciprocity and the Rawlsian conception of associations and institutions which it informs bring to the fore a different picture of human personality. The priority of the self which Rawls describes in Part I of *Theory* is gone. He has abandoned the mechanical view of a self that is always prior to its ends and proposes a far more complex assessment of the individual's character. "Moreover," he says, "the social system shapes the wants and aspirations that its citizens come to have" (259). "It [the social system] determines in part the sort of persons they want to be as well as the sort of persons they are" (259). This is precisely Sandel's reply to Rawls, but he does not acknowledge or fails to notice that it is already present in Rawls's own philosophy.

To put it differently, in Rawls's account of community, we do not find abstract parties and principles that are beyond any kind of contingencies. We find historical individuals who are part of a social tradition (525) and who require cooperation and social union for their completion: "it is only in active cooperation with others that one's powers reach fruition. Only in social union is the individual complete" (525). Thus, a well-ordered society is not only a social union of social unions pursuing "the good of community" (520), but also its members "have the common aim of cooperating together to realize their own and another's nature in ways allowed by the principles of justice" (527). This is a claim that expands considerably the scope of justice since a well-ordered society is not only a matter of allegiance to the principles of justice, but a communal enterprise to realize each member's nature. This vision of community suggests that the notion of pluralism underlying a Rawlsian community as described in *Theory* is not the same pluralism that characterizes actual liberal societies. In *Theory* Rawls's understanding of pluralism assumes a strong similarity of interests and values in such a way that each member is able, through a cooperation regulated by justice, to realize his own and another's nature.[17]

We are approaching an intriguing metamorphosis in Rawls's argument. What began as a conception of justice as the fundamental virtue of the basic structure of society ends up as a "social union of social unions" in which justice is the most fundamental virtue of the individual's life. "It follows," he says, "that the collective activity of justice is the preeminent form of human flourishing. For given favorable conditions, it is by maintaining these public arrangements that persons best express their nature and achieve the widest regulative excellences of which each is capable" (529).

Rawls's communitarianism turns out to rest on the monopoly that justice exercises over institutions and the individual's character (see Chapter 2).[18] This monopoly is, in fact, a central trait of the Rawlsian construction of human nature. The self's nature—and by this I mean the self's core—is not a complex of different virtues which may place different demands and conflicting claims on the individual's character. Nor is it a space of painful dilemmas. It is a uniform dimension that requires only justice to best express itself. One of Rawls's early formulations about the sense of justice may explain why justice is so central to the individual's nature. In the self's core, Rawls proposes, the foundation of our humanity is justice. Our true nature and our true self require us to be just, and if we disobey the precepts of justice, we "disfigure" ourselves. "Put another way," he said,

> one who lacks a sense of justice lacks certain fundamental attitudes and capacities included under the notion of *humanity*. Now the moral feelings are admittedly unpleasant, in some extended sense of unpleasant; but there is no way for us to avoid a liability to them without disfiguring ourselves. This liability is the price of love and trust, of friendship and affection, and of a devotion to institutions and traditions from which we have benefited and which serve the general interests of mankind.[19]

The "plurality" that Rawls's well-ordered society seeks to protect turns out to be more problematic than he suggests. The individual's attachments (associations) and aims (final ends) are plural. But the individuals who, in Rawls's account, are behind those attachments and aims are the same. They all regard justice as the regulating principle of their lives. They all aim at full cooperation over a complete life. They all realize their natures in the activities of other selves. They all belong to one or another association. I suggest that Rawls's conception of pluralism is restricted to those traits and characteristics that his account understands as external features of the self. The self's core, by contrast, conjures up an image of sameness that turns out to be the necessary requirement for the goal of harmony which Rawls relentlessly pursues.

My argument, however, is meant to propose a stronger claim than that his communitarianism undermines his pluralism. I suggest that the monopoly that justice exercises in Rawls's theory offers an impoverished vision of society. In other words, "the fact of pluralism" which Rawls rightly invokes suggests a more complex view of the ordering of the virtues in both the individual's character and in associations.[20]

Human nature is extremely complex. Through a complete life individuals may find themselves with different orderings of the moral excellences that define their character. To assume, as Rawls does, that the place of justice in the individual's character must be fixed—that it must occupy the first and foremost place—is to deny the complexities accompanying the changes of the individual's character and its quest for self-understanding. This fixity that Rawls attributes to justice in the individual's character might not be compatible with "the fact of pluralism" unless one assumes that pluralism refers not to the individual's character and its willingness to give justice an absolute priority, but to traits the individual chooses once he has accepted the primacy of justice. Such a vision of pluralism as a space of external traits surrounding, like appendages, a uniform human nature would render pluralism something quite different.

The complexity of the human condition makes it clear that human nature may require a plurality of orderings of the virtues as well as a plurality of associations, or even the absence of them, to realize itself. If we assume that individuals need a plurality of associations to realize their nature, it is likely that individuals will rank the importance of those associations on the ground of how they contribute, in their judgment, to that realization. A devout individual will certainly think that his church and the particular ordering of the virtues it presupposes are what best express his nature. Yet, a Rawlsian individual inhabiting a society regulated by justice as fairness would challenge him. Deep commitments rooted in comprehensive moral, religious, or philosophical doctrines, he might say in line with Rawls's essays after *Theory,* belong to the private sphere of individuals, not to the public sphere.[21] Those deep commitments arising from comprehensive doctrines are irrelevant, "politically speaking." Justice depends upon "intuitive ideas."

What the Rawlsian construction clearly suggests, then, is that individuals best express and realize their nature by accepting the intuitive ideas that constitute the foundation of justice and by complying with the rules of public institutions, since the primary concern of justice, allegedly, is the basic structure of society.[22] As Rawls says, "the desire to express our nature as a free and equal rational being can be fulfilled only by acting on the principles of right and justice as having first priority" (574). This is consistent with the monopoly that Rawls ascribes to justice, but it is certainly doubtful that many individuals will accept this account as representative of their character and dispositions. In other words, many individuals may disbelieve that compliance with the principles of justice and support for public institutions are more central to the best expression and realization of their nature than are their private associations and their comprehensive philosophical, moral, or religious doctrines.[23]

The centrality that justice possesses in both a Rawlsian personality and community explains Rawls's view that a genuine mature morality requires a relation, not to persons, but to institutions that embody principles of justice.[24] A genuine mature morality is thus a question of impersonal relations. This view, in Rawls's argument, is axiomatic. It is equally problematic. Many people may argue that a mature morality requires a relation to, and a concern for, people they know and care about deeply rather than people who are strangers. Rawls opposes this view and promotes instead "the love of mankind." On close scrutiny, however, this notion is nothing more that the individual's willingness to pay taxes so that public institutions will take care of distributing the social product equitably. Taxpayers will then feel that their taxes have benefited the least advantaged members of the community—members whom they do not even know. This is the epitome of a higher morality. The Rawlsian "love of mankind" and the "complete" moral development it purports to represent do not assume an immediate relation between individuals and strangers, but rather between individuals and the state; and through the state, individuals relate to strangers. The Rawlsian higher morality thus seems to be a statist conception: it needs to assume the centrality of the state as an aggregate of institutions that connect, through the distribution of social products, individuals with one another.

Replies and Counterreplies

A possible liberal reply might claim that only by accepting the priority of justice in social institutions as well as our lives do we avoid oppression and that those who invoke the complexity of human nature to dispense with that priority may be willing to engage in or defend oppressive practices. Such a reply seems unaware that Rawls himself may offer an argument to dispute it. He might leave aside his view of the development of the sense of justice and argue, in keeping with the first part of *Theory*, that the centrality of justice refers to social institutions rather than to the individual character. When those institutions are regulated by the principles of justice, he might claim, it is irrelevant whether some individuals may be prone to oppress others. A framework of rights and the distribution of the social product according to principles of justice would prevent them from carrying out their designs.

Although this response is valid from a Rawlsian perspective, I prefer to set it aside and address the reply on its own merits. I assume that most contemporary liberal theorists would not dispute the following assertion: many citizens of liberal societies do not accept the claim that justice is the virtue that best expresses their nature. In keeping with this assertion, I suggest that throughout a lifetime, a person may order and reorder the virtues orienting his or her character without thereby advocating oppression. A person may place a higher premium on love or truthfulness. That justice is not the first virtue of one's character does not imply that one advocates injustice.

In the context of institutions, Rawls claims that justice must be their first virtue. The reply I am considering asserts that without that priority we would be willing to defend oppression. From a liberal perspective, this contention ignores some pervasive conflicts arising from individual choices in the context of liberal societies. There is a conflict when a liberal discourse stands for personal and political rights and opportunities to devise a (rational) plan of life at the same time that it defends the right of individuals to participate in groups or engage in practices that, according to liberal standards, are oppressive.[25] A religious group, for example, may defend the subordination of women and hold principles that are oppressive in the light of liberalism; but individuals have the right to join that group, and the state should not interfere with their choices. Thus the priority of justice in social institutions may coexist with oppressive groups and practices provided the groups are organized and carried out on a voluntary basis.

The framework of rights and the distributive paradigm insinuate another problem more closely related to Rawls's conception of justice. Imagine a society whose social product is derived primarily from military industries. This society has a framework of rights and complies with Rawls's second principle: inequalities must benefit the most disadvantaged members of society. According to Rawls's standards, then, this society is just. In Rawls's account the strategy that creates the social product is not at stake. What is morally and politically relevant is the distribution that the strategy makes possible. Yet some people may find oppressive a society in which the moral character of its central economic activities is not deemed important in the decision of whether or not that society is just.[26] A society may become wealthier by producing and selling missiles, and its wealth may be distributed along Rawlsian principles, but the moral character of that society and its justice would be dubious. Along similar lines, a society may derive its wealth from the activities that its industries perform abroad. These industries may pay low salaries to, say, Guatemalan women or Mexican citizens, and low wages abroad may increase the profits those industries make and the taxes they pay at home. These same taxes are part of the social product that the state distributes according to Rawls's principles. Once again, the content of the practices underlying the production is irrelevant. And that society, whose social product depends on what many may consider the oppression of foreigners, would be just according to the Rawlsian paradigm.

My response to the possible liberal reply is threefold. First, the complexity of human nature may require different orderings of virtues without implying that if, for example, love replaces justice as the preeminent virtue of our character, we would be prone to oppress other persons. Second, a liberal order anchored in the priority of justice may coexist with oppressive groups and practices that ought to be tolerated in the name of individual freedom. Third, a Rawlsian society may carry out a just distribution of the social product in the light of Rawls's model, but that society may depend on strategies that some members may consider oppressive. So the claim that only by accepting the priority of justice—I take this to mean the Rawlsian conception of justice—do we avoid oppression, becomes unpersuasive.[27]

Sandel's Interpretation: A Rejoinder

My arguments thus far suggest that Rawls's analysis offers many complexities that in turn explain how one sided is Michael Sandel's critique of Rawls's paradigm. Sandel's critique concentrates on the original position and the social contract that Rawls derives from it. Yet the account of moral personality which Rawls presents in his discussion of associations, virtues, and moral psychology is conspicuously absent from Sandel's analysis.

In characterizing Rawls's view of community, Sandel argues that it "describes a possible aim of antecedently individuated selves, not an ingredient or constituent of their identity as such. This guarantees its subordinate status. . . . As a person's values and ends are always attributes and never constituents of the self, so a sense of community is only an attribute and never a constituent of a well-ordered society."[28]

Sandel's critique of Rawls's view of community relies on his understanding of the Rawlsian self—a self that, according to Sandel, is individuated in advance, whose identity cannot be engaged, and whose ends never fully constitute it. Just as these ends are external attributes that the self chooses, so also is community an external trait preceded by individuated subjects. The "Rawlsian self," Sandel says, "is not only a subject of possession, but an antecedently individuated subject, standing always at a certain distance from the interests it has. One consequence of this distance is to put the self beyond the reach of experience, to make it invulnerable, to fix its identity once and for all" (*LLJ*, 62).

This is the key to understanding Sandel's argument: his claim that the Rawlsian community presupposes "the antecedent individuation of the subject" (*LLJ*, 149) whose identity is fixed "once and for all." "But a self so thoroughly independent as this," he insists, "rules out . . . the possibility of any attachment (or obsession) able to reach beyond our values and sentiments to engage our identity itself. It rules out the possibility of a public life in which, for good or ill, the identity as well as the interests of the participants could be at stake" (*LLJ*, 62).

I believe Rawls's arguments offer a more nuanced picture than Sandel's interpretation might suggest. My discussion of Rawls's communitarianism argued that, in Rawls's theory, individuals are shaped by institutions and communities of interests, and if this is so, the "antecedent individuation" Sandel sees is not what Rawls describes. Moreover, this individuation is *one* of the moments of Rawls's philosophy concerning *one* aspect of the self, which, contrary to Sandel's claim, is not its identity.

In Rawls's view, Sandel argues, a person's identity is given in advance; it is "antecedently individuated" in such a way that it can never be reached by the self's attachments.[29] But Sandel conflates two different dimensions of the Rawlsian self. Rawls's analysis suggests a distinction between the self's *core* and the self's *identity*.[30] The former is constituted by the self's two capacities: a capacity for a sense of justice and a capacity for a conception of the good (505). The latter, the self's identity, is formed by those values, attachments, and ends that are acquired through associations and through a life plan that is formed gradually by those values that, in Sandel's view, cannot engage "our identity itself." Stated differently, it is the self's core, not its identity, which is independent of values and attachments. It is the self's core that is individuated in advance and fixed once and for all.

If my argument is correct, then the identity of individuals in the sense I have mentioned is neither prior to their ends nor incapable of being engaged and constituted by values and attachments. Quite the contrary, Rawls's account of institutions shaping the individual's attachments suggests that our identity is not beyond our values and attachments since those values and attachments help constitute it and since individuals shape their rational plans gradually (561). Once again, what is beyond our reach is the self's core and its two capacities. But how "individuated" is this core? A further exploration shows that the self's core—that is, its "moral personality"—is just a potentiality, something that is overlooked by Sandel's critique: "moral personality is here defined as a potentiality that is ordinarily realized in due course" (505). The original position relies on the potentiality of the parties. Their moral personality "refer[s] to a capacity and not to the realization of it" (509). Therefore, it is not clear why Sandel calls this potentiality an "individuated self" that not only possesses an identity but is beyond the reach of experiences and values. "Moreover," Rawls goes on, "regarding the potentiality as sufficient accords with the hypothetical nature of the original position, and with the idea that as far as possible the choice of principles should not be influenced by arbitrary contingencies" (509). In other words, this potentiality is necessary to explain the original position, not to justify a Rawlsian community.

When Rawls points out that the social system shapes the kind of persons individuals want to be and the sort of person they already are; when he insists that individuals develop the sense of justice in association with others; and, finally, when he argues that individuals need at least one community of shared interests to confirm their worth, he displaces the emphasis on a self that is always prior to its ends in favor of a community that contributes to the individual's identity.

Sandel disagrees. His critique of the Rawlsian community is predicated upon an unclarified distinction between *attributes* and *constituents*. In Rawls's view, he argues, community is an "attribute," not a "constituent." But if my argument is correct, this distinction is as doubtful as "the antecedent individuation of the subject" Sandel sees in Rawls's theory. A Rawlsian community is far from being a mere attribute. It is rather an arena of institutions, associations, and moral principles which makes possible harmony and stability and shapes the sort of persons individuals want to be and the sort of persons they already are. If the community provides standards of worthiness to judge and confirm the individual's self-esteem—the most important good—this community is constitutive of the individual's identity. Furthermore, by participating in a community of shared interests, Rawlsian individuals engage in a process of self-understanding. They come to know their nature as moral persons and, more importantly, they come to develop their sense of justice and the good of self-esteem in association with other individuals. "We need one another as partners in ways of life that are engaged in for their own sake, and the successes and enjoyments of others are necessary for and complimentary [*sic*] to our own good" (522–23).

In addition to his treatment of the Rawlsian self, a substantial part of Sandel's analysis relies on oppositions that he makes absolute without exploring the porousness of their boundaries. Thus, he opposes *attributes* to *constituents; feelings* to *self-understanding; choice* to *discovery.* In many instances, however, the boundaries separating these terms are not as sharp as Sandel leads us to believe. This is important because a substantial part of Sandel's argument is his claim that the Rawlsian self does not represent what we really are. Neither does Sandel's description. For a nonbeliever, for example, religion is an attribute he may certainly choose. But if he becomes a devout convert, the status of this attribute changes altogether. It is now a constituent, perhaps the most important one, of his identity. Likewise, if he is born into a religious fundamentalist group, religion is going to be not an attribute but a constituent of his character and identity. But if he, later in life, abandons the beliefs of his fundamentalist group and becomes indifferent to religious matters, religion as a constitutive element of his identity is transformed into an attribute from which he now exercises distance. This does not mean, of course, that his religious background and its implications are now erased from his life. This is, perhaps, impossible. It means that he has reordered the components of his identity. For all of Sandel's criticisms of a Rawlsian self whose bounds are allegedly fixed, his conception of attributes and constituents participates in the same "fixity" he ascribes to Rawls's view of the subject. Sandel does not recognize that the boundaries between attributes and constituents are porous, not fixed, whereby an attribute may become a constituent and vice versa.

The same argument holds for his distinction between choice and discovery. The same individual of the previous example may discover the attachments that tie him to his religious group. But if he decides to live by values other than those his group advocates, he is making a choice. Along the same lines, that individual may discover an attachment to his group on the basis of his socialization rather than the religious beliefs of that group. A well-known principle of Christian fundamentalist groups is that it is not sufficient to be born into a religious family. One must experience his own conversion, and this is a choice one makes, not an inherited discovery.

Just as he opposes attributes to constituents, Sandel opposes *the capacity for choice* to *the capacity for reflection* (*LLJ*, 153). He says: "But on Rawls' moral epistemology, the scope for reflection would appear seriously limited. Self-knowledge seems not to be a possibility in the relevant sense, for the bounds it would define are taken as given in advance, unreflectively, once and for all, by a principle of antecedent individuation" (*LLJ*, 153). Again, the core of Sandel's argument is his claim of an antecedent individuation. We have seen that this claim is unconvincing. But, more importantly, the opposition Sandel presents between choice and reflection is not persuasive. His argument is that the voluntarist dimension of agency requires choice; and the self, in this view, appears as external to its choices. The cognitive dimension of agency, by contrast, requires reflection. The identity of the subject appears "as the product rather than the premise of its agency" (*LLJ*, 152). Thus, the reflection Sandel proposes rules out any kind of choice. The self that is engaged in the cognitive dimension of its agency reflects upon itself, inquires "into its constituent nature" and acknowledges "its purposes as its own" (*LLJ*, 58).

There is no doubt that there is a reflection at work here. But we might distinguish between two types of reflection, which, while being active, have different goals. Let me call the first type *confirmatory reflection* and the second type *critical reflection*. In the first type, the individual reflects upon himself, his identity, his nature, to confirm and acknowledge what is already there. This reflection aims at a better self-understanding rather than a transformation or a reordering of the constituents that make him the sort of person he is. In the second type, the individual reflects upon himself, his identity, his nature, to acknowledge the attachments he wants to keep and to discard those he no longer finds relevant. In a confirmatory reflection, the individual acknowledges his identity. In a critical reflection, the individual is open to reconstitute it. Sandel's analysis, with its insistence on acknowledgment and discovery, stands for a confirmatory reflection, thus weakening his arguments. If that is the kind of reflection Sandel defends, it is better, so the liberal argument goes, to accept the unencumbered self of Rawls's philosophy, which at least provides a space for critique and distance of inherited values.

Sandel leads us to believe that in exercising reflection the individual does not exercise choice.[31] Sandel does not explore the possibility of choice *through* reflection—a reflection that allows the individual to choose new attachments, which may question the values he already has, or to discover consciously the principles that have constituted his identity.

Finally, and in keeping with a line of reasoning whose coherence seems to depend on absolute oppositions, Sandel opposes *will* to *self-understanding* (*LLJ*, 58, 152).[32] Self-understanding, presumably, does not attempt to make choices. It rather seeks a reexamination while being driven by an unexamined goal: to acknowledge ends that are already given (*LLJ*, 58) and attachments that are found (*LLJ*, 158). It is thus possible to turn Sandel's analysis against his own conceptions. He claims that the Rawlsian self is individuated in advance.

As I have argued, that is not the case with Rawls's theory, but it is what really happens with the Sandelian self. The Sandelian self is one individuated in advance by the attachments and constituents of its community. So the self does not exercise choice; it reflects upon what is already given. It does not construct attachments; it finds them. It does not use its will to choose traits that are outside it. It uses self-understanding to acknowledge what is already there in its inner dimension. Its will is confined to the inner life of the self rather than its external dimension. But even in the inner life, this will is one that acknowledges, not one that transforms. The unencumbered self is thus replaced by one so encumbered by its attachments that it seems incapable of exercising distance from them. It remains to be seen whether the Sandelian self is capable of offering a meaningful account of agency.

Conclusion

My inquiry is not meant to suggest that a Rawlsian community is free of all of the problems Sandel ascribes to it, but rather that Rawls's communitarianism suggests other problems that have not been fully explored and which require additional analyses. It is clear, however, that for all of Rawls's suspicions of the notion of society as "an organic whole with a life of its own distinct from and superior to that of all its members in their relations with one another" (264), Rawls's society resembles just that: an organic whole in which all individuals must be "fully cooperating member(s) of society over a complete life"[33]; who express their nature when complying with the dictates of only one virtue (justice); and who need the opinions of others to affirm their own worth. It is, then, a puzzle, why liberals who are sympathetic to Rawlsian tenets decry tight and close communities while holding fast to the not less tight and close vision of society of Rawls's communitarianism. Equally problematic is the realization that in the harmonious realm of a Rawlsian society there is no place for moral conflict. The individual does not face tragic dilemmas because his ends cohere with each other.[34] There are no conflicts within the individual or among individuals since all plans are part of the social plan of society.

Rawls's communitarianism as a utopia of harmony, cooperation, and a uniform human nature that best expresses itself by following the dictates of justice is a departure from Kant's vision of society. Kant envisions antagonisms as the cause of human progress and proposes the famous analogy of the forest.[35] Without competition, he argues, trees would grow feeble and bent; with conflicts, they will grow straight. Without antagonisms, Kant goes on, men would live an Arcadian and pastoral life. Rawls's account of community clearly suggests that he prefers the Arcadian life Kant rejects to the antagonisms he praises. The end result is thus a striking surprise: Rawls's communitarianism and its goal of harmony turn out to be not Kantian, but similar to the Platonic view of the relationship between the individual and the city.[36] Just as, in Plato, the individual's character must be in harmony, and this harmony is reflected in the state,[37] so also with Rawls's account: the harmony ruling the individual's plurality of ends finds its way in a social order where individual plans are part of a larger plan and where individuals are part of associations that in turn constitute a social union of social unions. Hence, there is harmony both in the individual's character and in society.

This picture seems to be at variance with Rawls's redescription of his project as political. And so it is. In his political version, the emphasis is no longer on strong communitarian bonds, and the priority of the right over the good, which was already compromised in his account of the principles of moral psychology, is eroded even further. But his view of justice as the regulating virtue of a person's character remains intact.

6

What Is Political about
Rawls's Political Liberalism

> In a well-governed state only a small fraction of persons may
> devote much of their time to politics. There are many other
> forms of human good. But this fraction, whatever its size, will
> most likely be drawn more or less equally from all sectors of
> society.
>
> —John Rawls, *A Theory of Justice*

Today, any student of Rawlsian philosophy might be struck by the political metamorphoses of Rawls's theory of justice. A reasonable perception is that Rawlsianism has become a moving target running for cover in political categories. Also supported by Rawls's texts is the claim that whenever a critic raises an important objection, Rawls attempts to circumvent it by ascribing a political character to the main features of his paradigm. The original position, for instance, is now a device of representation. The parties are not metaphysical creatures, but representatives of democratic citizens. Autonomy is no longer an ethical value, but a political one. The psychological "laws" governing the acquisition of the Rawlsian sense of justice are not psychological, but political.

In other words, the same paradigm that tried, at all costs, to go beyond contingent attributes to find an Archimedean point is now invoking politics—the very embodiment of contingency—to justify its theoretical enterprise. Contingency itself has experienced its own metamorphosis: it is no longer an arena from which one escapes, but a refuge to which one flees. What is political about political liberalism?

Chantal Mouffe has argued that Rawls's liberalism rejects "any possible idea of a common good" and entails the negation of politics.[1] Bonnie Honig claims that Rawlsian justice displaces politics with administration and reduces politics to technique.[2] William Connolly holds that liberalism is tied to a juridical vision of politics.[3] In this chapter I wish to discuss the political character of Rawls's views by examining his understanding of political liberalism.

Accounts of Politics and the Displacements of Rawlsian Justice

Let me present some understandings of politics to see what is the conception of politics, if any, underlying Rawlsian liberalism. Politics can be understood as:

1. a system of rules to realize the good of justice where justice is understood as the distribution of goods according to fair procedures;

2. the quest for, and the institutionalization of, common goods;

3. a practice that defines and encourages the quest for a public understanding of the human good;

4. the pursuit of glory (Machiavelli);

5. the pursuit of order (Hobbes);

6. the teaching of the virtues for the sake of the individual's character;

7. the teaching of the virtues for the sake of the public structure;

8. participation to realize the good of community (Dewey);

9. participation for its own sake;

10. the creation of state power;

11. a system of principles to address and, if possible, to solve conflicts;

12. a system of principles to avoid conflicts (conflicts that might threaten the stability of the political order are shunned);

13. a system of principles to accommodate different conceptions of the human good;

14. an arena of conflicting vocabularies where consensus is impossible (Lyotard).

Using these accounts of politics as a background, let us examine Rawls's view of political liberalism.

Rawls understands his political liberalism as a doctrine whose central goal is to make possible an agreement on a political conception of justice.[4] A political conception of justice is understood to be independent of comprehensive religious, moral, or philosophical doctrines.[5] The foundations of political justice lie in "intuitive ideas" that are dissociated from comprehensive religious, moral, or philosophical doctrines and which are found in the political culture of democratic societies. I assume that Rawls would not deny that these intuitive ideas, in their origins, could have been part of a larger religious, moral, or philosophical universe. But he might well argue that even were that the case, through a long process of historical maturation those ideas are completely independent of their comprehensive roots. They are now so embedded in the political culture of democratic societies that reasonable people can accept them as the starting point in the quest for an agreement on political justice.

A political conception of justice does not seek to reflect a truth metaphysically or philosophically conceived. Its goal is to provide a workable agreement by displaying what Rawls calls a "method of avoidance"[6]: political justice seeks, purposefully, to avoid the deep metaphysical questions that are part of a plural society and which are bound to remain so as a permanent feature of a modernity characterized by incommensurable and conflicting visions of the good. Rawls is at pains to show that although political justice is a working agreement, a kind of pragmatic solution to the diversity of modern societies, it does not follow that it is a modus vivendi justified or supported by prudential reasons.

Political justice is a moral conception[7] that is the end result of an overlapping consensus among reasonable religious, moral, or philosophical conceptions. A modus vivendi suggests a unstable truce among tired combatants who stop the fight to plot a better strategy against their enemies or to wait for a better opportunity to destroy them. Their reasons for supporting the truce are entirely prudential and based on self-interest, justified from their own perspective, but not necessarily from that of their opponents. Political justice, however, attempts to be a stable agreement among persons who are committed to being fully cooperating members of society over a complete life, who perceive their society as existing in perpetuity, and who see justice as settled once and for all. The reasons to justify political justice also contain an element of self-interest represented by the mutual advantages Rawlsian justice offers to the members of a "well-ordered" society, but they are moral reasons to the extent that they transcend the narrow scope of self-interest and propose a society in which culture and civilization will be preserved and advanced (285). Equally important, they are reasons to which reasonable people can assent.

A political conception of justice is politically neutral in the sense that it accommodates a variety of human flourishings and visions of the good compatible with justice, but it is not morally neutral. It is predicated upon two intuitive ideas that are morally partisan: 1) society as a fair system of cooperation, and 2) persons as free and equal.[8]

Before proceeding, it is perhaps worth noticing several modifications that Rawls's political liberalism has introduced into the original version of Rawlsian justice. First, in *Theory* Rawls stated, without arguing: "Being first virtues of human activities, truth and justice are uncompromising" (4). Likewise, the principles of justice were agreed upon on the basis of "true general beliefs about men and their place in society." As Rawls argued, "since principles are consented to in the light of true general beliefs about men and their place in society, the conception of justice adopted is acceptable on the basis of these facts" (454). The reader may notice that Rawls equates "true general beliefs about men and their place in society" with "facts." In political liberalism, however, the agreement is based not on truth, but on a working agreement that is validated by contingency, namely, by the shared fund of beliefs found in a democratic society. In political liberalism, truth is no longer an issue; what is really crucial is whether a political arrangement is workable.

Second, in Rawls's arguments in *Theory*, justice was based on rational choice (16). In political liberalism, justice depends on the political culture of a democratic society.[9]

Third, in *Theory*, Rawls was suspicious of common sense as a foundation for justice. Common sense was too precarious a ground upon which to base principles of justice, and he held that it was necessary to go behind common sense. "Moreover," he said, "it is essential to keep in mind the subordinate place of common sense norms. Doing this is sometimes difficult because they are familiar from everyday life and therefore they are likely to have a prominence in our thinking that their derivative status does not justify. None of these precepts can be plausibly raised to a first principle. . . . Common sense precepts are at the wrong level of generality. In order to find suitable first principles one must step behind them" (307, 308).

In "Justice as Fairness" Rawls is no longer behind common sense. He is instead digging into the political culture searching for intuitive ideas that can be organized into a coherent vision of justice. Thus, in his political liberalism, Rawls has apparently abandoned his qualms about common sense. The justification of political justice now depends on it. "As we have said," Rawls declares, "on matters of constitutional essentials and basic justice, the basic structure and its public policies are to be justifiable to all citizens, as the principle of political legitimacy requires. We add to this that in making these justifications we are to appeal only to presently accepted general beliefs and forms of reasoning found in common sense, and the methods and conclusions of science when these are not controversial."[10]

Fourth, in *Theory*, the parties were noumenal selves acting from a situation of independence (255). They are still independent of some contingent traits, but they now know that they are representatives of democratic citizens.[11]

Fifth, along similar lines, in the first version of Rawlsian justice the parties lacked knowledge of the generation to which they belonged. Now at least they know that their generation is a democratic one.

Sixth, the major conflicts that Rawls suggests in *Theory* arise from unequal distributive shares; in his political liberalism the only conflicts he addresses are those arising from different conceptions of the human good.

Seventh, in "Justice as Fairness" Rawls espoused an agreement among different comprehensive doctrines. In his latest version he has restricted this agreement to one among *reasonable* religious, moral, and philosophical outlooks.

Two of the most striking displacements in the transition from the arguments in *Theory* to Rawls's political liberalism refer to the status of the psychological laws justifying the stability of the Rawlsian order and the place of autonomy within justice as fairness. In *Theory* the psychological laws were seen as "true, or approximately so" (502). Rawlsian psychology was understood as natural[12] and as part of the facts about the world: "I have assumed that general facts about the world, including basic psychological principles, are known to the persons in the original position and relied upon by them in making their decisions" (456). Now the psychological laws are no longer true but philosophical. As he writes: "It is not a psychology originating in the science of human nature but rather a scheme of concepts and principles for expressing a certain political conception of the person and an ideal of citizenship."[13]

In *Theory* autonomy was a moral value informing a person's whole character, so much so that moral education was education for autonomy. Now, autonomy is envisioned as a political aspect of a person's public identity.[14]

Finally, in "The Basic Structure as Subject" and the "Dewey Lectures" Rawls argued that a person's "highest interest" was to exercise his capacity for justice. Moral persons, Rawls argued, "regard themselves as having a highest-order interest in regulating all their other interests, even their fundamental ones, by reason, that is, by rational and reasonable principles that are expressive of their autonomy."[15]

The only principles that, at that time, Rawls considered expressive of persons' autonomy were his two principles of justice.[16] In "Social Unity" and "Justice as Fairness" he dropped all references to a highest interest and wrote in the latter, in a footnote, about persons' "higher-order interest."[17] To the best of my knowledge, nowhere has Rawls explained why justice is no longer the highest interest but is instead on a par with conceptions of the good; persons now have a higher order interest in exercising both their capacity for a sense of justice and their capacity for a conception of the good. And he might accept the argument that his principles of justice may be completely irrelevant in the private domain of citizens.

Another metamorphosis pertains to the status of the first principle of justice in the evolution of Rawls's political thought. As far as I know, in *Theory* Rawls makes no claim that the first principle of justice—the principle of equal liberty—is settled once and for all. Quite the contrary, and paradoxically, the emphasis in *Theory* is on how Rawlsian public justice depends on the social conditions of a historical setting (152, 542). And so the lexical ordering of the two principles is subject to hospitable circumstances. In the political version, however, the status of equal liberty is set—that is, in his most metaphysical expression, namely, in his arguments in *Theory*, Rawlsian justice was sensitive to the force of contingency; in his political expression, contingency is excluded from the evaluation of the first principle, which is declared settled.

Here is the evolution of the status of the first principle of justice. In *Theory* this principle was exposed to material and historical circumstances. To the best of my knowledge, the only aspect of the first principle which was settled was liberty of conscience (206). In "Justice as Fairness" Rawls perceives the convictions that serve as grounds for the first principle to be "provisional fixed points." "We collect such settled convictions as the belief in religious toleration and the rejection of slavery and try to organize the basic ideas and principles implicit in these convictions into a coherent conception of justice. We can regard these convictions as provisional fixed points which any conception of justice must account for if it is to be reasonable for us."[18] In "Overlapping Consensus," however, Rawls announced, in a footnote, that the provisional fixed points had become established permanently. "In regard to equal liberty of conscience and rejection of slavery and serfdom," Rawls wrote, "this means that the equal basic liberties in the constitution that cover these matters are taken as fixed, settled once and for all."[19]

Before summarizing the major displacements in Rawls's arguments, it is worth noticing a puzzling aspect of his theory which, for reasons still unexplained, has not kept pace with the political transformation of Rawlsian justice. The priority of liberty which Rawls defended in *Theory* did not assume the centrality of property rights of the means of production. As he pointed out in "A Well-ordered Society," "liberties not on the list, for example, the right to own certain kinds of property (e.g., means of production), and freedom of contract as understood by the doctrine of laissez-faire, are not basic; and so they are not protected by the priority of the first principle."[20] One might reasonably expect that Rawls would have abandoned this view in the light of the grounds he uses to articulate his political liberalism. In other words, since Rawlsian political liberalism is based on the "settled convictions" of the political culture of the United States and its public traditions of interpretations, it is not possible to claim that property rights have not been central in the formation and development of that political culture, that the right to own the means of production and natural resources is not part of the settled convictions of the American society.

Intriguingly, Rawls still claims that property rights governing the ownership of means of production and natural resources are not included in the basic liberties.[21] It is clear, however, that he cannot invoke the political culture of the United States to derive his principles of justice and then suggest that in that culture the right to own means of production has not been preeminent. Notice that the argument is not whether Rawls is correct in his claim that the right to own the means of production and natural resources is not central to people exercising their two moral powers. The real issue is whether he can justify that exclusion in the light of the political culture he uses to support his view of justice (see Table 6.1).

In developing his political liberalism, Rawls engages in what might be termed a *hermeneutic* and *archaeological* enterprise. He does not claim to "discover" principles from nowhere; rather, his project is to bring to the surface ideas that are already in the political culture, in the funds of shared beliefs which sustain a common life in a democratic society. This is the archaeology. As he says, "We look, then, to our public political culture itself, including its main institutions and the historical traditions of their interpretation, as the shared fund of implicitly recognized basic ideas and principles."[22] Since his project is to find "a public basis of political agreement," "a conception of justice will only be able to achieve this aim if it provides a reasonable way of shaping into one coherent view the deeper bases of agreement embedded in the public political culture of a constitutional regime and acceptable to its most firmly held considered convictions."[23]

Once those bases of agreement are identified and unearthed, Rawls proceeds hermeneutically to articulate them into a political argument that presents what he considers a better alternative to existing practices and agreements. His argument suggests that even if existing agreements and practices are based on the same intuitive ideas as his, those ideas can lead to other unexplored possibili-

Table 6.1

Major displacements in transition from arguments advanced in *Theory*
to Rawls's views of political liberalism

Arguments presented *in* Theory	Arguments defining Rawls's political liberalism
Justice is based on rational choice.	Justice depends on the political culture of a democratic society.
Justice relies on "true" beliefs about men and their place in society.	Justice relies on intuitive ideas that are not true but workable.
Conflicts arise from unequal distributive shares.	Conflicts arise from incommensurable visions of the human good.
Parties are noumenal selves.	Parties are representatives of democratic citizens.
There is no place for common-sense notions in the elaboration of justice.	Common-sense notions play an important role.
Psychological laws are true.	Psychological laws are not true but philosophical.
Moral education is education for autonomy encompassing the individual's whole character.	Autonomy is seen as a political value, not an ethical ideal.
Parties have a highest interest in exercising their capacity for justice.	Parties have a higher interest in exercising their two capacities.

ties. They present a better picture of ourselves through just institutions that express the common good. He understands the common good as "certain general conditions that are in an appropriate sense equally to everyone's advantage" (246). The operation of the two principles of justice seeks, precisely, to contribute to the general advantage (158).

In its effort to articulate an agreement on the basis of existing values, Rawlsian justice seeks to settle questions of justice once and for all, an attempt that may deny Rawls's hermeneutic method of resorting to history and culture—the realm of contingency. But not necessarily. Contingency is neither destiny nor the abolition of human will. Even if the human condition is fragile, it does not follow that citizens are going to adopt a Greek notion of destiny and leave their institutions and values exposed to any assault that may come their way. Even well-known believers in the inevitability of decay, as Machiavelli was, attempted to arrest the tendency toward decay by cultivating civic virtues and invigorating public institutions.

Rawls is not a believer in historical necessity, but he is extremely aware of the dangers that contingency poses to his version of Kantian justice. Indeed, Rawlsian justice can be read as a deliberate effort to keep contingency at bay. Hence the original position; the exclusion of desert based on talents—which are part of the natural lottery and, accordingly, morally irrelevant in Rawls's view—and the establishment of perpetual constitutional essentials that seek to prevent, for example, the reemergence of slavery or religious wars. A Rawlsian society might well collapse, and new ways of enslavement might appear. As Sartre would say: "Tomorrow, Nazism will be the truth of man." But if something that unsettling were to happen, it would not be due to a lack of constitutional provision or to a Rawlsian willingness to accept Richard Rorty's liberal utopia where anything goes or to a tolerance of William Connolly's politics of paradox in which nothing (slavery, presumably, included) is settled. A pragmatist such as John Dewey would not oppose the construction of guardrails to sustain society. In my understanding of hermeneutics,[24] engaging in a contingent and interpretive journey neither denies nor invalidates the (prudential, perhaps; moral, more likely) virtue of foresight. Contingency and foresight are compatible.

Once justice as fairness is articulated, it goes to the public arena where it can be accepted as the end result of an overlapping consensus among reasonable moral, religious, or philosophical doctrines. It is worth noticing, in this regard, another important modification of Rawls's first version of an overlapping consensus.

In "Overlapping Consensus" Rawls implied that comprehensive doctrines had to be excluded from public deliberation. In the "Dewey Lectures" he proposed a distinction between the public and the private spheres of people's identity according to which comprehensive doctrines were allowed to reign supreme in one's private dimension as long as those doctrines were compatible with justice. In the public arena citizens were expected to invoke political values, which in Rawls's understanding of politics, are completely disconnected from comprehensive doctrines.

In his latest version, *Political Liberalism,* Rawls confines this rule of exclusion to what he calls *constitutional essentials,* the liberties enshrined in his first principle of justice. The second principle is still considered basic but is not part of the constitutional essentials. The end result is that—as a Hobbesian subject who is free to follow his judgment in all those areas in which the law is silent—Rawlsian citizens and legislators are free to speak their minds and invoke their comprehensive doctrines in public deliberations in all those areas that do not involve constitutional essentials. "Citizens and legislators," Rawls writes, "may properly vote their more comprehensive views when constitutional essentials and basic justice are not at stake; they need not justify by public reason why they vote as they do or make their grounds consistent and fit them into a coherent constitutional view over the whole range of their decisions."[25]

Rawlsian Justice and the Public Sphere

Let us now explore Rawls's political liberalism in the light of his view of moral personality and his claim that political liberalism is different from comprehensive doctrines as well as from those that are perfectionist, teleological, and utilitarian.

Rawlsian moral personality may be more understandable within the context of two major moments that appear in his philosophy. One is the moment of plurality and diversity, the moment in which Rawls stresses "the fact of pluralism" in modern democratic societies. The other is the moment of social unity, social concord, and stability. Both moments are in tension against each other, but I believe that the moment of unity has become Rawls's favorite. Indeed, all of his philosophical constructions can be read as an effort at social harmony as well as a theoretical drive to soften and, if possible, abolish the divisiveness of modernity. Even in his discussion of civil disobedience, Rawls asks dissenting minorities not to overburden the state by pressing claims it cannot address simultaneously.

The ideal toward which Rawls seems to strive is a society that substitutes social unity for dissention and social harmony for instability. These are the central goals of his politics. William Galston was right when several years ago he identified the unitarian and harmonious thread underlying Rawls's philosophy. "Specifically," Galston wrote, "Rawls believes in the possibility of a recognizably liberal society (and theory) in which all significant internal tensions have been overcome."[26]

From another perspective, the two moments of the Rawlsian philosophy can be understood as a conflict between the private and the public realms. The two powers of Rawls's moral personality—a capacity for a sense of justice and a capacity to form, to revise, and rationally pursue a conception of the good—are the foundations of the distinction between the public and private realms. The first power is meant to bring about a public agreement on justice; the second power is meant to define the individual's private identity. The private sphere, as the locus of conceptions of the good, is thus the realm of pluralism par excellence and hence a terrain of divisiveness and instability. The public sphere, by contrast, is the stage of consensus, the locus of stability, equilibrium, and agreement.[27]

The tensions between these two spheres might explain why Rawls invokes "the fact of pluralism" in the private sphere to justify his exclusion of comprehensive doctrines in the public one. In his view, comprehensive doctrines, whether fully or partially comprehensive, are relegated to the sphere of private subjectivity, where they might reign supreme. In the public realm, however, the quest for an overlapping consensus is the overriding concern. Rawls then proposes a divide between the public identity of individuals and their private subjectivity, their "personal affairs."[28] He suggests that their public identity requires citizens to see themselves "as free persons" with "the right to view their persons as independent and not identified with any particular system of ends."[29] In the private domain of "their personal affairs or within the internal life of associations," by contrast, citizens "may regard their ends and aspirations differently."[30] *Differently* means that they have attachments and commitments from which they cannot stand apart. In other words, in the private domain, citizens need not view themselves as independent of their final ends, whereas in the public sphere they must do so.[31] Hence a self becomes divided between the attachments of its private realm and the rules of its public one. The exclusion of comprehensive doctrines thus suggests a twofold independence for the individual: that from his final ends (his willingness to revise them) and that from his comprehensive doctrines (his willingness to exclude them in the public domain in order to arrive at a public consensus on justice).

I propose a hypothesis to account for the Rawlsian exclusion of comprehensive doctrines from public deliberations on justice. In his articles after *Theory*, Rawls has shifted the argument from the original position to the public realm of democratic societies. Now the parties of the original position have been replaced by citizens in search of an overlapping consensus. But the shadow of the original position looms large in Rawls's politics, and in both cases we have the red thread that defines his project: the exclusion of contingent traits to preserve contingent institutions that are conceived in perpetuity. This is the cornerstone upon which his effort at social harmony is built. And in Rawls's view, conceptions of the good are contingent attributes and, for that very reason, morally irrelevant. "That we have one conception of the good rather than another is not relevant from a moral standpoint. In acquiring it we are influenced by the same sort of contingencies that lead us to rule out [in the original position] a knowledge of our sex and class."[32] This explains why those conceptions are excluded from both the original position when the parties deliberate about justice and from the political realm when citizens seek an overlapping consensus on a political conception of justice.

Rawls conceives of the political as a space that ought to be free, as far as possible, of contingent attributes. Rawlsian political selves possess knowledge of their philosophical and moral beliefs, but they do not use it in the political sphere. Instead, this knowledge will be located in the private sphere where subjectivity reigns. The original position thus carries the day: the citizens of Rawls's overlapping consensus are modeled after the parties of the veil of ignorance, and the "fact of pluralism" is muted. It is rendered a "safe" fact to the extent that it is cornered into the private domain of individuals just as, in the original position, the parties' historicity is placed outside their reach.

This is an unmistaken trait of Rawls's philosophy: his philosophical method always abolishes tensions by placing them outside the sphere of deliberation. The end result betrays Rawls's conception of pluralism, with the parties or the citizens displaying a disturbing sameness. The parties in the original positions are *one* person, and the same holds true of the citizens of his overlapping consensus. They are defined by intuitive ideas that are settled convictions upon which everyone agrees; therefore, the citizens are also uniform embodiments of these ideas and convictions. They are not plural; they are the same.[33]

The Rawlsian construction of a public identity as a locus of intuitive ideas is thus difficult to understand, although it fits perfectly into Rawls's own categories. Social cooperation requires neat boundaries between the private and public dimensions of the individual's identity. And to justify his claims Rawls invokes the ghost of a not so remote era of religious conflicts.[34] He reminds us that "justice as fairness tries to construct a conception of justice that takes deep and unresolvable differences on matters of fundamental significance as a permanent condition of human life."[35] Yet—and faithful to his method—these unresolvable differences are ignored in the foundational act that establishes a consensus on justice. It is worth repeating that, as Rawls's latest version of political liberalism suggests, comprehensive doctrines are only excluded from the justification of constitutional essentials.

Rawls's paradigm thus invokes a "political liberalism" that is self-justified.

Rawlsian justice guarantees social unity to the extent that its premises are justified in advance. In other words, the political conception of justice defines what are just institutions, and citizens can evaluate such institutions "by citing what are recognized among them as valid and sufficient reasons singled out by that conception itself."[36] But we are in front of a circle, and it is not surprising that within the circular reasoning provided by that conception citizens will always arrive at an enduring consensus, thus securing "stability" and a "long-run equilibrium."[37]

More than circular reasoning is afoot here. As I discussed in Chapter 5, Rawls seeks a harmonious private personality with final ends cohering between each other, and the harmony of the Rawlsian private personality eventually finds expression in a harmonious public realm. Rawls's conception of private personality corresponds to his vision of the public domain. Both are predicated upon harmony, which may explain his understanding of the public sphere as a space from which divisive issues have been removed. He says:

> We appeal to a political conception of justice to distinguish between those questions that can be reasonably removed from the political agenda and those that cannot, all the while aiming for an overlapping consensus. Some questions still on the agenda will be controversial, at least to some degree; this is normal with political issues.
>
> Faced with the fact of pluralism, a liberal view removes from the political agenda the most divisive issues, pervasive uncertainty and serious contention about which must undermine the bases of social cooperation.[38]

This second statement is baffling and seems to strengthen Mouffe's contention that Rawls's paradigm represents the abolition of politics. I believe she is incorrect in her argument, but, to be sure, one must wonder what merit, if any, has a political conception whose capacity to reach a consensus depends on the exclusion of divisive issues.

Political Liberalism as a Comprehensive Doctrine

My hypothesis is that although Rawls distinguishes his political liberalism from both comprehensive doctrines and perfectionist, teleological, and utilitarian claims, he creates a paradigm that, by his own standards, is similar to a comprehensive doctrine as well as a political liberalism that possesses important traits of perfectionism and teleology.

Rawls's argument distinguishes between the claims of a *political* understanding of liberalism—the claim he endorses—and a *comprehensive* doctrine of liberalism—a claim he rejects. The latter, in his view, would impose a conception of the good over citizens, whereas a political understanding of liberalism would not.

Rawls illustrates the crucial difference between a comprehensive doctrine of liberalism and his own version of political liberalism by discussing the duties of a religious sect that lives in a liberal community but nevertheless rejects its values. Although the state should not impose a conception of the good over the members of that religious group, its children, Rawls claims, should be educated "to be fully cooperating members of society and . . . to be self-supporting."[39] In other words, members of religious groups that reject the values of a Rawlsian society are expected to accept the principles of justice informing that society and to be "fully cooperating members." It is possible to argue, in this regard, that this requirement of full cooperation is something more than an allegiance to the principles of justice. Full cooperation may entail accepting the social plan and goals of that society. If this is so, the option of withdrawal is not available to those individuals, Rawls's claims to the contrary notwithstanding.

Equally important, the children of those religious groups should be educated in the constitutional principles of the community, even though "justice as fairness does not seek to cultivate the distinctive virtues and values of the liberalisms of autonomy and individuality, or indeed of any other comprehensive doctrine. For in that case it would cease to be a form of political liberalism."[40] Nevertheless, Rawls goes on: "Justice as fairness honors, as far as it can, the claims of those who wish to withdraw from the modern world in accordance with the injunctions of their religion, provided only that they acknowledge the principles of the political conception of justice and appreciate its political ideals of person and society."[41]

There are two problems with Rawls's formulation. First, Rawls presupposes a consensus in a democratic culture as to the "ideals of person and society." That is hardly so. One must wonder, for instance, what kind of space would be available for the sort of community defended by Alasdair MacIntyre, a community that not only questions the validity of liberal ideals of individuals and society but also tries to bring about an alternative model of both.[42]

Second, and more importantly, it is not clear what the difference is between *cultivating* the values of autonomy and individuality (which Rawls does not ascribe to his political liberalism) and *acknowledging and appreciating* "the principles of the political conception of justice and . . . its political ideals of person and society" (which he does support). The boundaries between these requirements are tenuous. To put it differently, if the political ideals of persons and society in Rawls's conception of justice defend both autonomy and individuality, then acknowledging and appreciating those ideals are not substantially different from advocating and cultivating the values they presuppose, namely autonomy and individuality. If people should be educated in the principles of justice, is that not cultivating the values of autonomy and individuality which the principles of justice seek to nurture? It is difficult to find convincing explanations of Rawls's distinction between cultivating values and acknowledging them. If we want to acknowledge the moral character of some values we need to satisfy a previous condition: being educated in a way that leads us to appreciate those values.

Rawls considers the liberalisms of Kant and Mill as comprehensive doctrines, and the reasons he offers to reject them can be used as the standards to judge his own theory. Rawls excludes these liberalisms on the grounds that "they are both general and comprehensive moral doctrines: general in that they apply to a wide range of subjects, and comprehensive in that they include conceptions of what is of value in human life, ideals of personal virtue and character that are to inform our thought and conduct as a whole."[43]

Since these are the criteria distinguishing a comprehensive doctrine, the question we must explore is whether Rawls's political liberalism differs from them. His text suggests that it does not. Indeed, Rawls's political liberalism turns out to be another comprehensive conception disguised as a political one. It, too, "includes conceptions of what is of value in human life, ideals of personal virtue and character that are to inform our thought and conduct as a whole." Let us explore why.

First, consider *"what is of value in human life."* For the Rawlsian individual it is to hold a higher order interest, which is justice; to construct and pursue a rational plan; to have the possibility of revising it; and to possess a plurality of final ends.

Second, consider the *"ideals of personal virtue and character that are to inform our thought and conduct as a whole."* The Rawlsian individual is expected to respect rights, to be tolerant, to have a sense of fairness, to be self-supporting, and to be a fully cooperating member of society over a complete life.[44]

These features are virtues of a comprehensive philosophical doctrine—or at least as comprehensive as the definition Rawls offers of the liberalisms of Kant and Mill. Equally important, the higher order of justice is meant to be "supremely regulative as well as effective" in governing "deliberation and conduct."[45] There is no doubt that, in Rawls's account, the principles of justice imply an "ideal of personal virtue and character" which informs "our thought and conduct as a whole"; so much so that in *Theory* Rawls even said that individuals "best express their nature and achieve the widest regulative excellences of which each is capable" (529) when they follow the principles of justice and affirm the institutions embodying them. The outcome is that the boundaries separating the Rawlsian construct from a comprehensive doctrine become more and more blurred. Actually, Rawls says that the political conception of justice "is itself a moral conception," one that "is affirmed on moral grounds, that is, it includes conceptions of society and of citizens as persons, as well as principles of justice, and an account of the cooperative virtues through which those principles are embodied in human character and expressed in public life."[46]

This formulation perhaps provides us with a better sense of Rawls's philosophical method, which begins by Rawls offering definitions of opposite alternatives in such a way as to make them unacceptable for a democratic society, "given the fact of pluralism." That is the case, for example, with his definition of a *comprehensive philosophical doctrine*. Then he presents a sharp divide between those opposite stances and his model of justice as fairness. Having defined his possible interlocutors and distanced himself from them, he introduces elements of comprehensive doctrines into his own paradigm while assuming that the initial boundaries are intact. That is the case, I think, with the citation just quoted. Rawls's statement suggests that his political conception of justice includes 1) a conception of society and persons; 2) a notion of cooperative virtues; and 3) principles of justice which are embodied in human character and in public life. I suggest then that his political conception includes the same criteria—or at least a substantial part of the same principles—underlying the liberalisms of Kant and Mill: "ideals of personal virtue and character that are to inform our thought and conduct as a whole."

I do not intend for my argument to deny possible differences between the liberalism of Rawlsianism and those of Kant and Mill. Nor is it meant to underestimate the lengths to which Rawls has gone to distance his positions from views that might be divisive and thus disruptive of a potential agreement on justice. In the "Dewey Lectures," for instance, Rawls explicitly presented his view on what he later termed a *comprehensive doctrine*. In justice as fairness, he argued, citizens are supposed to be guided by "an executive and regulative highest-order desire to act from certain principles of justice in view of their connection with a conception of the person as free and equal."[47] This desire, which is "regulative and effective," is "to be a certain kind of person specified by the conception of fully autonomous citizens of a well-ordered society."[48] He wrote:

a moral conception assumes a wide role as part of public culture. Not only are its first principles embodied in political and social institutions and public traditions of their interpretation, but the derivation of citizens' rights, liberties, and opportunities invokes a certain conception of their person. In this way citizens are made aware of and educated to this conception.[49]

Rawls's argument thus suggested a comprehensive view where the value of autonomy was conceived as the dominant value defining the individual's identity. In his later work,[50] however, he clarified that political justice does not seek to promote any value associated with a comprehensive liberal doctrine. So his theory does not seek to promote autonomous Kantian or Millian citizens. However, the interest he presented in *Theory*—namely, in placing certain bounds "upon what is good," upon "what forms of character are morally worthy and so upon what kinds of persons men should be" (32)—is still present. Thus, in "Overlapping Consensus," he writes, "The focus of a political conception of justice is the framework of basic institutions and the principles, standards and precepts that apply to them, as well as how those norms are expressed in the character and attitudes of the members of society who realize its ideals."[51]

This argument suggests that the values implicit in a political conception of justice are rendered a necessary component of the individual's "character and attitudes." Better still: "even if political liberalism can be seen as neutral in procedure and in aim, it is important to emphasize that it may still affirm the superiority of certain forms of moral character and encourage certain moral virtues."[52] Rawlsian political liberalism is thus committed to at least a minimalist form of perfectionism in which certain forms of moral character and certain moral virtues are encouraged and affirmed.[53] This is certainly at variance with the claim he made in *Theory* that his paradigm did not determine individuals' ends as long as they were compatible with justice. But then Rawls is now aware that his theoretical system is not free of paradoxes.

The paradoxes are found not only in a denial of perfectionist claims while intimating a minimalist perfectionist project that a well-ordered society is bound to promote. More importantly, they also exist in one of the central claims that Rawls intended to present as a distinctive trait of justice as fairness: the priority of the right over the good. I wish to argue that in his political liberalism, this priority is no longer tenable.

In *Theory* Rawls distinguished teleological doctrines from deontological theories by arguing that the former define the good "independently from the right, and then the right is defined as that which maximizes the good" (24).[54] Justice as fairness, by contrast, is a deontological theory: it holds the priority of the right over the good (30, 31). It was clear, however, that the principles of justice pursued a minimalist vision of the good for the public structure expressed in the values of cooperation and stability as well as an idea of the good of individuals expressed in primary goods, self-esteem, and mutual advantages. In *Political Liberalism* the status of the priority of the right over the good seems to be substantially modified, if not abandoned altogether. In Rawls's recent version of political justice, the instrumental value of justice, already present in *Theory*, becomes more evident, and justice is presented explicitly as a means to a person's good.

> The situation is different with the sense of justice: for here the parties cannot invoke reasons founded on regarding the development and exercise of this capacity as part of a person's determinate conception of the good. They are restricted to reasons founded on regarding it *solely* as a means to a person's good.[55]
>
> The parties assess the traditional alternatives in accordance with how well they generate a publicly recognized sense of justice when the basic structure is known to satisfy the corresponding principles. In doing this they view the developed capacity for a sense of justice as a means to the good of those they represent. That is, a scheme of just social cooperation advances citizens' determinate conception of the good; and a scheme made stable by an effective public sense of justice is a better means to this end than a scheme which requires a severe and costly apparatus of penal sanctions, particularly when this apparatus is dangerous to the basic liberties.[56]
>
> For the parties in adopting the principles of justice which most effectively secure the development and exercise of the sense of justice are moved not from the desire to realize this moral power for its own sake, but rather view it as the best way to stabilize just social cooperation and thereby to advance the determinate conceptions of the good of the persons they represent.[57]

In *Theory* people's final ends were not relevant to the assessment of justice, and whether people were able to develop their second capacity—the capacity to pursue the good—was not important either. Justice was justified on the basis of external goals—cooperation and stability—but these goals referred to the public structure. In "Social Unity" Rawls introduced an important modification of his arguments: the justification of justice depended on whether people's life plans embodied ways of life worthy of human endeavors. "Just institutions," he said, "would have no point unless citizens had conceptions of the good they strove to realize and these conceptions defined ways of life fully worthy of human endeavour" (184).

In his most recent formulation, *Political Liberalism,* justice has a completely instrumental value enjoining both individuals' conceptions of the good and the public structure. Rawls's reasoning seems to be the following: justice provides stability—a stable and just social cooperation—and stability allows individuals to advance their determinate conceptions of the good. But if the goal and justification of justice are a stable social order allowing individuals to pursue their visions of the good, then the right is not derived independently of the good. Quite the contrary, the good is what justifies the right, and the right is derived from a goal that is rooted in our good.

Better still, "the most stable conception of justice [is] congruent with and unconditionally concerned with our good, and rooted not in abnegation but in affirmation of our person."[58] The phrase *unconditionally concerned with our good* is open to two possible interpretations. It might suggest, as the common understanding of the word *unconditional* makes clear, that in its concern with our good, the principles of justice do not present any constraint or condition to the good. Or the word might mean that justice is unconditionally at the service of the good. In both cases, the claim that justice is "unconditionally concerned with our good" might suggest a subordinate status for justice.

From "We the People" to "We the Justices"

I suggest that Rawls's doctrine is deeply political in 1) his attempt to articulate a conception of justice on the basis of values that are part of the history and culture of constitutional democracies; 2) his effort to provide a wide space for the accommodation of conflicting understandings of the human good; 3) his goal of promoting the political values of cooperation, stability, and order through the regulation or avoidance of conflicts.

Several of the conceptions of politics I identified earlier are compatible with the Rawlsian view of political liberalism. Central to the understanding of political liberalism are the conceptions of politics as: a system of rules to realize the good of justice (conception 1); the quest for, and the institutionalization of, common goods (conception 2); the pursuit of civil order (conception 5); the creation of state power (conception 10); a system of principles to address and, if possible, to solve conflicts (conception 11); a system of principles to avoid conflicts (conception 12); and a system of principles to accommodate different conceptions of the human good (conception 13).

Compatible with the liberal view, but not necessarily central to it, are conceptions of politics as: the teaching of the virtues for the sake of the public structure (conception 7); participation to realize the good of the community (conception 8); and participation for its own sake (conception 9). Rawlsian political liberalism excludes politics as: a practice that defines and encourages the quest for a public agreement on the human good (conception 3); the pursuit of glory (conception 4); the teaching of the virtues for the sake of the individual's character (conception 6); and an arena of conflicting vocabularies where consensus is impossible (conception 14).

In the light of what I have said, Chantal Mouffe's claim that justice as fairness lacks a vision of the common good is textually false, and her claim that Rawlsian liberalism abolishes politics is not persuasive. In her view, the political is a space of conflicts. But Rawls relegates conflicts to the private sphere, and the political becomes a realm ruled by consensus. "Therefore," Mouffe concludes, "Rawls's 'well-ordered society' rests on the elimination of the very idea of the political."[59] But this view suggests only one definition of politics: an arena of conflictive claims which is bound to remain that way. Intriguingly, Mouffe envisions the political as a space of diversity and conflicts but predicates her view upon one understanding of politics which attempts to exclude all other possible understandings. It is true that Rawls's conception of the public/political sphere is ruled by his concern for a stable order—the ideal is order in perpetuity. But it is not true that Rawlsian politics is free of conflicts, even if that is his deepest goal. My discussion suggests the following.

1. There are no conflicts about the principles of justice because the principles have been already chosen.

2. There are no conflicts about the grounds of justice pertaining to constitutional essentials since those grounds are political, the end result of intuitive ideas upon which everybody agrees.

3. In all those areas that are not constitutional essentials, there are conflicts, and comprehensive doctrines are allowed to play a role.

Rawlsian politics, however, is so concerned with the exclusion of divisive issues that might threaten the stability of a well-ordered society and so interested in removing any contingency that might impair the orderly application of the principles of justice that it might engender a passive citizenry, one willing to silence its criticisms rather than risk the instability of the political order.

Rawls's political liberalism does exclude certain visions of politics, particularly an agonistic one in which the political is an arena of permanent conflicts wherein any attempt to solve, regulate, or deflate those conflicts negates politics. But this view, which, intriguingly, is also supported by thinkers—Mouffe, included—who emphasize our shared understandings, does not monopolize the understanding of politics and seems to be at variance with common sense.

Honig's claim that Rawlsian justice displaces politics in favor of administrative procedures is partially true. The quest for an agreement on a political conception of justice is not an administrative procedure; it is a hermeneutic journey that resorts to the ideas and traditions of a constitutional democracy to articulate a coherent and persuasive idea of political justice. However, the implementation of Rawlsian justice requires a huge administrative apparatus, and Rawls seems to prefer a stable system of rules to distribute the social product. The outcome is that justice becomes an administrative and juridical issue, and citizens become recipients of the primary goods regulated and administered by the public structure.

Although Mouffe's criticism is not supported by Rawls's idea of political liberalism and Honig's argument is only partly true, Connolly's view that Rawlsian liberalism is predicated upon a juridical vision of politics is confirmed. Rawls's political liberalism is an arena of public deliberation where legal arguments, lawyers, and judges have the final say in setting controversies. And MacIntyre's claim that lawyers are the priests of liberal modernity is equally confirmed. Rawls goes so far as to imply that "We the People" is no longer relevant once the Constitution is in place and a legal tradition has been formed.

> The Court could say, then, that an amendment to repeal the First Amendment and replace it with its opposite fundamentally contradicts the constitutional tradition of the oldest democratic regime in the world. It is therefore invalid. Does this mean that the Bill of Rights and the other amendments are entrenched? Well, they are entrenched in the sense of being validated by long historical practice. . . . The successful practice of [constitutional] ideas and principles place restrictions on what can now count as an amendment, whatever was true at the beginning.[60]

This argument has two important implications. The first is that the Constitution no longer depends on the authority of We the People. It has acquired an authority of its own. The second implication is that *what is* (a tradition of legal interpretation) has become the standards to judge *what ought to be.* I suspect that this claim has nothing to do with the Kantian tradition. It is rather the Rawlsian version of Hegel's historicity.

In Rawls's political liberalism, the people, like the parties to the original position, appear at the founding moment when the Constitution is enacted and ratified. After that, judges replace the people, and public officials replace the citizens who were represented in the original position. The people have no authority to overthrow the Constitution, which is now in the hands of the final arbiters of constitutional meaning, namely, the political appointees who become justices. And the citizens have no say in determining what are the greatest benefits of the second principle of justice. Those benefits are determined by public administrators. Rawlsian justice and the end of history go hand in hand.

There are two important exclusions from Rawls's politics. First, the possibility of exploring an agreement on a political conception of the human good is gone. Second, Sheldon Wolin's understanding of politics as the public deliberation about power has no place within the confines of Rawlsian political liberalism.[61] In the Rawlsian paradigm, there is no discussion of power; the Rawlsian assumption, seemingly, is that if his two principles of justice are in place, there is no need to examine the nature of power. Power, I suppose, is regulated and watched over, but an examination of its nature—that maze of technology, secrets, and political practices which outgrew the constitutional framework and which is what Wolin calls the *megastate*—is unavailable.[62]

Also unavailable is an examination of the disciplinary character that may exist in a society ordered along Rawlsian lines. Political liberalism is, then, vulnerable to the dangers of conservatism which are usually associated with the ideas liberalism fought to replace. But liberalism is now a triumphant doctrine. It has created a world in its own image. It must colonize its adversaries ("Romantics can be liberals," in Charles Larmore's phrase). And the fourth founding of the American Republic (Declaration—Constitution—Civil War—Rawls's political liberalism) needs an orderly system where lawyers can argue their cases; Rortyans can read their novels and enjoy the culture of irony; Rawlsian citizens can pay their taxes and show their cooperation and their love of mankind; and potential rebels can take the daily dosage of their prescribed and publicly endorsed medication, the Prozac that is a metaphor for the end of history which political liberalism, so proudly, has inaugurated.

7

Envy, Nature,
and Full Autonomy

Since the original agreement is final and made in perpetuity,
there is no second chance.

—John Rawls, *A Theory of Justice*

Previous chapters have explored issues that suggest inner tensions in the
Rawlsian arguments or claims that might be opposed by the political culture
of constitutional democracies or their citizens' judgment. Stability and the role
of nature within justice as fairness are the main themes of the present chapter,
but I should begin with a problem that is directly related to Rawls's view of
order and which he resolves in an innovative and intriguing way. I refer to the
problem of envy.

A Note on Envy;
or, Why Shopping Malls Matter

If there is a conflict that acquires a rather grotesque character in Rawlsian justice it is his discussion of envy in *Theory*, just a few pages after the spirit of
Humboldt has inspired and led him to present his ode to the idea of social
union. The emphasis in Section 79 of *Theory* is on connectedness, on each per-

son participating "in the total sum of the realized natural assets of the others" (523), and on cooperation, which is the only foundation for bringing one's powers into fruition (525 n, 571). "So the members of a well-ordered society have the common aim of cooperating together to realize their own and another's nature in ways allowed by the principles of justice" (527).

In Section 81 Humboldt disappears, Rawls recovers his senses, and his reasoning depicts his project as an effort to patch up any possible fissure through which instability may bring havoc to his edifice. This time he is building dams against the power of envy. As we may know, envy is not a problem in the original position, but it is a danger in an actual society. How does Rawls cope with it? Given his discussion in Section 79, his arguments come as a surprise, and one is hard pressed to account for the obvious tensions in his reasoning.

According to Rawls, there is no room for envy in his well-ordered society because people, after all, are morally equal even if they are economically and socially unequal. This claim is the equivalent of the religious view that we are all God's children, a ground that has not been successful in preventing envy, but one that will not deter Rawls's hope of arresting it. Yet, if envy happens to be a threat given the large inequalities that may exist in the Rawlsian order, his solution is the Federalist way: since society is divided into different associations, the visibility of inequalities will no longer be a political problem (536) just as, in Madison's reasoning, the prospect of a tyrannical majority disappears as soon as society is fragmented into different factions.

Thus the communality of Section 79 suffers a humiliating defeat in Section 81, just five to seven pages later, where we no longer hear of the "common end" of realizing each other's nature, or how the actions of others complement our good, or how we all benefit from a division of labor aimed at mutual aid. Now the argument is about separation, fragmentation, and isolation. Rawls's views must be quoted in full.

> Although in theory the difference principle permits indefinitely large inequalities in return for small gains to the less favored, the spread of income and wealth should not be excessive in practice, given the requisite background institutions. . . . Moreover the plurality of associations in a well-ordered society, each with its secure internal life, tends to reduce the visibility, or at least the painful visibility, of variations in men's prospects. For we tend to compare our circumstances with others in the same or in a similar group as ourselves, or in positions that we regard as relevant to our aspirations. The various associations in society tend to divide it into so many noncomparing groups, the discrepancies between these divisions not attracting the kind of attention which unsettles the lives of those less well placed. (536–37)

Rawls's ideal society, then, is one in which the painful visibility of large inequalities is concealed from the view of the worst-off lest they entertain the disruptive feeling of envy. The communality of Section 79 vanishes, and the Rawlsian order turns out to be one in which inequalities are hidden, almost clandestine, encoded in a network of many noncomparing groups whose discrepancies in wealth and status are not supposed to attract "the kind of attention which unsettles the lives of those less well placed." In Section 79 we realize our nature in cooperation with others; in Section 81 we learn that these others are people who belong to our own economic and social status. The disadvantaged are not supposed to commingle with privileged people: there is a wall of separation between the groups. In Section 79 the language is universal; in 81 it is class coded.[1]

Why Rawls must resort to secrecy and fragmentation in his effort to avoid envy, however, is a mystery. He also claims that in his well-ordered society people's self-esteem will depend not on income or status, but on a public acceptance of the principles of justice (544, 545). He also says that once his principles are in place, justice is "whatever it is." Both claims are denied by this politics of hiding. Yet, if these claims are true, as Rawls believes they are, why does he emphasize removing from public sight the painful visibility of social inequalities when they are already justified by his view of justice? Most plausible is that Rawls wishes not to take any chances with actual persons, not even with his Kantian creatures who have reached the "highest" level of moral development when they pay their taxes. We are given a paradox of inequalities that are publicly justified and privately hidden, a paradox that bodes ill for Rawls's own idea of publicity. As in Rousseau's community,[2] the members of a Rawlsian well-ordered society "follow and know of one another," a knowledge that his politics of noncomparing groups explicitly denies.

> If we take seriously the idea of a social union and of society as a social union of such unions, then surely publicity is a natural condition. It helps to establish that a well-ordered society is one activity in the sense that its members follow and know of one another, that they follow the same regulative conception. (582)

But envy disrupts Rawls's best intentions. Rawlsian citizens should not know what takes place among groups of privileged persons, and Rawls must deal with the contingencies associated with the circumstances of life. He does not take chances.

Rawls's argument about fragmentation is similar to the shopping mall culture of liberal modernity. Malls are the best expressions of democracy and of the Rawlsian recipe against envy. In a mall all individuals can see and even put on the commodities displayed. And even if only a few people are able to buy the goods, the rest will not know because those who are able to afford, for example, expensive clothes, are members of associations (private clubs, all-male fraternities, the bar, political-action committees) to which the others do not belong. The closest the groups may come to encountering each other is at an AA meeting, in a setting where all are clinically equal; all are patients who may not be inclined to the comparisons Rawls wants to avoid in order to prevent envy.

Parking lots exemplify the fictions of equality in the same way as do shopping malls, particularly when a Yugo can display its shrieking armor side by side with a Jaguar, thus illustrating the equal chances both have to a parking space. That a person finds a parking space close to the mall entrance demonstrates luck, accident, or contingency, not moral superiority.

In a line to buy a theater ticket (now I apply freely, but legitimately, Rawls's arguments) "the principles of justice are acknowledged" (537). All must be treated as equal citizens. If the man behind you looks like a successful banker and you are on welfare, you need not envy him. You have the firm and secure guarantee of Rawlsian justice that his success does not indicate that he is "more deserving from a moral point of view" (536). It just happened that way. And after all, he is paying the taxes that support your welfare programs. Accordingly, he is showing the "love of mankind." Better still, you are in front of him in the line, a fact that shows how, in a public forum, "this ignoring of differences in wealth and circumstance is made easier by the fact that when citizens do meet one another, as they must in public affairs at least, the principles of equal justice are acknowledged. Moreover in everyday life the natural duties are honored so that the more advantaged do not make an ostentatious display [a claim that, incidentally, violates the first principle of Rawlsian justice] of their higher estate calculated [this is the key word] to demean the condition of those who have less" (537). The more advantaged may display their wealth ostentatiously, not because they calculate to demean others, but because they are that way: ostentatious, flamboyant, Hollywoodesque. Returning to you in the theater line: you are ahead of the banker. He must wait for you to count five dollars in pennies to buy your ticket (there is only one cashier). His look or status as a successful banker does not entitle him to a privileged pass or treatment. You and he are equal moral persons. And Rawls's arguments on how his principles avoid the tendency toward envy even when large inequalities are permitted by his version of justice are, to put it mildly, amusing.

Precarious Stability

Envy, then, remains a problem that challenges the prospects of a stable order in justice as fairness. Rawls, however, insists that his two principles of justice offer a more stable conception than does utilitarianism. A careful look at his arguments shows that he has not proven his case.

Rawls claims that the "three psychological laws" are a better foundation for stability than utility is (498, 499). "For suppose," he writes, "that certain institutions are adopted on the public understanding that the greater advantages of some counterbalance the lesser losses of others. Why should the acceptance of the principle of utility (in either form) by the more fortunate inspire the less advantaged to have friendly feelings toward them?" (499–500). This is why utilitarianism needs to stress the importance of sympathy and relies on altruistic inclinations, which are weaker than those that "the three psychological laws formulated as reciprocity principles" make possible; "a marked capacity for sympathetic identification," he concludes, "seems relatively rare" (500).

How do his arguments about fair equality of opportunity measure up to the standard he applies to utilitarianism? The reader is invited to look at his argument in *Theory* (298–302). Rawls discusses the arguments advanced by Keynes, Burke, and Hegel, respectively: that before the First World War injustices could not be removed without worsening the conditions of the laboring man (Keynes); that the rule of aristocratic families contributes to the general welfare (Burke); and that restrictions of fair equality of opportunity are necessary to ensure the political hegemony of a landed class "especially suited to political rule" (Hegel) (300). Burke's and Hegel's defenses of inequality, Rawls holds, are inconsistent "with the priority of fair opportunity over the difference principle" (300). For that defense to be consistent with fair equality of opportunity we need to examine the prospects of the most disadvantaged. If removing those inequalities worsens the conditions of the least favored members, then those inequalities are justified (301).[3]

In other words, in Rawls's account of fair equality of opportunity, some people might have a larger share of the social product if this arrangement improves the lot of the less fortunate members of society, or if the elimination of such an arrangement "would so interfere with the social system and the operations of the economy that in the long run anyway the opportunities of the disadvantaged would be even more limited" (301).[4] In a strict interpretation of the Rawlsian paradigm, then, improving the lot of the most disadvantaged is not even necessary to justify inequalities. It suffices to show that their conditions and opportunities, whatever they are, would be even more limited if the inequalities of the social system were abolished.

Rawls's discussion of the difference principle contains a similar justification of the better prospects that members of the "entrepreneurial class" might have in a "property-owning democracy," a justification that is strikingly similar to the conservative version of trickle-down economics.

> Their better prospects act as incentives so that the economic process is more efficient, innovation proceeds at a faster pace, and so on. Eventually the resulting material benefits spread throughout the system and to the least advantaged. I shall not consider how far these things are true. The point is that something of this kind must be argued if these inequalities are to be just by the difference principle. (78)

As indicated in Chapter 4, a Rawlsian society might thus have the following arrangement:

1. One group enjoys a larger share of the social product by virtue of their power to provide benefits to the most disadvantaged through their economic activities. Their rate of taxation, theoretically at least, could even be zero.

2. The most disadvantaged receive the greatest benefits from society and without paying taxes.

3. Middle sectors bear the brunt of taxes.

It is then clear that "the greater advantages of some counterbalance the lesser losses of others," which is, precisely, his description of the principle of utility (500). In this case, however, the lesser losses would be borne not only by the most disadvantaged but also by middle sectors. If any change threatened to throw middle sectors into the ranks of the most disadvantaged, then, following Rawls, the inequalities they now suffer are preferable to the more limited opportunities they might have as members of the most disadvantaged. It is worth noting, however, that in the light of Rawls's understanding of rationality, some members of the middle sectors might prefer to become members of the most disadvantaged: their prospects would be more modest, but they would receive the greatest benefits from society.

Let me return to the Rawlsian view of the difference principle and the claim that inequalities are justified when they improve the lot or are to the advantage of the worst-off (303). Rawls clearly suggests that people are expected to see whatever improvement the least advantaged may obtain as a fulfillment of the difference principle. Recall that justice is "whatever it is." Furthermore, the greatest benefits are a very elusive category to be defined by public institutions intent on maintaining civil peace. It is especially important to note that Rawls does not specify a correlation between the larger share of the better-off and the greatest benefits of the worse-off. Accordingly, as he admits readily when saying that his idea of justice might be compatible with large inequalities (531),[5] the larger share of the better-off may correspond to an insignificant improvement for the worse-off. And this would be just because Rawlsian justice is whatever turns out from the application of the principles of justice (275, 282).

If we subject the Rawlsian paradigm to the same question (reformulated) which Rawls asks of utilitarians, we ask: Why should the acceptance of the principles of Rawlsian justice by the more fortunate "inspire the less advantaged to have friendly feelings toward them?" (500). Rawlsianism does not provide a persuasive answer, particularly when the greatest benefits for the most disadvantaged are not substantial. And they are not, since, in the case of that group, justice as fairness is committed to offering a social minimum that is redescribed as the greatest benefits. In this sense Rawls's consistent effort to show that justice as fairness is more stable than a system based on the principle of utility fails, and Rawlsian stability lies on the same precarious ground where he finds utilitarianism.

In utilitarianism, he argues, "allegiance to the social system may demand that some should forgo advantages for the sake of the greater good of the whole. Thus the scheme will not be stable unless those who must make sacrifices strongly identify with interests broader than their own. But this is not easy to bring about" (177–78). Rawlsian justice faces the same problem. The better-off, both the upper-class and middle sectors, may have to sacrifice advantages in the name of "the greater good of the whole" expressed in cooperation. They might have to identify not only with the greater good of the whole but also with the greater good of a particular group expressed in the greatest benefits.[6] The worse-off might have to condone the privileges of the more fortunate members of society as the necessary condition for their benefits, however meager those benefits might be.

"What the principle of utility asks," Rawls goes on, "is precisely a sacrifice of [life] prospects. We are to accept the greater advantages of others as a sufficient reason for lower expectations over the whole course of our life. This is surely an extreme demand" (178). Sure it is. But members of the middle class, too, might have to sacrifice their life prospects to sustain a government committed to maximizing the long-term expectations of the most disadvantaged. They might have to accept "the greater advantages of others"—the members of the upper classes whose economic activities are deemed necessary to the benefits, however insignificant, of the least advantaged as well as to a stable order. And they might have to live with "lower expectations over the whole course of [their] life" on the ground that this is the price to pay for stability and cooperation from both the upper classes and the most disadvantaged. This is surely an extreme demand too.

My conclusion is warranted: since justice as fairness is "whatever it is" once Rawls's principles are in operation, and since reciprocity might represent a meager improvement for the most disadvantaged, justice as fairness ultimately relies on the same principle that, in Rawls's view, characterizes utilitarianism: sympathy. Justice as fairness may finally depend on the same "marked capacity for sympathetic identification" which, by Rawls's own admission, "seems relatively rare" (500) and is "not easy to bring about" (178). The most disadvantaged and middle sectors would have to display a rather high dosage of sympathetic identification with the better-off whose larger share of the social product is the condition of the limited, but at least real, benefits they are obtaining. Or, in Rawls's Kantianism, they would have to identify, not even with persons but with Rawlsian public institutions provided we believe Rawls's moral psychology and its claim that identification with the principles of justice embodied in public institutions represents the highest level of moral maturity.

Another option is available within the theoretical assumptions of justice as fairness. Rawlsianism may end up relying on neither reciprocity nor sympathy, but on the Hobbesian claim that the only alternative available to justice as fairness is a state of nature. The principles of justice, Rawls claims, "are collectively rational; everyone may expect to improve his situation if all comply with these principles, at least in comparison with what his prospects would be in the absence of any agreement" (497). In "the absence of any agreement" the alternative would be a Hobbesian chaos. In this case Rawlsianism would call citizens to reconcile themselves with the given since the prospects of its replacement would open the possibility of even greater inequalities and dangers: the replacement of existing inequalities may constitute the "day of reckoning" (303) Rawlsian justice is committed to avoiding.

The bottom line is that even though Rawls sees reciprocity as a stronger foundation for stability than utility, he does not specify it—which might be, in any case, a burdensome task. For example: does reciprocity mean that if the share of the better-off increases by X percent, the greatest benefits of the most disadvantaged ought to increase by the same percent? Or does any improvement in the status of the most disadvantaged count as a fulfillment of the reciprocity principle? Rawls does not address these issues, but his argument clearly suggests that he understands reciprocity as formulated by the second question.

Hence, in those circumstances in which large inequalities reign supreme under the cover of Rawlsian justice, the stability of Rawlsian justice, by his own account, is on precarious ground. It must resort to sympathy and altruistic inclinations, perceived by Rawls as rare occurrences and unreliable foundations for a well-ordered society.

Circles, and How Nature
Supports the Constitution

One feature that certainly does contribute to the stability of the Rawlsian order is the persistent circular character of Rawls's reasoning. Often his mode of argumentation proceeds along the following model: the principles of justice regulate, or define, or provide criteria for X (an activity, a public policy, a vision of the human good). X then is defined by reference to those principles. The end result is stability. Circles are round; and utilitarianism, no doubt, could resort to the same strategy to justify its beliefs. In this section I want to summarize some of the circles that stand out in Rawlsian justice.

1. Justice as fairness takes the given structure of society (a constitutional democracy), the given conventions about cooperation (as expressed in intuitive ideas), and the given social status of citizens and then designs a conception of justice which seeks to provide grounds of legitimacy to the political order. The public structure must provide equal rights, fair equality of opportunity, and all-purpose means. The better-off must pay taxes to provide the greatest benefits to the worse-off; this is the price of cooperation and social stability. Citizens, in turn, must revise and adjust their ends taking into account "their present and foreseeable situation." A public conception of justice

> includes what we may call a social division of responsibility: society, the citizens as a collective body, accepts the responsibility for maintaining the equal basic liberties and fair equality of opportunity, and for providing a fair share of the other primary goods for everyone within this framework, while citizens (as individuals) and associations accept the responsibility for revising and adjusting their ends and aspirations in view of the all-purpose means they can expect, given their present and foreseeable situation.[7]

The phrase *in view of the all-purpose means they can expect, given their present and foreseeable situation* is ambiguous. Are the all-purpose means they can expect those that society is *able* to give them or those that society, given a particular institutional setting, can offer to them? I assume that Rawls refers to the latter, that *their present situation* refers to people's circumstances within a particular society with particular institutions.

As is characteristic of Rawls's arguments, we face a circle: a given social structure determines the individuals' present situation and puts some constraints on their life plans and ends. Individuals then adjust their life plans and ends to their present and foreseeable situation.[8] Society establishes some boundaries to what individuals can reasonably expect, and individuals do not place unreasonable demands on society. The final result is stability and cooperation. As Rawls says in "Social Structure," "The social structure also limits people's ambitions and hopes in different ways; for they will with reason view themselves in part according to their position in it and take account of the means and opportunities they can realistically expect."[9] Rawls goes on: "So an economic regime, say, is not only an institutional scheme for satisfying existing desires and aspirations but a way of fashioning desires and aspirations in the future."[10] In other words, the economic system is expected to shape people's realistic expectations and to fashion their future desires and aspirations.

Presenting this circle in another way: the public structure places limits on the ends that would be financially acceptable, and people adjust their ends to satisfy the criterion of financial acceptability, which the public structure preordains. This accommodation is called *justice*. The public structure certifies itself as just.

2. In Rawlsian justice each person is entitled to receive his due, and this due is defined by the public system of rules and institutions. A just scheme "allots to each what he is entitled to as defined by the scheme itself. The principles of justice for institutions and individuals establish that doing this is fair" (313). The public system thus determines a person's due and then proceeds to provide it. This is fairness plus stability.

3. The Rawlsian conception of public reason encompasses "the good of the public and matters of fundamental justice." The content of public reason, namely, the content of "the good of the public and matters of fundamental justice," is "given by the ideals and principles expressed by society's conception of political justice."[11] In other words, matters of fundamental justice are given by society's conception of political justice. Justice defines justice.

4. Rawls finds "intuitive ideas" in the political culture of the American society, and these ideas serve as foundations for a conception of justice which justifies that political culture. In his "Reply to Habermas" he goes further and includes *Theory* as part of the grounds that support the central ideas of his own system. The fundamental ideas of Rawls's political liberalism, he writes, "all belong to the category of the political and are familiar from the public politi-

cal culture of a democratic society and its traditions of interpretation of the constitution and basic laws, as well as of its leading historical documents and widely known political writings."[12]

5. Rawlsian justice determines the criteria to judge its legitimacy and then uses those criteria to certify itself as legitimate.

6. Rawls's idea of "social cooperation over a complete life" implies that "we can also take responsibility for our ends, that is, that we can adjust our ends so that they can be pursued by the means we can reasonably expect to acquire given our prospects and situation in society."[13] To put it differently, social circumstances determine what one can anticipate from the social structure.

The circularity of Rawls's reasoning is not, however, the ultimate ground to support his belief in the stability of his system. The ultimate ground of stability and loyalty to the Rawlsian order is found in nature. In Chapter 2 I showed how the parties' willingness to accept the Rawlsian principles of justice arises from a natural duty of justice. From this natural duty emerges an institutionalized justice, which is the Rawlsian contract as stipulated by the two principles. From this institutionalized justice arise the constitutional forms of a democratic society. It follows, or it ought to follow, that our duty to obey the Constitution is derived from the public, institutionalized agreement on justice, since the Constitution is based on our explicit agreement. This ought to follow, but it does not. Seemingly, Rawls does not regard institutions as a strong foundation for our allegiance to the Constitution. And so he oversteps his own system of public justice and places our loyalty to the Constitution not on an obligation defined by an institution (the two principles)—which is, in any event, an artificial construction—but on a natural duty. "Thus we have a natural duty to comply with the constitution, say, or with the basic laws regulating property (assuming them to be just)" (344). Rawls is consistent: he does not take chances with actual persons. So instead of the linkage of natural duty → institutionalized justice → allegiance to the Constitution, we have natural duty → loyalty to the Constitution.

The support of the Constitution is thus not mediated by institutional forms. In Rawlsian justice, nature and obedience are linked directly. An institution, after all, defines particular obligations, whereas a natural duty is unconditional and does not require consent. This is, to say the least, extremely confusing since the Constitution derives from the explicit consent of citizens, not from a natural duty that holds regardless of a person's voluntary acts. Apparently, the Constitution is derived from consent; however, once in place, it—like the Rawlsian contract—no longer depends on the people. This is precisely the argument that Rawls presents in *Political Liberalism* (see Chapter 6).

Rawls does say, however, that "justice as fairness holds that natural duties and obligations arise only in virtue of ethical principles. These principles are those that would be chosen in the original position" (348). The problem with this claim is that the natural duty of justice is given before the two principles of Rawlsian justice are chosen, and these two principles are the only ethical principles Rawls allows in his system. That is to say, natural duties cannot arise from ethical principles since those principles—the two principles—depend on the natural duty of justice.

Let me pursue further the link between nature and constitutional loyalty. "The natural duty of justice," Rawls writes in *Theory*, "is the primary basis of our political ties to a constitutional regime" (376). In Section 52 Rawls says that "all obligations arise from the principle of fairness" (342), a principle according to which a person is obligated "to do his part as defined by the rules of an institution when two conditions are met: first, the institution is just (or fair) . . . and second, one has voluntarily accepted the benefits of the arrangement or taken advantage of the opportunities it offers to further one's interests" (111–12).

I assume, then, that it is reasonable to construct the following argument.

1. All obligations arise from the principle of fairness.

2. The principle of fairness refers to institutions.

3. The Constitution is an institution.

4. Ergo, our allegiance to the Constitution stems from an obligation justified and articulated by the principle of fairness, namely, an obligation articulated by institutions.

In this case the principles of Rawlsian justice would be the institutional foundation determining our allegiance to the Constitution. This reasoning is sound, but Rawls's zeal for stability leads him to reject it. Our obedience to the Constitution does not arise from the principle of fairness, but from a natural duty, which is preinstitutional. Before Rawlsian justice is chosen or acknowledged, we have a natural duty of justice. Before the Constitution is written, we have a natural duty to support it.

It is thus not a small irony of Rawlsian justice that despite all of its effort to escape contingency and to provide a firm anchor to a well-ordered society, it ultimately relies on nature. Rawls stands for a natural duty of justice; a natural duty to support the Constitution (344); a natural duty of civility which calls us to show restraint and "not to invoke the faults of social arrangements as a too ready excuse for not complying with them, nor to exploit inevitable loopholes in the rules to advance our interests" (355). We even discover in Rawls—a philosopher who is always devising innovative ways to avoid political deliberations in the public realm—that we have a "natural political virtue."[14] The four dimensions of Rawlsian nature are:

- Natural duty of justice
- Natural duty to support the Constitution
- Natural duty of civility
- Natural political virtue

When we put together *nature* (the central ground of Rawlsian justice), the *reasonable* (a set of external restrictions guaranteeing the moral character of the original position), and *institutions* (the embodiment of justice and public reason), we might see justice as fairness as a theoretical and political project that consistently excludes actual persons from its operations. Judges are the exception, but then Rawls claims that the reasonable is strongest at the judicial stage.[15]

Full Autonomy and the Priority of Liberty

The effacement of actual persons (or at least actual citizens) climaxes in Rawls's view of full autonomy. In the "Dewey Lectures" Rawls defines *full autonomy* as that of citizens who "affirm and act from the first principles of justice."[16] In *Political Liberalism* he clarifies this view by arguing that "it is in [the citizens'] public recognition and informed application of the principles of justice in their political life, and as their effective sense of justice directs, that citizens achieve full autonomy."[17]

Although clear enough, Rawls's view of full autonomy is open to several questions. If citizens are fully autonomous when complying with the principles of justice in the public realm, do they need to be autonomous in the nonpublic areas of their lives? If full autonomy is achieved only in the public realm and by paying alliance to public principles of justice, does this mean that the public sphere is more important than the private sphere in the constitution of a person's autonomy?

Notice that compliance with the principles of justice in the public realm does not mean participation in political affairs as a preeminent good. Rawls explicitly rejects the republican tradition. What it does mean is the public respect of rights (the first principle) and the willingness to pay taxes (the cornerstone of the second principle). So, in Rawlsian justice, respect for rights and paying taxes—actions that we can carry out as private citizens—are the standards by which to judge full autonomy. Actions that belong to our private conceptions of the good, such as a commitment to participating in society's public affairs or a willingness to examine the ideas of the good embodied in private associations, make people, in Rawls's view, partially autonomous.

It follows then that in the important aspect of autonomy, the public sphere is preeminent in the constitution of a person's identity as an autonomous agent. It remains to be seen whether this view is compatible with our "considered judgments." And it is equally undecided whether or not Rawls can reconcile his defense of the neutrality of political liberalism regarding incommensurable visions of the human good and the claim that full autonomy must be located in the public identity of persons as exemplified by their adherence to the principles of Rawlsian justice.

Common sense might be welcome here. And common sense highlights the difficulties facing a politically neutral doctrine that privileges a person's public dimension in the area of autonomy while it assumes that no ideal of autonomy in that person's private domain will provide the grounds for full autonomy. Rawls might certainly reply that a person could still pursue autonomy as an ethical value defining his private commitments. But since that person has already achieved full autonomy by accepting Rawls's principles of justice, it is not clear why he would still need ethical autonomy.

I am not saying that Rawls's redefinition of autonomy as a political value is invalid. What I propose is that his conceptualization is confusing when, after narrowing the scope of autonomy to two practices (respect for rights and paying taxes), he then proceeds to call it *full autonomy*. A conceptual clarification might help the Rawlsian argument here. For example, Rawls can claim that he no longer understands autonomy as a philosophical or ethical ideal that defines a person's whole life. His view that autonomy is only political is a more limited sense of it. Accordingly, people might display their political autonomy by respecting rights and paying taxes while pursuing other more robust versions of autonomy in their private quests according to their own likings.

In other words, political autonomy is just a partial and limited expression of autonomy, which does not preclude citizens from articulating and following other views of autonomy which might make them fully autonomous. This is a reasonable avenue, but Rawls does not show any sign of considering it. Rawlsian full autonomy is possible only in the public domain and by supporting the public principles of Rawlsian justice. It is as though one part of his philosophy were deeply aware that the original Kantian enterprise is now floating adrift with no anchor other than the contingent political culture of a democratic society, while another part of his paradigm still longs for a Kantian foundation that is no longer there. As I will show in the next chapter, Kantian selves are very much alive in Rawls's political liberalism, but Rawls seems to sense that the political redefinition of his project has left it vulnerable to the contingencies he once sought to avoid. The part of his philosophy yearning for Kantian consolations wishes to call law-abiding citizens fully autonomous. And in *Political Liberalism* he even suggests, without further elaboration, that fully autonomous citizens undergo a Kantian metamorphosis and pursue justice for its own sake.

In *Political Liberalism* Rawls argues that the parties are moved not by the desire to realize their sense of justice for its own sake but by their interest in a stable cooperation that is necessary "to advance the determinate conceptions of the good of the persons they represent."[18] Fully autonomous citizens, by contrast, are expected to pursue justice for its own sake. Here is his argument:

> Thus the basic liberties enable the two principles of justice to meet more effectively than the other alternatives the requirements for self-respect. Once again, note that at no point in the parties' reasoning are they concerned with the development and exercise of the sense of justice for its own sake; although, of course, this is not true of fully autonomous citizens in a well-ordered society.[19]

Put another way, Kantian parties, who are independent of social circumstances, are nevertheless moved by the external interests they wish to obtain for the persons they represent; by contrast, Rawlsian citizens, who are embedded in the historicity of their society, pursue justice for its own sake. Presumably, the argument is that they have reached the highest level of moral maturity, whereby they are no longer concerned with the material benefits they can expect from their compliance with Rawlsian justice. Now they respect rights and pay their taxes for their own sake.

This understanding is dubious both philosophically and politically. Philosophically, it is so because Rawlsian individuals comply with justice to the extent that they expect other persons to do the same. This is the principle of reciprocity (494, 499). Politically, Rawls's claim about "full autonomy" is dubious because citizens might have a reasonable interest in receiving advantages from their public institutions. Yet, Rawls now suggests that what started as a project for mutual advantages has evolved into a Kantian exercise in which citizens act on the principles of Rawlsian justice regardless of the material benefits they anticipate. Such a sudden transformation of Rawlsian creatures is hard to explain. If they calculated in the original position, when they did not have the full picture in terms of relevant information, we can imagine what they will do in an actual society where, potentially, they can see where their taxes go and what they receive in return.

In Rawls's view, *full autonomy* refers to public persons, whereas the *priority of liberty* refers to private ones. But in the priority of liberty, the only liberties that are central to the first principle of justice are those of *conscience*—the only liberty that is settled in *Theory* (206)—and of *movement* and *occupational choice*. Since Rawls talks about the settled character of the liberty of conscience when writing about religion, it is reasonable to infer that the basic liberty he wants to protect is that of persons, as private individuals, to practice and express their religious or any metaphysical beliefs. This is, essentially, a private matter. Other liberties that are part of the political culture of the American society are not central. The right to own means of production and natural resources, for instance, is not central to Rawlsian justice. Nor is the right to participate in the political affairs of society. The right to free speech is not inalienable, particularly when it is used for "socially wasteful"[20] advertising. The Rawlsian priority of liberty, in short, exalts the private realm of the individual's conscience and his freedom to choose his occupation, two hallmarks of modern European revolutions. His view of full autonomy, by contrast, seems to privilege the public realm. Citizens are fully autonomous when they follow public principles of justice.

This reading, however, is not entirely accurate. Full autonomy is realized when people pay their taxes, and strictly speaking, this is not a public act, but a private act of private persons, which happens to possess a public significance. The point is worth repeating: a Rawlsian society is one of private persons who are connected through the state. Governmental bodies will make citizens autonomous by defining the rights they ought to respect and specifying the taxes they ought to pay. This is the ultimate meaning of full autonomy in the context of the statism encouraged by justice as fairness.

8

Farewell to
Rawlsian Justice

We cannot have things both ways.

But we must try to postpone the day of reckoning as long as
possible, and try to arrange society so that it never comes.
—John Rawls, *A Theory of Justice*

The contractarian liberalism informing the Rawlsian paradigm has never
been an invigorating philosophy. It is, and has been, a modus vivendi that
grows in the soil of tired combatants.

Rawlsian justice is no exception. It arrived on the scene in 1971, a few years
after the civil protests and social unrest that had threatened the façade of
American democracy during the 1960s, had weakened, and eventually died
out. The boisterous protests of oppressed citizens became the muted deliberations of Rawls's ventriloquism. The murdered were resurrected, and victims
and victimizers alike were transformed into the fictitious entities of the original position founding a society *sub specie aeternitatis.*

Despite its explicit goal of erasing justified anger, state persecution, and
class and race resentment before arriving at the essential core of Kantian creatures—a capacity for choice—Rawls's theory was resilient, probably because it
gave liberalism an intimation of an unfulfilled project that went back to the
Enlightenment: the presentation and justification of universal principles without the dangerous presence of Klan members or Black Panthers. But the Kant-

ian choosers and the Hobbesian calculators at the heart of the Rawlsian universe never understood each other. And they had to part company and go their separate ways.

The Kantian choosers became representatives of democratic citizens, thus introducing a significant dosage of contingency into the purity of the Rawlsian deliberation. And the Hobbesian calculators, now knowing who they were representing—shoppers who are energized by strolling in malls, overburdened by mortgage payments, and always on the lookout to reduce their taxes—kept thinking about the costs involved in their commitment to Rawlsian justice. Rawlsian justice, we should recall, is a duty when it does not represent a high cost to us, and "while we have a natural duty to bring about a great good . . . if we can do so relatively easily, we are released from this duty when the cost to ourselves is considerable" (117).

As they examine the costs, the calculators have two options: define the greatest benefits that the most disadvantaged expect in such a way that they would be nil, or define those benefits as too high for their inclinations, thereby suspending the deliberations of the original position and informing the parties that their term as representatives is over. Apparently, Rawls did not realize that the love of mankind and the costs to ourselves which are implied in his view of justice are different and conflicting. Like Kantian choosers and Hobbesian calculators, they are meant to go their separate ways.

Rawlsian justice has its own dosage of fortitude, though, and Rawls may have an argument at hand. He wants to free us from the stress of calculating costs by placing us in his original position, a strategy that only adds confusion to his theory. Claiming that justice is a matter of cost while excluding information needed to make the determination of that cost meaningful is simply incomprehensible.

Rawls's possible reply that the agreement of the original position complies with our "considered judgments" makes clear that his notion of considered judgments and his idea of fairness are at odds with what many citizens of democratic societies think. These citizens are not abstract entities choosing in a vacuum; they are parents or single mothers, or senior citizens, or middle-class individuals, or rich persons. They are also taxpayers. Their jobs might be uncertain. Their prospects of saving for the education of their children may be gloomy. And they may have projects in which the well-being of their children and relatives is more important than the solidarity among strangers, which is part and parcel of Rawlsian justice. So they might believe that their "natural duty" to bring about a great good (assuming that Rawlsian justice fits this category) is so onerous that they should be released from it. This position assumes, of course, that the Kantian claim to represent the highest expression of moral development and the belief that people will help strangers because of a devotion to the principles of right are disputable at best and false at worse.[1]

I have discussed so far some of the problems that may justify why people should be released from the Rawlsian paradigm not necessarily because they are Hobbesian calculators—although many of them are—but because Rawls's theory is riddled by tensions that call not for amendments, as he suggests in *Political Liberalism*, but for a farewell.

Let us explore here whether Rawlsian justice can be justified in the light of its own standard, which is coherence, and then examine Rawls's goal of reconciling social conflicts as well as the possibility that, with his political liberalism, justice as fairness turns out to be an exhausted project.

The Question of Coherence and Summary of Problems

Rawls conceives of justification as "a matter of the mutual support of many considerations, of everything fitting together into one coherent view" (579). By its own standard, Rawlsian justice cannot be justified. It is not coherent. Let me show why.

Pure Procedures and Outcomes

Justice as fairness is a question of following some procedures, and the outcomes will be just no matter what they are (275, 282). In a well-ordered society "the distribution of material means is left to take care of itself in accordance with the idea of pure procedural justice" (545; see also 86ff.). But Rawls also advocates an activist government that redistributes wealth and property continually to prevent apathy and resentment. If justice is a matter of pure procedures that have, as their backdrop, just institutions, what is the justification of the subsequent redistribution of property after the pure procedures are followed properly?

This tension is aggravated further by Rawls's claim that disagreements about the difference principle—the cornerstone of the Rawlsian edifice—should be settled by the political process (372–73). His redistributive policies are compounded even more by his presumption that when the first principle of justice, the principle of equal liberty, is "fully honored," "other injustices, while possibly persistent and significant, will not get out of hand" (373).

Unfortunately, this formulation suggests a typical Rawlsian problem in which a theoretical assumption is explicitly contradicted by Rawlsian policies. Why must wealth and property be distributed as widely as possible when the presumption is that when the basic liberties are protected through the first principle, other injustices, though possibly significant, "will not get out of hand?" And if other injustices "will not get out of hand," then it is not necessary to tamper with the principle of equal and formal liberties. The politics of hiding will keep the "painful visibility" of inequalities out of sight, and the Rawlsian public order will be secured.

On closer examination, Rawls's arguments are fully consistent with his paramount goal: a stable society. The claim that compliance with the first principle will spread stability to all areas of social life is presented in the context of his discussion of civil disobedience, and it serves as the ground to support his view that civil disobedience is justified primarily when the principle of equal liberty is violated (373). This claim coheres with the centrality of public order to the extent that, from the state's perspective, it is precisely this principle that is less burdensome to follow. In modern liberal societies a state's recognition of the formal character of personal liberties requires no major effort. This formal character is already part of the vocabularies and the political culture of modern democracies.

By contrast, it is the issue of material benefits—what some call *entitlements*—which lies at the core of deep disagreements that may invite acts of civil disobedience from those who feel left behind or from others who are taxed to buy the cooperation of the most disadvantaged. But civil disobedience arising from dissension over entitlements has no place in a Rawlsian society. People are expected to accept their due as defined by state institutions.

The tension between pure procedures and redistributive policies evokes an additional ramification. "The general conception of justice," Rawls writes, "imposes no restrictions on what sort of inequalities are permissible; it only requires that everyone's position be improved" (62; see also 64 and 65). I have already discussed some problems with this formulation in Chapter 4. Here it is sufficient to indicate that this view is denied by Rawls's arguments, specifically his defense of redistributive policies aimed at keeping wealth within permissible levels. Rawls clearly suggests that certain inequalities of property and wealth are restricted, even if everyone's condition is improved. He goes so far as to claim that "there is a maximum gain permitted to the most favored on the assumption that, even if the difference principle would allow it, there would be unjust effects on the political system and the like excluded by the priority of liberty" (81).

In short, Rawls claims that society is well organized when his two principles of justice are in operation. Basic liberties are respected; and the most disadvantaged receive the greatest benefits from society, with their long-term expectations improved. But Rawls has also consistently rejected the wide disparities of wealth and property in his view of a well-ordered society. In other words, compliance with the principles of Rawlsian justice is not enough. Society must possess a certain level of equality in property and wealth, even while Rawlsian justice may be compatible with large inequalities.

A possible solution to this quagmire resides in the Aristotelian median. Rawls values equality; but too much equality will destroy the necessary incentives to increase the social product, thus reducing the benefits expected by the most disadvantaged. Likewise, inequality is also a necessary incentive; but too much inequality produces resentment and instability. The Rawlsian formula thus stands for equality, but not too much equality; and for inequality, but not too much inequality. As I indicated in Chapter 4, Rawls accepts that the ideal median point of justice as fairness might be the end result of "plain hunch" (278).

Principles, Consequences, and the Kantian Self

The parties must evaluate the principles of justice in light of their consequences (138) and assess the possible effects of that justice (454). However, those consequences must be anticipated under conditions—the original position—which are hardly hospitable to a fair examination of the effects of justice. These issues are compounded when we add in the perpetual character of the Rawlsian contract. Rawls's arguments make clear that contingent attributes are "morally irrelevant" (first claim) or "politically irrelevant" (political claim).[2] But in either version, Rawls continues to rely on the metaphysical self of his Kantianism, a self that can agree on justice only by separating from its surrounding circumstances and attachments and by displaying its capacity to make choices from a contingency-free situation.

How, then, can we account for the claim of Rawls's revised project that the parties derive justice from the political culture of democratic societies, and that, consequently, Rawls's doctrine is political, not metaphysical? This claim is partly true. The parties arrive at Rawlsian justice by using two "intuitive ideas"[3] that have been "Kantianized," that is, "Rawlsianized": purified from any comprehensive traces. The political culture Rawls now invokes is constituted by the parties' knowledge of the people they represent (the original position is a "device of representation") and by the two intuitive ideas. The first condition was already present in *Theory* in Rawls's discussion of the Constitutional Convention (195–201). The second condition—the intuitive ideas—can be construed as the general knowledge of human life and society which the parties have possessed all along.[4] So the political redefinition of Rawlsian justice still requires the Kantian self despite Rawls's assurances that his doctrine does not build on any comprehensive view. The Kantian self that Sandel unmasked—and which Rawls allegedly debunked by redefining his project as political—is alive and well. It is now disguised as a democratic citizen whose contingent attributes are still irrelevant, "politically speaking." Rawls has shifted the ground of irrelevance from moral to political. But the crux of his argument remains: the Kantian self is stubborn, and contingent attributes are still irrelevant.

Despite the claim that consequences are important, Rawls desires a perpetual contract. He seems to draw an analogy between the rational plan for individuals and justice as fairness, which embodies a collective rationality for the whole society. In both instances there is no place for self-reproach (422–23). There is no second chance. But this view betrays a dogmatic project—one that is hardly compatible with the considered convictions and judgments of democratic citizens.

Priority of Basic Liberties

Rawls insists that justice as fairness does not compromise the priority of the basic liberties. Neither the welfare of society nor greater economic advantages compensate for lesser liberties: "a departure from the institutions of equal liberty required by the first principle cannot be justified by, or compensated for, by greater social and economic advantages" (61; see also 15, 28). Rawlsian justice does not exchange the basic liberties of citizens for economic benefits, but it is willing to make trade-offs for them. To clarify: in justice as fairness the worth of liberty is bound to be unequal permanently because economic and social inequalities—the preconditions of an unequal worth of liberty—are deemed necessary for cooperation and greater benefits. An equal distribution of primary goods is rejected as "irrational."[5] Rawls does say that the worth of liberty ought to be maximized to the least advantaged (205); but, logically, this maximization should never reach a substantial degree of equality, not to mention perfect equality. An equal worth of liberty for all citizens requires a strict egalitarianism, which Rawls has rejected in advance.

In *Theory* Rawls explicitly says that the "lesser worth of liberty is . . . compensated for, since the capacity of the less fortunate members of society to achieve their aims would be even less were they not to accept the existing inequalities whenever the difference principle is satisfied" (204). My argument here is that the trade-offs that he bans between basic liberties and greater economic advantages are allowed to play an important role when the worth of liberty is at stake. And this means that, at least temporarily, the freedoms of some individuals are sacrificed in the name of the welfare of society or of other citizens. A Rawlsian society might impose heavy taxes on the most disadvantaged on the ground that those taxes are indispensable to create the industrial and technological bases necessary for economic growth. This economic growth, in turn, will produce the economic resources needed to maximize the expectations of the least advantaged members in the long run. Rawls writes: "Each member of society is thought to have an inviolability founded on justice or, as some say, on natural right, which even the welfare of every one else cannot override. Justice denies that the loss of freedom for some is made right by a greater good shared by others" (28). This is an unfulfilled promise. In the previous example, a greater good that others will share in the long run makes right the tax burden of the most disadvantaged in the present in the name of a future progress. Or, it might well be that Rawlsian justice is only relevant for rich societies that are expected to remain rich.

Self-realization in the Activities of Others
People are supposed to realize themselves in the activities of many others and to know of one another. But both goals are denied explicitly by the existence of noncomparing groups, some of whom hide their privileges to avoid arousing envy in the most disadvantaged.

Sympathy and Identification
Rawlsian justice claims not to rely on sympathy, but ultimately it depends on the same strong identification it ascribes to utilitarianism (see Chapter 7).

Fair Value of Political Liberties
Rawls includes the fair value of the political liberties in the first principle of justice when, in his own arguments, the exercise of these liberties is not central in the articulation of a person's conception of the human good. In responding to the charge that the basic liberties were formal, Rawls introduced an important modification into the original version of justice as fairness. Not only did he emphasize that the worth of liberty ought to be maximized, but, more importantly, he argued that the fair value of the political liberties should be part of the first principle. His goal was to bring forward a coherent combination of liberty and equality supported by considered convictions. "But to achieve this fit with our considered convictions," he wrote, "we must take an important further step and treat the equal political liberties in a special way. This is done by including in the first principle of justice the guarantee that the

political liberties, and only these liberties, are secured by what I have called their 'fair value.'"[6] The meaning of this guarantee is that the worth of the political liberties to all citizens "must be approximately equal, or at least sufficiently equal, in the sense that everyone has a fair opportunity to hold public office and to influence the outcome of political decisions."[7] The inclusion of this guarantee follows from an explicit recognition that the social and economic inequalities permitted by the second principle of justice might allow some citizens to exclude others from the political process.[8]

This guarantee is certainly an important modification of Rawlsian justice. It is also suspect. By Rawls's own admission, freedom of movement and of choice of occupation are liberties whose exercise is more central than the political liberties in the articulation of a person's conception of the good. "Given the size of a modern state," he says, "the exercise of the political liberties is bound to have a lesser place in the conception of the good of most citizens than the exercise of the other basic liberties."[9] If this is so, why is the fair value of liberties that are more central to a person's idea of the human good *not* included in the first principle?

As shown in Chapter 6, in the original position the parties invoke reasons that treat justice "solely as a means to a person's good."[10] It is clear that freedom of movement, choice of occupation, and fair equality of opportunity to provide for a person's education, health care, and all the other goods encompassed by what Rawls calls "the long-term expectations" are more fundamental in the construction of a person's conception of the human good than the political liberties. Why, then, are the difference principle and fair equality of opportunity not included in the first principle of Rawlsian justice? What about the fair value of other basic liberties that are closely connected to the difference principle?

To be sure, Rawls does argue that freedom of movement and choice of occupation are "constitutional essentials." But he concludes that legislation providing the material foundations to exercise those liberties is outside the framework of a political conception of justice.[11] His reasoning hinges on a divide he establishes between basic liberties and the material conditions that make them possible. Freedom to choose an occupation, for example, may require a high level of education whose boundaries might be specified by a political conception of justice. In justice as fairness, however, the freedom to choose an occupation is a central liberty, but the difference principle, which makes it possible, is not a constitutional essential. It is instead a principle whose contours will be determined by the political process. As I have shown in Chapter

4, this separation is problematic, particularly when we take into account that the difference principle is the real foundation of the Rawlsian paradigm (see Table 8.1).

Rawls's explanation as to why only the fair value of the political liberties is part of the first principle is that a wider guarantee in the sense of a more egalitarian distribution of primary goods is unnecessary "since it does not permit society to meet certain essential requirements of social organization, and to take advantage of considerations of efficiency, and much else."[12] A more plausible interpretation is found in the umbilical cord between the Rawlsian paradigm to the Aristotelian mold. Rawls seeks the median, and he finds it by including the fair value of the political liberties in the first principle but leaving the rest of the basic liberties at the mercy of the difference principle and the political process.

In other words, justice as fairness seeks to maximize the worth of the basic liberties, but this maximization was never meant to approach a strict equality or one that might jeopardize "certain essential requirements of social organization" and "consideration of efficiency," which presumably were not part of the parties' deliberations in the original position. They arose instead from the philosophical and political framework that guided their maker.

As I have argued, Rawlsian justice is a balancing act that requires inequality, but not too much of it, as well as equality, but not too much of it either. Rawls envisions this median as a "natural focal point between merely formal liberty on the one side and some kind of wider guarantee for all basic liberties on the other."[13] But there is nothing "natural" in the Rawlsian median, unless we treat as natural Rawls's reluctance to say explicitly that a society designed to advance the good of its members might require a greater equality than he is willing to allow. This leads my argument to what is perhaps the most intriguing paradox of justice as fairness.

Maximum and Minimum

Justice as fairness is committed to maximizing the primary goods, the worth of liberty, and the long-term expectations of its most disadvantaged members not through a social maximum, but through a social minimum (276).[14] And even though the difference principle ought to regulate the implementation of this social minimum, its establishment is outside the scope of a political conception of justice. Each society must define it. A theory of justice which maximizes the long-term expectations of its most disadvantaged and hence its own legitimacy by offering a social minimum is reminiscent of Rawls's view that we

Table 8.1

Rawls's understanding of basic liberties and constitutional essentials

	Basic liberties			Constitutional essentials	
Included[1]	Basic, but having less intrinsic value[2]	Excluded	Included	Excluded
Liberty of conscience	Political liberties	Right to own means of production and natural resources[3]	Basic liberties plus social minimum to address basic needs[4]	Fair equality of opportunity
Political liberties and freedom of association				Difference principle[5]
Freedoms specified by the liberty and integrity of the person (freedom of movement, freedom to choose an occupation)				
Rights and liberties covered by the rule of law				

1. *Political Liberalism*, 291.
2. Ibid., 299.
3. Ibid., 298.
4. Ibid., 228.
5. Ibid., 228–29.

have a natural duty of justice when the cost to ourselves is not too high. It might also be an eloquent expression of efficiency or a reflection of the Rawlsian-Kantian commitment to a gradual and possibly long process of reforms to bring the institutions of the modern state into line with Rawlsian justice. Patience, it appears, is an important virtue of Rawlsian citizens.

These paradoxes are actually inner tensions between:

1. pure procedures and redistributive policies in that Rawlsian justice is not whatever turns out from the application of pure procedures;

2. pure procedures and the claim that disagreements about the difference principle should be addressed by the political process;

3. the request for an examination of the consequences of justice and the demand to make that assessment from the perspective of the original position—in which the knowledge many people might find necessary to make that evaluation is excluded—and the creation of a perpetual contract in which there is no room for reexamination[15];

4. the rejection of trade-offs between equal liberties and economic advantages and the acceptability of them between the worth of liberty and economic and social welfare;

5. people realizing their nature through—and in—other people and those same people facing the politics of hiding;

6. the rejection of sympathy as a ground for stability and the dependence upon it;

7. maximizing the worth of the political liberties when the exercise of these liberties is not central to a person's view of the human good;

8. maximizing the long-term expectations of the most disadvantaged through a social minimum.

Serious as these might be, other problems face Rawlsian justice. In justice as fairness we have the following situation:

1. The fair share of primary goods depends on productivity, the saving principle, administrative procedures defining what the greatest benefits are, and competition from the products and technology of foreign markets. Rawls's system refers to a "self-contained national community" (457), but because his principles of justice require "the conditions of our life as we know it" (454) and because competition from foreign markets is part of those conditions, competition must be included in any assessment of Rawlsian justice.

2. The worth of liberty is unequal.

3. The worth of the fair equality of opportunity is unequal (my hypothesis). All citizens are entitled to education (formal character of the principle of fair equality of opportunity [FEO]). But it does not follow that the quality of education will be the same for all persons. All citizens are entitled to medical care (formal character of the FEO principle). It does not follow that the quality of medical care will be the same for all citizens. All citizens are entitled to legal representation before a court of justice (formal character of the FEO principle). But the quality of that legal representation will not be the same for all citizens. And so on.

So in Rawlsian justice, the worth of liberty is unequal. The worth of the fair equality of opportunity is also unequal. And a citizen's fair share of primary goods depends upon productivity, efficiency, the saving principle, and foreign competition. Rawls himself states that a well-ordered society is compatible with large inequalities. He also says that these disparities will not last—an unpersuasive claim. Given a private property structure that Rawls is committed to preserving and given a public system that is expected to decide what constitutes the greatest benefits for the most disadvantaged, justice as fairness might well become a meager economic benefits program for the most disadvantaged. Taking into account all of the previous constraints, the stability of the social order, of course, may compensate for the limited economic benefits that society is expected to provide.

Rawls might look at that prospect against the background of the American society and decide that this society is not yet ready for justice as fairness; that the lexical arrangement of his system must be altered to address the contingencies of the American order.[16] A redistribution of property must be carried out before the priority of liberty can be secured firmly.

The principle of maturity is unavailable to Rawls, though; in the United States, he claims, there are "reasonably favorable conditions" for the priority of the basic liberties.[17] It is clear by now that agreement on moral equality and cooperation (the "intuitive ideas" of Rawls's political project) does not necessarily lead to Rawlsian justice.[18] Rawlsianism is a hope chained to its own premises. The political context traps justice as fairness, and the question of cost dooms it.

If stability plus meager economic benefits are what Rawlsian justice can offer, and if this possible outcome is, as I think it is, the most likely to occur, then justice as fairness has stretched the limits of common sense unreasonably by claiming to be the blueprint for a well-ordered society conceived in perpetuity. The first principle of Rawlsian justice does not differ from the classical liberal view or from the present constitutional arrangement of the United States. The principle of fair equality of opportunity seems to be compatible with existing legislation. The difference principle, which I take to be the most important contribution of Rawlsian justice, is compatible with large inequalities that might be the same ones we already have. A society ordered along Rawlsian lines could well be the same society in which we live, and justice as fairness can thus serve as a legitimation of the status quo—an outcome that comes as no surprise if we are aware of the umbilical cord tying Rawls's arguments with the Aristotelian median.

Bidding Farewell

The problem with justice as fairness, then, is not so much the ontological feasibility of the original position. Nor is it the status of the parties that are, according to Sandel, incapable of moral agency. Even less is the possibility of finding political grounds to justify the principles of justice. The problems suggested by my discussion are far broader and deeper.

1. Justice as fairness has no persuasive power in its attempt to present meager economic benefits plus stability as the hallmarks of a well-ordered society and even less in its effort to present that society as one conceived in perpetuity.

2. The most feasible outcome of justice as fairness—marginal economic benefits plus a stable social order—questions the Rawlsian premise that, in the original position, citizens' representatives will agree on the two principles of Rawlsian justice as the best option for a well-ordered society where they can display their rationality and maximize their ends in life.

3. Rawlsian justice embodies a conflict between the principle of stability and the principle of mutual advantages. People might be unwilling to sacrifice what they have—for example, income they must divert to pay increased taxes—in order to obtain more stability, particularly when stability turns out to be the mutual advantages they ought to expect from a Rawlsian society.

4. Justice as fairness has, at its root, a tension between the moral character of the first principle and the Hobbesian and prudential status of the second principle, particularly the difference principle, while ascribing a moral character to both principles and demanding from all citizens compliance with, and acceptance of, that moral character.

5. It is unclear from which theoretical resources the Rawlsian paradigm addresses an issue that impairs Rawls's political redefinition of justice. What happens when the settled convictions that Rawls invokes lead to outcomes that are not only controversial but also—and more importantly—are rejected by other settled convictions of the same political culture from which Rawls drew his conclusions? Rawlsian justice entails two possible outcomes that are at variance with the political culture underlying and justifying justice as fairness: the creation of a powerful state responsible for the administration of justice, and the erosion of personal accountability.

The Rawlsian paradigm is predicated upon the assumption that if the grounds of his principles are settled, their outcomes will also be settled and uncontroversial. All citizens, accordingly, are expected to accept those outcomes. But agreement on justificatory grounds does not necessarily entail agreement on the policies and principles built upon those grounds. One thing does not follow from the other. If the principles of justice which Rawls derives from settled convictions lead to controversial outcomes, the least responsible citizens can do is to treat those principles as preliminary and temporary resting places instead of "once and for all" principles. But this Rawls does not allow. His principles are meant to be perpetual.

6. A well-ordered society that privileges order and abhors controversial issues may ultimately be composed of a passive herd of Hobbesian subjects.

7. In one reading, at least, Rawlsian justice seems to exclude citizens from the assessment of the mutual advantages and the greatest benefits they expect from society. Ideally, public administrators will design procedures to distribute the social product and to determine the greatest benefits. The Supreme Court, the embodiment of public reason, will certify those procedures as just.

8. Justice as fairness encourages unaccountability on the part of the most disadvantaged. Society must pay for the actions of the worse-off, but the latter do not carry any financial responsibility toward society.

9. Although the first principle of Rawlsian justice refers to individuals, the difference principle refers to a group and requires that the long-term expectations of the most disadvantaged be maximized. To the best of my knowledge, however, nowhere does Rawls say that the long-term expectations of the worse-off will be maximized in their lifetime.

My argument suggests that in a Rawlsian society, the conditions of the group might be improved but not necessarily the conditions of individuals within that group. As a group, African Americans and Hispanics have more access to education and health care now than they did fifty or twenty-five years ago. It does not follow, however, that a majority of them, and not even a substantial minority, is now educated or employed.

It is thus reasonable to pose the following question: how individualistic is this theory when the advantages of the group compensate for the disadvantages of particular individuals? In this case some of the long-term expectations of African Americans and Hispanics as a group have improved, and, accordingly, society can claim that it is complying with Rawlsian justice. But how long must the most disadvantaged wait for improvements in their long-term expectations?

Given problem 3, my discussion suggests that the legitimacy of justice as fairness treads on precarious grounds since many people may not accept the claim that their mutual advantages will be received in the form of public stability. Given problem 4, the Rawlsian paradigm should give up its efforts at a universal agreement on justice and at a universal acceptance of its moral character. Since Rawls himself acknowledges that the former is impossible and that it is necessary to settle for an agreement anchored in a "reasonable" pluralism, it is unclear why he continues to expect universal agreement with his principles. Because Rawlsian justice entails the legitimation of inequalities that might be large, it is unreasonable, in the light of the political culture of democratic societies, to demand citizens' acceptance of the moral character of those inequalities unless order is conceived as a paramount and moral goal whose attainment and preservation turn any policy supporting it into a moral one, including policies that leave large inequalities intact.

It would be more consistent to jettison the Kantian view of the priority of the right and to examine justice not from the perspective of Kantian reason but from a Hobbesian concern for a stable public order. The principle of fairness, after all, is not only Kantian, but Hobbesian, and Rawls's principle of maturity shows that justice ought to bend its knees to the demands of order.

Given problem 5, justice as fairness should stop trying to settle, once and for all, the principles of justice. Given problems 6 and 7, justice as fairness ought to redefine autonomy to accord with the dominant values of the Rawlsian order. Autonomous thinking is not expected to be rebellious, but instead cooperative over a complete life. Given problems 1 and 2, the appealing power of justice as fairness is reduced to the importance of order and to the Hobbesian justification of inequalities. The importance of order claims that because justice as fairness is congruent with the political culture of a constitutional democracy, it is in a better position to gather popular support and to maintain it. The Hobbesian justification holds that inequalities would be even worse in the absence of the difference principle.

To sum up: given problem 4, justice as fairness should abandon its universality, that all citizens should agree with Rawls's principles of justice. Given problem 5, Rawlsian justice should give up eternity, that justice is conceived in perpetuity. Given problems 6 and 7, it should redefine autonomy in the light of the Hobbesian discourse whose emphasis on order, stability, and eternity fits the Rawlsian project. Given problems 8 and 9, it should relinquish its claim to be in accord with the considered judgments of democratic citizens. Given problems 1, 2, and 3, we would do better by going beyond Rawls.

Justice as Reconciliation

Rawlsian justice is the modern offspring of a liberal tradition whose signature was its bewilderment at social conflicts and its obsession with public order. No wonder Rawls envisions persons as rational selves partaking of an almost Hobbesian nature: they need institutions to educate and constrain them. Left to their own inclinations, individuals will likely prefer their own rational calculations, which is why they need the reasonable in the form of "an established public world," the warranty against the chaos that Hobbes found so dreadful. "Without an established public world," Rawls argues, "the reasonable may be suspended and we may be left largely with the rational, although the reasonable always binds *in foro interno*, to use Hobbes's phrase."[19] Rawlsianism must then be understood as a project whose deepest goal is reconciliation through a state that moralizes the existing order by remedying its imperfections through distributive policies.[20] This is his solution to a Hobbesian predicament.

Rawls conceives of the principles of justice as "the kernel of political morality. They not only specify the terms of cooperation between persons but they define a pact of reconciliation between diverse religions and moral beliefs, and the forms of culture to which they belong" (221). But this "pact of reconciliation" extends well beyond different religious and moral beliefs and the cultural setting that contextualizes them. Rawlsian reconciliation spreads through the crevices of the social body and calls citizens to take a second look at their social world. A philosophical enterprise that began exalting, as a core feature, the individual's freedom from social accidents and contingency is, at bottom, a project that asks its interlocutors to reconcile themselves with the circumstances of life. They accomplish this through a principle of distribution in which almost everything is apportioned: talents, liberties, primary goods, benefits, inequalities, misfortunes (381), and hardships—all are evaluated and assigned a particular place by the Rawlsian state. Exploring the pervasive codification of Rawlsian justice, readers of *Theory* might be inclined to believe that Rawlsian justice is a genuine critique of the status quo and perhaps even a radical indictment of natural and social inequalities. Rawlsianism, indeed, takes pains to reject nature and the cumulative weight of inequalities as grounds for a legitimate society. But such a reading, though dominant, rests on a misunderstanding probably fueled by the first account of the difference principle in the first part of *Theory.*

Ultimately, the principles of justice as fairness seek reconciliation with nature, human life, and social inequalities. Rawlsian justice is a strategy of containment reminiscent of the foresight Machiavelli wanted rulers to display. The difference principle is a redefinition of the grounds of inequalities (511). And the central purpose of Rawlsian justice is an effort to build banks against Fortune so that contingency "can more easily be accepted." For all of its "unnatural" and "unhistorical" character, the original position becomes a gathering where some entities reconcile themselves with the contingencies they do not know and with the idea that their actual society can be justified. It is just a question of redefining when inequalities are legitimate, something which, as Rawls shows, does not cost too much.

Hear Rawls once again on the question of reconciliation:

The acknowledgment of the difference principle redefines the grounds for social inequalities as conceived in the system of liberal equality; and when the principles of fraternity and redress are allowed their appropriate weight, the natural distribution of assets and the contingencies of social circumstances can more easily be accepted. We are more ready to dwell upon our good fortune now that these differences are made to work to our advantage, rather than to be downcast by how much better off me might have been had we had an equal chance along with others if only all social barriers had been removed. The conception of justice, should it be truly effective and publicly recognized as such, seems more likely than its rivals to transform our perspective on the social world and to reconcile us to the dispositions of the natural order and the conditions of human life. (511–12)

Rawlsianism does not pursue the removal of all social barriers. It is an arrangement in which the unavoidable inequalities of nature and social circumstances are regulated by state institutions to provide the greatest benefits to the most likely victims of those inequalities: the least advantaged. At the same time, although the validity of the claim of Rawlsian justice—to be better equipped than its rivals to transform people's view of the social world— may be dubious at best, it is evident that Rawlsianism does entail a flattening of our perspective on the social world. We need only the circles of Rawlsian reasoning to remember that the social system determines what we can expect, and our goals must be "realistic." The Kantian self that once relished its universality and distance from history is now mired in the formulas and procedures of public accountants.

In the name of realism and cooperation, Rawls calls the potential subjects of his well-ordered society to lower their expectations and to be reasonable, with *reasonableness* defined by the public structure. Once this operation is successful—that is, once people's ideas are flattened by a Rawlsian society—the remaining goals of Rawls's order will follow naturally. The least advantaged will accept the benefits certified by the state as the "greatest," and they will reconcile themselves to "the dispositions of the natural order and the conditions of human life." The end of history, so conspicuous in the political version of Rawlsian justice, was already intimated in Rawls's deepest goals in *Theory.*

Rawlsian justice was never meant to be a radical departure from the status quo. It was a struggling effort to look at the circumstances of human life in the quest for shelter under a public system of justice, which explains why injustices are not abolished, but redistributed, and the "inevitable imperfections of a constitutional system" ought to be shared "equitably" (355). "Accepting these hardships is simply recognizing and being willing to work within the limits imposed by the circumstances of human life" (355).

The search for a moderate alternative to the tribulations and vicissitudes of the human condition makes Rawls extremely sensitive to the crucial distinction between a utopia and a feasible project, between an ideal leading a philosophical inquiry and a nonideal model orienting a political and practical project. Strictly speaking, Rawlsian justice is not a utopia (just as the Hobbesian commonwealth was not one). It is rather a set of guiding principles that insist on their feasibility as an order that may represent "the least unjust scheme" and constitute "a balance of imperfections, an adjustment of compensating injustices" in Rawls's math in which "two wrongs can make a right." "In practice," Rawls writes,

> we must usually choose between several unjust, or second best, arrangements; and then we look to nonideal theory to find the least unjust scheme. Sometimes this scheme will include measures and policies that a perfectly just system would reject. Two wrongs can make a right in the sense that the best available arrangement may contain a balance of imperfections, an adjustment of compensating injustices. (279)

The intimation that Rawlsian justice is, at its core, a balance of imperfections is a lingering presence whose best expression is found in the distinction between a *just society* and a *nearly just society*, one in which the boundaries separating these two concepts conjure the image of a pending and imminent evaporation. In the Rawlsian paradigm a just society and a nearly just society are probably one and the same.

In *Theory* Rawls defines a nearly just society as one that "has some form of democratic government, although serious injustices may nevertheless exist" (382; see also 363). The United States fits this definition.

My conclusion is warranted: the balance of imperfections to which we should look in practice is probably fulfilled in the North American society, which is perhaps why Rawls allows a place for his tamed and domesticated version of civil disobedience. Civil disobedience is justified only in a nearly just society and is practiced by people who accept the legitimacy of the existing institutions and whose actions accept the principle of fidelity to law. They are not militant. They are, most likely, defendants looking for a Rawlsian lawyer who will exhaust all avenues available within the political system. When those avenues are closed, the lawyer will plead his case all the way to the Supreme Court. Should this court write a decision, Rawlsian civil disobedients will examine the reasons offered by the justices and apply to them the standard of public reason. "To check whether we are following public reason we might ask: how would our argument strike us presented in the form of a supreme court opinion? Reasonable? Outrageous?"[21]

Rawls understands civil disobedience as "one of the stabilizing devices of a constitutional system" (383). This view stands to reason once we acknowledge the "due restraint and sound judgment" that ought to be present in acts of Rawlsian civil disobedience. Rawls's claim to the contrary notwithstanding, it is clear that in a nearly just society the burden of stability rests not with the government or an oppressive majority but with the oppressed groups. They ought to show restraint so that the political order is not disrupted. In one page Rawls repeats the same argument twice. "It is conceivable, however, even if it is unlikely, that there should be many groups with an equally sound case . . . for being civilly disobedient; but that, if they were all to act in this way, serious disorder would follow which might well undermine the efficacy of the just constitution" (374). If many groups, each one having strong justifications for their actions, engage simultaneously in acts of civil disobedience, "lasting injury may result to the just constitution to which they each recognize a natural duty of justice" (374).[22] Minority groups, accordingly, ought to coordinate "their actions so that while each has an opportunity to exercise its right, the limits on the degree of civil disobedience are not exceeded" (375).

In *Theory* Rawlsianism suggests that the United States is a nearly just society, one in which stability is a preeminent value, so much so that oppressed minorities must show restraint when engaging in acts of civil disobedience, coordinating their actions and taking care not to destabilize the political order. They have to spend "a decent period of time" making "reasonable political appeals in the normal way" (384)—presumably, and as already suggested, through liberal lawyers pleading their case before the courts—and "care must be taken to see" that the mode of public address represented by civil disobedience is understood by the wider community (376), as though oppressed minorities had in their power the capacity to dispel the superstitions, fantasies, and outright prejudices that very often blind those who enjoy, either materially or psychologically, the oppression of others.

The problem is that one reads Rawls's theory of civil disobedience—which renders it an exercise of orderly conduct—and one imagines next a decent philosopher writing in the sixties from an Ivy League university. Then one remembers the dogs biting the flesh of Blacks in the South, bullets piercing the chests of civil rights workers, and a political system mired in obscene spectacles of political banality. And deep inside our moral consciousness an inarticulated something might revolt at the well-intentioned argument that calls for restraint in the face of crass oppression under the pretense that society recognizes formal liberties and has welfare programs that are destined, sometime down the road, to maximize the long-term expectations of the most disadvantaged—which must assume, logically, that the actual lives of the most disadvantaged will outlast their long-term expectations. Neither then nor now is this a reasonable premise.

The reconciliation Rawls expects does not square with the undeniable metaphysical aspects of justice as fairness. Yet, against Sandel's reading, the metaphysical project of *Theory* is so embedded in the historicity and contingencies of social life that, despite Rawls's consistent effort to free his paradigm from uncertainties, they keep assaulting his project in unexpected ways.

It is not a small irony that Rawls's solutions to two important issues of justice as fairness are reduced to hunches: in determining whether the difference principle (the centerpiece of Rawlsianism) is satisfied (372) and in deciding whether the level of acceptable wealth has not transgressed the boundaries of Rawlsian stability (278). On a similar note, it is puzzling that Rawls leaves pending an aspect that, in his own account, is a necessary component of his social contract. His theory seeks to harmonize cooperation and self-interest. Cooperation is managed by the state's tax machinery; but self-interest, an issue that refers directly to individuals, is left unaddressed. "Eventually, of course, for a complete contractarian account of right, we would have to work out from the standpoint of the original position what is to count as reasonable self-interest. But I shall not pursue this question here" (439). As far as I know, Rawls has never returned to this notion, and given his distrust of actual persons, there are no good reasons to believe he ever will. A Rawlsian circle, of course, might always be available; self-interest is defined by compliance with the principles of Rawlsian justice from the perspective of the original position, and so on.

Reconciliation or Exhaustion?

The importance of contingency explains why the Rawlsian paradigm has always displayed a marked sensitivity to how circumstances may constrain the establishment of just institutions. This profound awareness of contingency was present in *Theory*, and the fragility of human institutions is a concern suggested in *Political Liberalism*.

In *Theory* Rawls argued that the priority of the first principle depended on whether society satisfied the necessary material conditions and, presumably, the moral development required by his view of justice (542, 543). In his political version, Rawls's contingency sensors led him to an unexpected turn: he lowered his expectations in a significant way, thereby contributing to the sense of uneasiness which seems to grip Rawlsian justice. For instance, each political attribute he ascribes to justice as fairness can be read as a reality check. But a passage in *Political Liberalism* presents an argument that obscures this pattern; it is unclear whether that argument is another reality check or a sign of exhaustion in a paradigm that attempts to patch up inner fissures that are now wider than ever. Exhausted or not, in *Political Liberalism,* Rawls surrenders any attempt to put the difference principle in operation by restricting his view of justice to constitutional essentials and basic justice, wherein *basic justice* apparently means basic needs.

There are two passages whose implications I would like to explore. The reader might recall my discussion in Chapter 4 in which I referred to Rawls's claim about the disagreement surrounding issues of social and economic equality. I concluded that Rawls's view did not fit into his larger project to the extent that, for him, justice is "whatever it is" once his principles are in place. Now I want to return to Rawls's initial claim, repeated more explicitly in *Political Liberalism,* in order to probe its possible implications. He writes:

> Whether the constitutional essentials covering the basic freedoms are satisfied is more or less visible on the face of constitutional arrangements and how these can be seen to work in practice. But whether the aims of the principles covering social and economic inequalities are realized is far more difficult to ascertain. These matters are nearly always open to wide differences of reasonable opinion; they rest on complicated inferences and intuitive judgments that require us to assess complex social and economic information about topics poorly understood. Thus, although questions of both kinds are to be discussed in terms of political values, we can expect more agreement about whether the principles for the basic rights and liberties are realized than about whether the principles for social and economic justice are realized.[23]

This passage suggests that a Rawlsian society will probably not agree on whether the difference principle is achieved, an important twist whose consequences bode ill for justice as fairness. How, then, will citizens know that they are receiving the greatest benefits from society? How can public institutions expect cooperation when the central foundation of that cooperation, namely, the mutual advantages that the difference principle makes possible, is uncertain and bound to spawn disagreements? If willing cooperation is suddenly dubious, how can this society be stable?

The recognition of the difference principle as part of the sphere of public deliberation and disagreements questions my interpretation about the administrative character of Rawlsian justice. But it does more than that. It brings havoc to the Rawlsian paradigm. If citizens entered the Rawlsian contract in the hope of setting up institutions for reciprocal advantages, if citizens are creatures who prefer a larger share of primary goods to a lesser one, if citizens conceived of a well-ordered society as "one designed to advance the good of its members" (453) and in which a person's good is determined by his rational plan, and if these same citizens do not agree on whether the difference principle is honored, then they will not support a Rawlsian society in which these basic goals are uncertain.

As we already know, the first principle of Rawlsian justice is beyond the reach of contingency; constitutional essentials are settled once and for all.[24] By contrast, the difference principle, the cornerstone of justice as fairness, is contingent through and through, and a Rawlsian society is unlikely to agree on whether the public structure is addressing social and economic inequalities in a proper manner.[25] This is probably the last drop needed to drown Rawlsian justice in its own paradoxes. It does not go alone, though: it drags with it Sandel's reading, which never recognized the importance of contingency in the Rawlsian paradigm.

The second passage opens other problems. Rawls writes:

> These considerations explain why freedom of movement and free choice of occupation and a social minimum covering citizens' basic needs count as constitutional essentials while the principle of fair opportunity and the difference principle do not.
>
> Here I remark that if a political conception of justice covers the constitutional essentials and matters of basic justice—for the present this is all we aim for—it is already of enormous importance even if it has little to say about many economic and social issues that legislative bodies must regularly consider. To resolve these more particular and detailed issues it is often more reasonable to go beyond the political conception and the values its principles express, and to invoke nonpolitical values that such a view does not include. But so long as there is firm agreement on the constitutional essentials and established political procedures are reasonably regarded as fair, willing political and social cooperation between free and equal citizens can normally be maintained.[26]

This passage, taken together with Rawls's claim about the disagreement surrounding the difference principle, suggests that he equates matters pertaining to the difference principle—matters that "are nearly always open to wide differences of reasonable opinion"[27]—with those "more particular and detailed issues" that "legislative bodies must regularly consider."[28] The last sentence of the previous passage is particularly telling. It suggests that Rawlsian individuals have undergone a radical transformation from the psychological make-up that defined their identity in the original position. They appear to have shed their concern for mutual advantages along with their interest in a larger share of primary goods. They are now content if constitutional essentials, that is, formal rights and political procedures, are fair. Yet, nothing in Rawls's text justifies this transformation.

These two passages bring forward three issues:

1. Deliberations about the difference principle could invoke nonpolitical values and, logically, even arguments derived from comprehensive doctrines. A possible reconciliation of the reference to nonpolitical values with Rawls's exclusion of comprehensive doctrines from public deliberations on justice may be that the justification of the difference principle must invoke political values (e.g., stability and cooperation). But the actual implementation of the difference principle may resort to comprehensive doctrines to determine whether the difference principle is honored by the public structure. A person whose life is ruled by a comprehensive doctrine that emphasizes egalitarianism may justify the difference principle by using political values; but, following his comprehensive doctrine, he may argue that such a principle is honored only when a strict equality is reached. In this case, political agreement on the justification of the difference principle is rather shallow. The difference principle is justified on political grounds, but disagreements will arise as to the best way to put it into practice, and the actual achievement of this principle will be subject to conflicts and measured by criteria provided by comprehensive doctrines. This is hardly an encouraging sign for stability.

2. Rawls's "political conception covers the constitutional essentials and matters of basic justice" in which *basic justice* refers to the satisfaction of basic needs. Rawls adds that "for the present this is all we aim for"[29]—a phrase whose meaning is not open to ambiguity. It means that, at this present moment in the history of the United States, Rawlsian justice has lowered its expectations to constitutional essentials and basic justice (basic needs). The term *basic justice* no longer refers to the difference principle since the explicit meaning of the phrase is that Rawls is restricting the scope of his view of justice to issues which, he claims, are "more urgent" and "far easier" to settle.[30] These are the issues covered, in his view, by the first principle of justice.

3. This lowering of expectations is ominous in three central areas of Rawlsian justice. First, the satisfaction of basic needs is completely different from the difference principle. Accordingly, that satisfaction is unable to maximize the primary goods, which are the preconditions for the fulfillment of rational

plans. Rawlsian justice is unconcerned with the actual fulfillment of rational plans, but it is committed to maximizing the primary goods offered by the public structure. As it stands now, this promise is bound to remain unfulfilled. Second, the satisfaction of basic needs is unable to maximize the long-term expectations of the least advantaged, which is the very standard of legitimacy of justice as fairness. Third, the satisfaction of basic needs is also unable to maximize the worth of liberty. In *Theory* Rawls argued that "the difference principle is basic throughout" (83). In his political version, this principle is now held in abeyance.

If justice as fairness is compatible with the status quo even when the difference principle is operating, we can imagine how Rawlsian justice looks when the satisfaction of basic needs replaces the difference principle. The goal of a well-ordered society along Rawlsian lines has been postponed. It remains to be seen whether Rawls will continue to describe America as a "nearly just society," which was the language he used in *Theory*. On closer examination, however, the goal of a well-ordered society has not been deferred; it is already present in the institutions of the U.S. constitutional system.

Both Ways

The key to understanding the shortcomings of justice as fairness is that in both a philosophical and political sense, Rawlsian justice wants to have it both ways.

Rawlsian justice attempted to reconcile a Kantian concern for choice and freedom from accident with a Hobbesian/utilitarian vocabulary of maximization (143, 412). It did not work. Rawlsian justice is uncompromising, but we must support it when it does not represent a high cost to us. If cost is central when determining our allegiance to justice, we can imagine its role in determining our possible opposition to injustice. We have a concern for autonomy coupled with a strong state apparatus that makes administrative decisions on behalf of its citizens. We have Kantian parties who relish their independence from social accidents while trying to advance their prudential interests that are expressions, precisely, of the world of contingency. And so we find, at the very beginning of the theoretical enterprise, a conflict between Kantian morality and prudential calculations. And Rawls wants to have it both ways. He cannot.

Rawlsian justice desires inequalities and political legitimacy. It seeks inequalities and cooperation. And it asks for inequalities and moral support for justice. It recognizes that an overlapping consensus must be based on a rea-

sonable pluralism, but it claims that all citizens should accept the moral validity of Rawlsian justice. It stands for self-sufficiency while proposing a principle that promotes passivity. It advocates the priority of liberty while defending
a strong welfare state responsible for providing the greatest benefits to, and dis-
ciplining, the least advantaged. It defends the political value of autonomy
while limiting its actual exercise in the public realm. It claims that in a well-
ordered society "fully autonomous" citizens pursue justice for its own sake. It
also argues that justice is a means to citizens' determinate conception of the
good.

In short, Rawls wants justice and interests: private individuals ruled by the
utilitarian principle of satisfying "more of [their] desires rather than less" (143)
and public individuals devoted to the ideas of liberty and choice. He seeks private utilitarians and public Kantians. This pervasive interest in having it both
ways is found throughout the Rawlsian project with surprising frequency and
unsurprising outcomes: weakened arguments exposed to the political danger
Rawls tried to avoid all along—the unpersuasive nature of justice as fairness.

The language of costs, specifically, comes with a price, and in the end we
are mired in the status quo. Rawls is caught in a conflicting triad: his desire for
a well-ordered society, his cost-dependent justice, and the Kantian fear of radical change. This triad is self-defeating, and the well-ordered society of Rawlsian justice becomes a rearticulation of the grounds that can be used to legitimize the status quo (511). If this is not the case—if the reading proposed here
is wrong, and justice as fairness ultimately stands for a radical change of present structures of power and property—it still faces its own wall: to defend justice when the cost is not too high. Because the notion of high costs, presumably, is one for the individual to decide—I assume that Rawls will not claim
that his public system of rules will be authorized in the original position to
determine what constitutes a "high cost" for individuals when justice is at
stake—we remain in the status quo, hardly a surprise since Rawlsian liberalism and its spiritual ancestors in the Kantian and Hobbesian traditions were
never meant to be an invigorating philosophy. The opposite holds true. They
were, as Rawls might say, stabilizing strategies to cope with the passions and
contingencies associated with the human condition, particularly those that
may spur citizens to prefer a day of reckoning to Rawls's math (two wrongs can
make a right) or to the balance of imperfections which his version of justice
requests.

Conclusions

Let me recapitulate some major conclusions of my investigation.

Priority of Right over the Good

This is an ontological impossibility. Rawlsian justice depends on reasons that are derived solely from the good of the persons the parties represent.

Priority of the Self over Its Ends

This is another ontological impossibility. The Rawlsian self is constituted by the principles of justice, and these principles depend on other people's willingness to be just. As I show in Chapter 5, the principles that allow the Rawlsian self to be prior are themselves not prior.

Original Position

By Rawls's own admission, we already know that it is a place to calculate the prudential interests of its participants (584). But it is something else: a gathering of Kantian ghosts (defined by a capacity for choice), imbued with a Hobbesian fear (defined by the possibility of being part of the most disadvantaged), and willing to arrive at utilitarian outcomes (e.g., sacrificing the interest of some groups) justified with the ground of stability.

Difference Principle

This is a novel way to buy the prudential cooperation of the least advantaged.

Rawlsian Well-ordered Society

As a utopia of harmony, it is not meaningful. As an articulation of the first principle of justice, it presents the same formal character of the classical liberal social contract and adds nothing new to the central liberties of the liberal tradition. As a principle of fair equality of opportunity, it does not add much to what the American system already provides. As a defense of the second principle of justice, it is compatible even with present inequalities. Thus justice as fairness must be seen as a decent and failed attempt in a long succession of theoretical and political projects that have attempted to provide a paradigm for a harmonious order defined as a well-ordered society.

There is a crucial difference, though. Previous utopias of harmony, with the exception of rabid conservative blueprints, endeavored to transform the given. Rawlsian liberalism is one of the few philosophical projects in human history in which an articulation of present ideas and institutions (in which even the status quo can remain intact while changing the justifying grounds for its legitimacy—the second principle) is presented as the model of a well-ordered society. This is hardly the path toward a transformation of the embedded inequalities that are part and parcel of liberal societies, constitutional democracies included.

That such a meager project as Rawlsianism has decreed the end of history by certifying the status quo as the well-ordered society—that elusive and unfulfilled goal of Western political philosophy until Rawls came along and redescribed the political culture of the United States—is a monument to the blindness toward its own limitations. Or it could be that liberalism had dwarfed its own horizon whereby history has, in fact, ended. The venerable, rational, and universal self of the Enlightenment is now a dutiful citizen showing his highest rationality and his deepest love of mankind through a state-constituted act of rational self-determination: his tax forms. This is not, after all, a small accomplishment. The end of history, indeed.

My arguments, if correct, present justice as fairness in a light quite different from the dominant readings of Rawls's views. I have not argued against the feasibility of its construction (the original position) or of its justification (the overlapping consensus of Rawls's political liberalism). My discussion identifies a principle of inequalities which invests the status quo with a moral character and demands from us compliance with the given. I have also argued that there is a utilitarian bent in the Rawlsian paradigm. My arguments, then, have deflated the credentials of Rawlsianism to be the blueprint for a well-ordered society conceived in perpetuity. This is enough to justify the title of this chapter and to bid farewell to Rawlsian justice.

Notes

Chapter 1.   Liberal Tribulations and Modern Malaises

1. Kant, *The Metaphysics of Morals*, 24, 44, 100–101.

2. See Woottons, "Introduction," in *Political Writings of John Locke*. Locke and Rousseau defended the right of revolution, but neither of them is prominent in the dominant versions of contemporary liberal theory.

3. Thomas Jefferson to William S. Smith, November 13, 1787.

4. Hobbes, *Leviathan*.

5. I am thinking here of "Idea for a Universal History with a Cosmopolitan Purpose," "Perpetual Peace," and "Theory and Practice" in *Kant's Political Writings*. See also Kant's *Groundwork of the Metaphysic of Morals*.

6. Tocqueville, *Democracy in America*.

7. However, as I argue in Chapter 4, there is a good dose of Hobbesian fear in the original Rawlsian position.

8. See Wolin's excellent discussion of Hobbes in *Politics and Vision*, Chapter 8.

9. Dworkin, "What is Equality? Part 2: Equality of Resources." Hereafter cited as "Equality of Resources."

10. Ibid., 285.

11. Dworkin, "What is Equality? Part 3: The Place of Liberty."

12. Rawls, *A Theory of Justice*, 4. Hereafter cited as *Theory*.

13. Rawls, "Justice as Fairness: Political Not Metaphysical." Hereafter cited as "Justice as Fairness."

14. Rawls, "Kantian Constructivism in Moral Theory." Hereafter cited as the "Dewey Lectures."

15. Mill, *On Liberty*.

16. MacIntyre, "Is Patriotism a Virtue?"

17. Biener, *What's the Matter with Liberalism?*, 39–97.

18. The postmodern pitch seems to annoy liberals, but they apparently do not know how to respond to it. Those who have ventured to take up the postmodern challenge have not provided more than unconvincing assertions. Thus, two theorists who sympathize with Rawlsian tenets, Will Kymlicka and Stephen Macedo, rushed to attack Richard Rorty for his alleged acceptance of what society takes as morality. Unfortunately, they did not realize that Rawls's principles had become Rortyan and that justice as fairness relies on a shared fund of values. In other words, Rawlsian justice depended on what society regards as morally acceptable principles of cooperation.

19. See Connolly, *Identity\Difference.* See also *The Ethos of Pluralization.*

20. Hobbes, *Leviathan,* Chapters 4 and 5.

21. "No-one," Kant writes, "can compel me to be happy in accordance with his conception of the welfare of others, for each may seek his happiness in whatever way he sees fit, so long as he does not infringe upon the freedom of others to pursue a similar end which can be reconciled with the freedom of everyone else within a workable general law—i.e. he must accord to others the same right as he enjoys himself" ("Theory and Practice," in *Kant's Political Writings,* 74).

22. Mill, *On Liberty,* Chapter 1.

23. See Galston, "Defending Liberalism."

24. See in this regard Moore, *Foundations of Liberalism.*

25. See Larmore, "Political Liberalism." See also *Patterns of Moral Complexity.*

26. See, for example, Stephen Macedo's characterization of MacIntyre's views as "idealistic communitarianism" and "humorously dire" conclusions. *Liberal Virtues,* 19, 16.

27. MacIntyre, *After Virtue,* 204.

28. Macedo, *Liberal Virtues,* 15.

29. See Kymlicka, "Liberalism and Communitarianism," 191–92.

30. Ibid., 190. Kymlicka writes: "What is central to the liberal view is not that we can *perceive* a self prior to its ends, but that we understand ourselves to be prior to our ends, *in the sense that no end or goal is exempt from possible re-examination.*"

31. Sandel, *Liberalism and the Limits of Justice.*

32. MacIntyre, *After Virtue.* See Chapters 15 and 16.

33. Hart, "Rawls on Liberty and Its Priority," 230–52; Neal, "Justice as Fairness."

Chapter 2. Rawls's Project

1. Unless indicated otherwise, page numbers in parentheses refer to *A Theory of Justice.*

2. "Dewey Lectures," 528.

3. Ibid., 532.

4. *Political Liberalism,* 291.

5. Rawls, "Social Unity and Primary Goods," 162. Hereafter cited as "Social Unity."

6. Ibid.

7. Ibid., 164. See also *Theory,* 320.

8. "Justice as Fairness."

9. Ibid., 228, 229.

10. See Rawls, "The Idea of an Overlapping Consensus." Hereafter cited as "Overlapping Consensus."

11. Ibid., 15–17.

12. For Rawls's discussion of pure procedural justice see *Theory,* 83ff.

13. In "The Basic Structure as Subject" Rawls writes the following: "The objection that the difference principle enjoins continuous corrections of particular distributions and capricious interference with private transactions is based on a misunderstanding" (65). The state's interference with private transactions is not capricious: it must comply with one criterion: maximizing the long-term expectations of the most disadvan-

taged. But it could be continuous if the contingencies of the social world make that interference necessary. Rawls goes on: "Again, the two principles of justice do not insist that the actual distribution conform at any given time (or over time) to any observable pattern, say equality, or that the degree of inequality computed from the distribution fall within a certain range, say of values of the Gini coefficient. What is enjoined is that (permissible) inequalities should make a certain functional contribution to the expectations of the least favored, where this functional contribution results from the working of the system of entitlements set up in public institutions." To the best of my knowledge, Rawls has not defined what he means by a *functional contribution,* although it is clear that any criteria of functionality will be determined by the Rawlsian state.

14. Ibid., 56.

15. Ibid.

16. Ibid., 53.

17. This view is confirmed by Rawls in "Reply to Habermas," 164. He writes: "In justice as fairness, we adopt in thought and subsequent practice a constitution in which, as I have said, we may or may not embed the basic liberties, thereby subjecting parliamentary legislation to certain constitutional constraints as one of the ways to discipline and regulate the presupposed state power.

18. "Basic Structure," 54.

19. Marx and Engels, *The German Ideology,* 52–57.

20. I discuss the political character of justice as fairness in Chapter 6.

21. I address the central place of associations in Rawlsian justice in Chapter 5.

22. In *Political Liberalism* his assurance has been replaced by a sense of fragility and contingency.

23. He insists, of course, "that this larger plan does not establish a dominant end" (528). But the issue here is that even the individual's private endeavors were expected to be in line with the common aim of each one realizing his own and other people's nature (527), a goal that seems more appropriate to monastic life than to a democratic setting.

24. Cf. *Theory,* 563.

25. My argument here, however, is not the same as that advanced by Sandel, who disentangled the metaphysical bearings of an unencumbered self. My argument refers to the metaphysical conception of justice as the preeminent form of human flourishing and as the best form that allows us to realize our nature as moral persons.

26. See "Justice as Fairness," 238.

27. Ibid., 239.

28. This argument is presented immediately after claiming that the principles of justice "are consented to in the light of true general beliefs about men and their place in society" (*Theory,* 454). Rawls does not realize that these true general beliefs about men rely on metaphysical assumptions.

29. Already in *Theory,* Rawls defined *political principles* as "the principles of justice which regulate the constitution and social institutions generally" (365). Other references to the political character of Rawlsian justice are found on pages 377, 378, 384, 385, 454. See also the "Dewey Lectures," 519, 540–43.

30. Insofar as a moral sense is concerned, I think the exception is Hobbes. It is not

clear whether his mechanistic account of man allows for the idea of a moral sense. See Riley, *Will and Political Legitimacy*, 23–60.

31. See also *Theory*, 509: "I have said that the minimal requirements defining moral personality refer to a capacity and not to the realization of it."

32. "Dewey Lectures," 547.

33. "Basic Structure," 61. Rawls's suggestion that a person can be a moral agent while lacking character is puzzling.

34. Admittedly, Rawls's reasoning is confusing at times. At different times he discusses *choosing, acknowledging*, and *describing*. Thus he holds that "the description of [the parties'] nature enters into the reasoning by which these principles are selected" (505). This is quite different. A description of our nature as possessing some natural sentiments is not the same as choosing the natural duty of justice.

35. "The appropriateness of moral sentiments to our nature is determined by the principles that would be consented to in the original position" (*Theory*, 490).

36. "Once the principles of right and justice are on hand, the full theory of goodness as rationality can in fact cover these judgments" (*Theory*, 434).

37. Rawlsian justice seems to be its own foundation. Even though it relies on a thin conception of the good expressed in the claim that people prefer more primary goods to pursue their more determinate visions of the good—whatever they are—it holds that it is derived independently of circumstances. It also relies on a natural sense of justice. Excluding these two minimal conditions, Rawlsian justice claims to be its own source.

38. On this issue, Bernard Yack writes: "Kantian liberals like Kant and Rawls . . . add another claim against their opponents. Those who fail to accept their conclusion are not only irrational, they are also untrue to themselves, that is, to their true identities as free and equal moral actors. Kantian liberals argue that if we make rational judgments from the standpoint provided by our shared identity, then we will choose liberal principles and practices" ("The Problem with Kantian Liberalism," 234–35).

39. Rawls's claim that justice as fairness is similar to a natural rights theory is not supported by his reasoning. See *Theory*, 505–6. In the "Dewey Lectures" he writes: "The point is that a theory of human nature is not part of the framework of the original position, except as such theories limit the feasibility of the ideals of person and society embedded in that framework. Rather, a theory of human nature is an element to be filled in, depending upon the general facts about human beings and the workings of society which we allow to the parties in their deliberations" (535). My argument here is that justice as fairness does not produce a theory of human nature. Rather, Rawls's project attempts to *create* human nature through the two principles of justice.

40. "If we answered love with hate, or came to dislike those who acted fairly toward us, or were averse to activities that furthered our good, a community would soon dissolve. Beings with a different psychology either have never existed or must soon have disappeared in the course of evolution" (*Theory*, 495).

41. "There is no race or recognized group of human beings that lacks this attribute [a capacity for moral personality, which includes the capacity for justice]. Only scattered individuals are without this capacity, or its realization to the minimum degree, and the failure to realize it is the consequence of unjust and impoverished social circumstances, or fortuitous contingencies" (*Theory*, 506).

42. This equality cannot be moral since morality requires the two principles of justice.

43. It is confusing to claim that natural duties hold regardless of institutional arrangements (114) and the claim that, in the original position, the parties "would agree to principles defining the natural duties which as formulated hold unconditionally" (116). If natural duties are preinstitutional, then they are predeliberation, and it is not clear why they must be "defined."

44. Note the distinction between *acknowledging* and *agreeing*. To *acknowledge* something implies that it was already there, whereas *agreeing* connotes that something is constructed or arrived at through deliberation.

45. One issue to note here is that the choice of a natural duty of justice is not Kantian. In the Kantian tradition we do not choose to be just, nor do we deliberate about it. Justice is an expression of the Moral Law, which is given by reason. From another perspective, however, one might argue that the Rawlsian parties are abstract rational creatures who, through reason, are given themselves their own nature. This possible contention is legitimate; but from a Kantian perspective, it is unacceptable. The Rawlsian vision of reason in the original position is premoral, whereas Kantian reason is entirely moral.

46. Keeping this implication in mind, one is able to understand why individuals' fulfillment of their life plans is irrelevant for justice as fairness, whereas the fulfillment of the social plan encompassing society and whose goals are stability, cooperation, and order, is *the* essential trait of Rawls's paradigm. I address these issues in Chapters 3 and 4.

47. In Chapter 5 I suggest that the priority of the right over the good is unpersuasive in the light of Rawls's own arguments.

48. "Saving is demanded as a condition of bringing about the full realization of just institutions and the fair value of liberty" (*Theory*, 290).

Chapter 3. Well-being and Political Calculus

1. Even though Rawlsian justice seeks to maximize people's well-being, it still excludes well-being from any evaluation of justice. Rawls's reasoning is that justice ought to be the end result of a deliberation free of contingent attributes and that any subsequent assessment of justice should not invoke contingent grounds such as well-being, conceptions of the good, and social status.

2. See, for example, Beiner's *What's the Matter with Liberalism?* and Moore's *Foundations of Liberalism*, 165–205.

3. For a discussion of utilitarianism, see Kymlicka, *Contemporary Political Philosophy*, 9–49; Griffin, "Modern Utilitarianism."

4. "Social Unity," 169. See also "A Well-ordered Society," 14.

5. See, in this regard, *Theory*, 324. On page 327 he writes: "In fact, the principles of justice do not even mention the amount or the distribution of welfare but refer only to the distribution of liberties and the other primary goods."

6. This would be an argument along Millian lines.

7. Yet that metaphysics is incompatible with the principle of the individual judg-

ment, which holds that it is the individual who should decide, according to his or her own lights, whether life is rewarding or not. If the theory imposes choice as the central criterion by which a life is defined as rewarding, that assumption undermines individual judgment in the same way as do role values derived from traditions. Choice, like values defined by traditions, would lie beyond critical scrutiny and would form the underlying ground on which judgment is supposed to operate.

8. Kant, *Groundwork of the Metaphysic of Morals.*

9. This is Rawls's argument in "Fairness to Goodness."

10. Another conception of well-being is as an index of objective needs that all people have and which should be satisfied before one pursues a more detailed life plan. These needs include food, shelter, clothes, education, and so on.

11. "Social Unity," 184.

12. Ibid.

13. *Political Liberalism,* 319.

14. "Social Unity," 169.

15. Ibid., 181.

16. This may explain why Rawls rejects Sen's view of capabilities. See Sen, "Capability and Well-being." For a critique of Sen's views see Cohen, "Equality of What?"

17. I think this word is probably a typographical error. The context and the next sentence clearly suggest that Rawls is talking about greater *inequalities.*

18. In "Social Unity" he addresses again the question of why justice as fairness does not propose "an equal share of *all* primary goods [as] the sole principle of justice." Rawls responds: "although the parties in the original position know that the persons they represent require primary goods, it does not follow that it is rational for the parties as their representatives to agree to such a strict principle of equality" (173, Rawls's emphasis). This principle of strict equality is seen as incompatible with the main goal of justice as fairness, which is to create a society to be a cooperative venture for mutual advantage. Rawlsian principles of justice are meant to express "a rational agreement" ("Social Unity," 173), and rationality, in Rawls's account, includes the desire to maximize one's personal ends (see the "Dewey Lectures").

19. Even in *Theory* Rawls claims that a strict egalitarianism would be the end result of envy, a feeling that is not present in the original position (538ff.).

20. Hobbes, *Leviathan,* 135.

21. *Political Liberalism,* 326.

22. However, since the better-off may believe that their interests are sacrificed to maximize the benefits of the worse-off, they may feel that their well-being has been limited and that Rawlsian justice—Rawls's claims to the contrary notwithstanding— sacrifices the well-being of some members on behalf of the well-being of others.

23. See Connolly, "The Dilemma of Legitimacy."

24. The distinctiveness of persons is violated when there is an external and universal imposition of specific desires, beliefs, or practices that all persons ought to accept. This is the problem that Rawls, among others, perceives in utilitarianism. The distinctiveness of persons is erased when the specific attachments, commitments, or life plans defining one's identity are excluded from the understanding of personhood. This is Sandel's critique of the Rawlsian self.

25. Nussbaum, "Aristotelian Social Democracy," 203–52.

26. This is not the same as indifference to any notion of well-being since, when individuals are allowed the means to actualize their two moral powers, presumably they are also realizing their well-being.

27. The three capacities defining the Rawlsian self are: a capacity to make choices, a capacity for justice, and a capacity for a conception of the good.

28. This is, incidentally, another Hobbesian trait of the Rawlsian contract.

29. Although I develop this position in Chapter 4, it suffices to mention here that when well-being is at stake, the difference principle is more important than the first principle of justice.

30. The context of these remarks is Rawls's discussion of civil disobedience in Section 57 of *Theory*. He says, first, that civil disobedience should be restricted to "serious infringements" of the principle of equal liberty and to "blatant violations" of the principle of fair equality of opportunity (372). But then he excludes the principle of fair equality of opportunity and concludes that "the violation of the first principle of justice is . . . the more appropriate object of civil disobedience" (373). His contention about why the difference principle might require the political process is relevant in my discussion about the legitimacy of taking to the political arena the decision as to the acceptability of the level of mutual advantages in the Rawlsian order.

31. *Political Liberalism*, 227–30; "Overlapping Consensus," 14 n. 22. See also *Political Liberalism*, 151 n. 16.

32. Rawls's own discussion of considered judgments seems to oppose this aspect of his theory.

33. See, in this regard, Sen, "Capability and Well-being."

34. Rawls might say that justice as fairness does not maximize the well-being of the most disadvantaged. I submit that, by maximizing the primary goods, which are the preconditions of well-being, justice as fairness maximizes the conditions that make well-being possible.

35. Or, Rawlsian policy makers may say that their doctrine was meant to apply to situations of abundance, but it is inadequate to tackle this scenario.

36. A utilitarian government can maximize: the citizens' share of primary goods; the benefits for the most disadvantaged; their long-term expectations; and the stability of society with the explicit goal of maximizing the preferences of the greatest number. Rawls's reasoning is different. Since neither the maximization of preferences nor the actual fulfillment of persons' rational plans was part of the agreement on justice, Rawlsian justice is not utilitarian.

In a typical Kantian fashion Rawls believes he can overcome utilitarian dangers by designing a Kantian procedure. It does not occur to him that the Kantian procedure is *already* sacrificing a person's preferences by declaring them morally and politically irrelevant. Rawls abolishes all preferences, desires, and specific ends and conceives of that abolition as the foundation of fairness. Because people do not know their preferences or life plans, they must scurry for cover under the difference principle. In other words, Rawls conquers utilitarianism not by maximizing the preferences of the greatest number, but by abolishing the preferences of the total number.

A person devoid of knowledge, desires, and inclinations becomes an abstract entity, ready to agree to principles that might have utilitarian outcomes. But those outcomes would be accidental; and if society complies with Rawlsian justice, the consequences are fair. Moreover, justice is judged not by outcomes but by its adherence to procedures.

My argument is that these distinctions are morally and politically specious. In the original position Rawlsian justice abolishes all preferences by invoking a standard of fairness which assumes the validity of the Kantian view of selfhood. He then envisions that view as politically neutral. That validity is not justified with arguments; it is given in advance.

In an actual society Rawlsian justice is willing to sacrifice a person's desires and interests and then to justify that sacrifice with the fiction of the original position, the morality of that action. This denies the principle of reciprocity: one gives a fair share to society and expects a fair share from society. If, by contrast, personal interests are sacrificed, it is dubious that an individual will regard that outcome as an expression of reciprocity much less fair. This is not a problem for Rawls, though. In his arguments the Hobbesian calculators of the original position become disciplined Kantians in an actual society and accept the claim that compliance with Rawlsian justice represents the highest level of moral development. They further accept the claim that their self-esteem will be based not on material possessions but on Rawls's system of justice. This does not agree with the society we know and the individuals it produces, but the Rawlsian system is confident in the strength of its reasoning.

37. "Theory and Practice" in *Kant's Political Writings*, 61–92.

Chapter 4.   Conflicts of the Heart: The First versus the Second Principle of Rawlsian Justice

1. In *Theories of Justice* Brian Barry offers a similar argument. He poses a conflict between two versions of justice which he sees in Rawls's work: justice as impartiality and justice as mutual advantages. In Barry's view justice as mutual advantages is not moral. It is rather the end result of gambling. My argument is that the psychological make-up of the parties in the original position makes impossible the appeal to moral reasons, which explains why the natural duty of justice is so central to Rawlsian justice.

2. In his discussion of interpersonal comparisons Rawls writes: "the clearest basis for interpersonal comparisons is in terms of primary goods, things that every rational person is presumed to want whatever else he wants. The more we ascend to the higher aims and aspects of the persons and try to assess their worth to us, the more tenuous the procedure becomes . . . the worth to a person of the circumstances of others simply cannot be assessed" (174, 175). The only interpersonal comparisons Rawls considers meaningful refer to primary goods, but he offers good reasons to reject comparisons that take into account another person's character and system of ends (*Theory*, 174).

When a Rawlsian agent imagines himself as a representative member of the most disadvantaged, this projection into the other's situation does not refer to that person's total circumstances. We need to know our determinate conception of the good to judge another person's situations. In the original position we lack that knowledge. Similarly, we cannot fully adopt the standpoint of the most disadvantaged because we do not know their conception of the good; nor do we know ours. And without that information it is impossible to evaluate a person's total situation.

"Now the combination of mutual disinterest and the veil of ignorance achieves the same purpose as benevolence. For this combination of conditions forces each person in the original position to take the good of others into account" (*Theory,* 148). But "the parties aim to advance their own interests" (*Theory,* 163). It is unclear how the parties can take into account the good of others when their only concern is to advance their own interests rather than those of others. Equally unclear is how they can do so without knowing the conception of the good of either party.

3. Okin defends this view in *Justice, Gender, and the Family.* She writes: "The veil of ignorance is such a demanding stipulation that it converts what would, without it, be self-interest into equal concern for others, including others who are very different from ourselves. Those in the original position cannot think from the position of *nobody,* as is suggested by those critics who then conclude that Rawls's theory depends upon a 'disembodied' concept of the self. They must, rather, think from the perspective of *everybody,* in the sense of *each in turn.* To do this requires, at the very least, both strong empathy and a preparedness to listen carefully to the very different points of view of others" (100–101, Okin's emphasis).

Okin's attempt to put to rest Sandel's criticisms is superficial, and her discovery of "strong empathy" in the original position is contradicted by Rawls's own texts. Rawls claims that we cannot evaluate a person's system of ends "without any reference to the details of our conception of our good." Here is Rawls's argument: "It suffices to observe here that what we cannot do is to evaluate another person's total circumstances, his objective situation plus his character and system of ends, without any reference to the details of our conception of our good. If we are to judge these things from our standpoint at all, we must know what our plan of life is. The worth to us of the circumstances of others is not, as the constructed expectation assumes, its value to them (*Theory,* 174).

In the original position, however, we lack knowledge of our life plan, and accordingly, we cannot take into account another person's system of ends which, presumably, embody their good. We therefore cannot take into consideration the good of others beyond the rather innocuous claim that all of them need primary goods. We might well agree that all of them need water and food, thus showing that we are "concerned" with their good. See Rawls's arguments in *Theory,* 171–75; they contradict Okin's reading.

4. Are there calculations in the original position? Rawls is unclear in this regard. He says: "The parties have no basis for determining the probable nature of their society, or their place in it. Thus they have strong reasons for being wary of probability calculations if any other course is open to them" (Theory, 155). But he also says: "As far as possible the choice of a conception of justice should depend on a rational assessment of accepting risks unaffected by peculiar individual preferences for taking chances one way or the other" (*Theory,* 172). "Judgments of probability must have some objective basis in the known facts about society if they are to be rational grounds of decision in the special situation of the original position" (*Theory,* 173). If the Rawlsian parties engage in a choice-making process, if their judgment of probability ought to rely on the known facts about society, and if they must consider the possible risks of their actions, then it is clear that calculations are part of the moral make-up of Rawlsian selves.

5. See Rawls's argument in *Theory,* 301–2.

6. Wolff offers a similar view in *Understanding Rawls*, 163.

7. As I show in Chapter 5, Rawls's communitarianism requires an even stronger identification with the interests of others.

8. "A person," Rawls says, "is choosing once and for all the standards which are to govern his life prospects." I might add that he is also choosing the standards that are going to maximize his life prospects. Otherwise, individuals would not agree to the principle that primary goods must be maximized, nor would they necessarily accept the principle of the greatest benefits for the most disadvantaged. But because they want to maximize their prospects in life, they maximize the preconditions of their life plans: the primary goods.

9. Rawls goes on: "We can, however, define ethical variations of the initial situation by supposing the parties to be influenced by moral considerations. It is a mistake to object that the notion of the original agreement would no longer be ethically neutral. For this notion already includes moral features and must do so, for example, the formal conditions on principles and the veil of ignorance. I have simply divided up the description of the original position so that these elements do not occur in the characterization of the parties, although even here there might be a question as to what counts as a moral element and what does not. There is no need to settle this problem" (*Theory*, 584–85). Rawls's claim that ethical variations of the original position may suppose the parties "to be influenced by moral considerations," is impossible. There is no morality in the original position. Moral considerations are built upon either the principles of right or a person's vision of the good, neither of which is available to the parties at the start of their deliberations.

10. The link between prudence and rational self-interest is also mentioned by Green in "Equality since Rawls."

11. *Political Liberalism*, 305–7.

12. Ibid., 51.

13. Ibid., 50.

14. Ibid., 52.

15. Ibid.

16. Ibid., 306.

17. In the third part of *Theory* Rawls spells out his communitarianism and defends cooperation as an indispensable component of our development as human beings. I have argued elsewhere that there is a tension between the first part of *Theory*, in which the principles of rights are derived independently of visions of the good, and the third part, in which even the sense of justice depends on our socialization. The most important good of Rawlsian selves, self-esteem, depends on communities of shared interests. See my essay "Rawls's Communitarianism." A revised version of this article is presented in Chapter 5. Rawls himself has argued that there is a tension between the first and third parts of *Theory* (see *Political Liberalism*, xv–xvii). He does so, not on the grounds I have mentioned, but on the ground that the third part suggests a comprehensive liberal doctrine, whereas a political agreement on justice does not depend on such, nor does it rely on comprehensive values. Rawls has renounced the comprehensive overtones of his theory, and, presumably, cooperation is no longer tied to the development of our humanity. Cooperation is rather to be understood as a political value, which is represented by the mutual advantages it makes possible. In other words, mutual advan-

tages require cooperation, and cooperation leads to mutual advantages. In the original position both are prudential.

18. *A Discourse on the Origin of Inequality*, in Rousseau, *The Social Contract and The Discourses*, Part II.

19. In this sense Rawlsian justice ought to be conceived as a two-stage process. In the first stage inequalities are justified by providing the greatest benefits to the most disadvantaged and leaving intact the existing inequalities. In the second stage the state ought to reduce the existing inequalities to an acceptable level. How this stage is compatible with the first principle of justice is not clear.

20. We have seen that the Rawlsian order is predicated upon prudential calculations that somehow acquire a moral character.

21. It is paradoxical that a theory allegedly assuming the centrality of persons ends up with an order in which the morality of actual persons is irrelevant in the assessment of society as a moral enterprise. For all its claims to the contrary notwithstanding, Rawlsian justice is deeply suspicious of *actual* moral persons. It is instead morally appealing only to public functionaries and to people who may prefer for the state to meet their needs through allocation, stabilization, transfer, and distribution branches (*Theory*, 276–77). In the original position there are no actual persons. In a Rawlsian society actual persons are excluded, as far as possible, from the administrative procedures required by the difference principle. Justice is "whatever it is" (*Theory*, 282).

22. "A Well-ordered Society," 16.

23. Ibid.

24. This argument is suggested by Rawls's discussion of fair equality of opportunity. See *Theory*, 301–2. I return to this issue in Chapter 8.

25. An intriguing solution but one that, given Rawls's reasoning, should not be excluded altogether is that the status of expectations (whether they are rising) is determined by the state, just as it determines what the greatest benefits are. In this case the judgment of a person or a group of persons on whether their expectations are rising is irrelevant. That judgment would be an administrative decision.

26. It is worth noticing that, in Marxist theory, the particular interests of the proletariat are universal. In Rawls's theory, by contrast, the interests of the disadvantaged are always particular and bound to remain so.

27. From a Marxist perspective, the workers might still be interested in abolishing the control of the bourgeoisie over the means of production, but that position depends on the Marxist metaphysics of history. In any case such an option violates the first principle of Rawlsian justice.

28. In *Theory* Rawls presents another of his important assumptions. "If we further suppose that social cooperation among those who respect each other and themselves as manifest in their institutions is likely to be more effective and harmonious, the general level of expectations, assuming we could estimate it, may be higher when the two principles of justice are satisfied than one might otherwise have thought" (180). This assumption is rather intriguing.

29. If this is the case, people may claim that the original position was unfair. It did not allow them to know how much they would care about this interest that happens to take a religious form.

30. See, for example, "Social Unity."

31. It is worth asking why, if these obligations are so important, they are treated as morally irrelevant (Rawls's initial argument) or politically irrelevant (the claim he presents in *Political Liberalism*).

32. "Furthermore," Rawls writes, "liberty of conscience is to be limited only when there is a reasonable expectation that not doing so will damage the public order which the government should maintain. This expectation must be based on evidence and ways of reasoning acceptable to all" (*Theory*, 213).

33. According to Rawls, the parties would not accept the principle of utility because "their freedom would be subject to the calculus of social interests and they would be authorizing its restriction if this would lead to a greater net balance of satisfaction" (*Theory*, 207). What happens, however, when a religious belief protected by the first principle of justice is an obstacle to cooperation, stability, and the goals of maximizing the long-term expectations of the most disadvantaged? Because Rawlsian justice is independent of contingent attributes (and Rawls treats religion as a contingent feature), it could be argued that it has precedence over religious beliefs. Rawlsian citizens might well be willing to restrict their freedom if this maximizes the greatest benefits and the long-term expectations of the least fortunate members. When these two maximizations are at stake, "the calculus of social interests" is welcome into the Rawlsian paradigm.

Note that Rawlsian citizens are not restricting their liberties for the sake of greater economic gains or a greater satisfaction. They do so for the sake of a stronger cooperation, a goal that justice as fairness explicitly pursues. Therefore, this restriction would be compatible with Rawlsian justice. If the parties want to maintain the lexical ordering of the two principles, they undermine the bases of cooperation and stability which were already agreed to in the original position. The issue, then, is not that the principle of utility is willing to limit freedom, but Rawlsian justice is not. The real issue is that their justifications for restricting freedom are different: a greater net of satisfaction (utility), a more stable cooperation that allows the system to "generate its own support" (261).

34. See Bernard Williams, "Consequentialism and Integrity," 20–50.

35. Machiavelli, *The Discourses,* Book 1, Chapter 4.

36. Ibid., Book 1, Chapters 7, 52, and 55; Book 3, Chapter 28.

37. The problem of alienation opens up other problems to the extent that unacceptable levels of wealth may not be its only causes. The Rawlsian public structure in which the citizens' judgment plays no role in the determination of mutual advantages and the greatest benefits might also have an alienating effect. But this Rawls does not accept. If public institutions affirm a person's good, that person will support those institutions. Yet, if public institutions affirm my good through administrative procedures that exclude me, I may feel that I should have a say in those procedures. In justice as fairness, however, my autonomy is not meant to enter governmental offices.

38. Justice as fairness is predicated upon an Aristotelian perspective on the limits of equality, which is presented in Chapter 8.

39. Rawlsian justice claims that persons are responsible for their ends in life compatible with the principles of justice. In the example I have been presenting, the wealthy individual is not violating the equal liberties of others, and he is complying with the second principle through taxes. But somehow his wealth is an alienating factor in the community, and the state ought to take steps to prevent a stampede of citizens with-

drawing from civic duties (Tocqueville's fear) to protest their disappointment with the level of wealth of other individuals.

40. In justice as fairness the right to own property is not part of the basic liberties, but a person's liberty of conscience is.

Chapter 5. Rawls's Communitarianism

1. In "Beyond Liberalism and Communitarianism" Doppelt argues that "Rawls's framework can be understood as a 'communitarian liberalism'" (281). But his focus is different from mine. Okin discusses the role of feeling in Rawls's account of justice, but she does not address Rawls's vision of community. See her "Reason and Feeling in Thinking about Justice." Nickel focuses on political community in "Rawls on Political Community and Principles of Justice."

2. Although Rawls's articles after *Theory* include important developments and, in some cases, modifications of his previous arguments, I believe that his account of community has not altered substantially.

3. "Dewey Lectures," 529.

4. The Rawlsian community is a space of harmony and transparency which assumes that men have a natural inclination toward unity. Justice seems to be a natural capacity, a built-in mechanism for human sociability. Rawls insists, a "stable conception of justice . . . elicits men's natural sentiments of unity and fellow feeling" (502). It is thus possible to apply to Rawls's philosophy his own description of Mill's theory: "one of a person's natural wants is that there should be harmony between his feelings and those of his fellow citizens" (502).

5. Along the same lines, he also argues that the soundness of our convictions depends upon a common perspective. "The acceptance of the principles of right and justice forges the bonds of civic friendship and establishes the basis of community amidst the disparities that persist. . . . But unless there existed a common perspective, the assumption of which narrowed differences of opinion, reasoning and argument would be pointless and we would have no rational grounds for believing in the soundness of our convictions" (517–18). This assertion suggests that even though the theory is individualistic, the conception of rationality informing it is social. In other words, the common perspective turns out to be a set of beliefs accepted by a community. This is another instance of Rawls's communitarianism.

6. See, for example, Kymlicka's "Liberalism and Communitarianism."

7. This turn of Rawls's communitarianism shows how mistaken is the attempt to present the liberal communitarian debate as a conflict between society and the individual's judgment. For this misconstruction, see Kymlicka's "Liberalism and Communitarianism." It could be argued, however, that the self is still prior to its ends in the sense that it can revise them. Rawls himself claims that "free persons conceive of themselves as beings who can revise and alter their final ends and who give first priority to preserving their liberty in these matters" ("Reply to Alexander and Musgrave," 641).

Kymlicka ("Liberalism and Communitarianism," 15–17) uses this view to present the principle of reexamination as an important feature of Rawls's liberalism. I think that Kymlicka's interpretation relies on an extremely selective reading of Rawls's texts, which fails to explore several important tensions in Rawls's arguments. Two grounds dispute Kymlicka's view: the Rawlsian view of a rational plan and Rawls's communitarianism.

In Rawls's theory a rational plan and the person's conception of the good are bound together. "The rational plan for a person determines his good" (408). More importantly, he goes on, "we are to see our life as one whole, the activities of one rational subject spread out in time. . . . The intrinsic importance that we assign to different parts of our life should be the same at every moment of time. These values should depend upon the whole plan itself as far as we can determine it and should not be affected by the contingencies of our present perspective" (420). This claim is certainly at variance with the principle of reexamination and with Rawls's own claim that free persons have an interest in revising their final ends.

Rawls's conception of a community of shared interests is the other ground that disputes the principle of reexamination. For Rawls, self-esteem and the conception of the good require a community of shared interests where the individual confirms his own worth. Therefore, the individual's membership in that community must also be part of his conception of the good. This individual depends on the standards his associates accept to confirm his own worth, develop his excellences, and complete his own nature. Accordingly, he is not one who is always willing to reexamine his conception of the good. That reexamination may lead him to adopt a conception of the good, which his associates may not accept. He would thus lose their support. And if that happens, he loses not only some friends but also the external source of his self-esteem.

A Millian or an Emersonian self would be willing to stand up for its moral independence regardless of what a community of shared interests may do. But it is not clear that a Rawlsian self is equally willing to risk its self-esteem in order to preserve its moral independence. Rawls's arguments, then, suggest a tension between the self's moral independence and its self-esteem, and the latter, after all, is the most important good. Kymlicka's analysis does not explore these tensions in the Rawlsian construction of the self.

8. Dworkin, "In Defense of Equality."

9. Kateb, "Democratic Individuality and the Meaning of Rights."

10. It would be worth exploring whether a Rawlsian community contributes to the same docility that Kateb ascribes to communitarianism. See his "Individualism, Communitarianism, and Docility."

11. It is possible to argue that a person may decide to join other groups, thus showing that he or she is prior to communal standards of self-esteem. Two arguments reply to this contention. First, if the self depends on others to affirm its worth, it may be willing to compromise rather than to leave a group that helps it to constitute its identity. Second, even if the self leaves its group, there is one from which it cannot escape, the group that gave it its first experience with the principles of justice: its family. A self that is always open to the possibility of leaving its group is not a Rawlsian self; it is one that is more in line with Mill's account of individuality. In *Liberalism, Community, and Culture* Kymlicka subscribes to this notion that the Rawlsian self is always willing to examine its ends, and, for instance, its membership in a group. See my discussion in note 7.

12. Those instances in which attachments are given, not formed, seem to be excluded.

13. It is possible to argue that the principles of reciprocity, as Rawls understands them, do not necessarily apply to other virtues like love, excellence, and courage. Love, for example, does not depend on the other's willingness to reciprocate. People tend to love their relatives and friends even when they do not appreciate that sentiment.

14. Or as Rawls puts it: [the three laws of moral psychology] "characterize transformations of our pattern of final ends that arise from our recognizing the manner in which institutions and the actions of others affect our good" (494).

15. This seeming twist of the Rawlsian discourse may bring up an intriguing problem: how can selves choose principles of justice in the original position when they have not even developed a sense of justice, which requires institutions and the influence of "the actions of others" to arise? I will not address this problem here.

16. Rawls himself suggests this reading when he says: "Thus, a conception of the good normally consists of a more or less determinate scheme of final ends, that is, ends we want to realize for their own sake, as well as of attachments to other persons and loyalties to various groups and associations. These attachments and loyalties give rise to affections and devotions, and therefore the flourishing of the persons and associations who are the objects of these sentiments is also part of our conception of the good" ("Justice as Fairness," 233–34).

17. As indicated in Chapter 2, Rawls no longer advocates this view of a pluralistic society.

18. He claims, a "conception of justice is but one part of a moral view" (512). But in Rawls's philosophy justice is the most important component of morality. At other moments he says that justice defines "the moral point of view" (491).

19. Rawls, "The Sense of Justice," 299.

20. When Rawls refers to associations as "an institutional setting" that is "just" (491), it is unclear whether he is referring to his two principles of justice or whether the justice that associations embody is different from Rawls's two principles.

21. Rawls, "The Priority of Right and Ideas of the Good," hereafter cited as "The Priority of Right." See also "Overlapping Consensus."

22. In his articles after *Theory* Rawls has not modified this position. Justice is a highest order interest that ought to regulate our character and public life. See "Overlapping Consensus."

23. In Rawls's political liberalism this problem has become more complicated. Now individuals are presented as having both a public and a nonpublic identity. Justice must define the individual's public identity, but comprehensive doctrines may define his private identity. However, those doctrines must comply with the principles of justice. Again, many citizens may question the priority that justice enjoys in the definition of their nonpublic identity.

24. This position, it should be said in passing, is in tension with his conception of justice as reciprocity: we expect the other person to respond in kind. But in a Rawlsian society, our expectation is mediated by institutions.

25. This is not necessarily Rawls's case, but it is a well-known scenario in liberal societies.

26. A possible liberal reply is that such a conception of oppression is not rational, and such a society is not oppressive. But the Rawlsian view of rationality and oppres-

sion is only one among many; and even in liberal societies there is hardly a consensus on it.

27. It is worth noticing that an alternative view of society such as that propounded, respectively, by MacIntyre, Walzer, and Kateb, does not rely on the fixed place of justice. It is not by any means clear that such a society would be an oppressive setting.

28. Sandel, *Liberalism and the Limits of Justice*, 64; hereafter cited as *LLJ*.

29. Okin ("Reason and Feeling," 245–46) critiques this idea, but her aim is to defend the original position, not to see how Rawls's communitarianism may challenge Sandel's interpretation.

30. Sandel hints at this distinction in his discussion of desert, but he does not develop it. *LLJ*, 82–95

31. According to him, the self cannot choose "that which is already given (this would be unintelligible)." *LLJ*, 58. But if the individual reflects upon what is given and reaffirms it, he is clearly making a choice, even though, for Sandel, this is "unintelligible." It is so if we assume the fixity of the oppositions he presents.

32. Sandel consistently insists on these kinds of opposition. In a recent article he posed: "What then is the resemblance between heterosexual intimacies on the one hand, and homosexual intimacies on the other, such that both are entitled to a constitutional right of privacy?" He answered: "This question might be answered in at least two different ways—one voluntarist, the other substantive. The first argues from the autonomy the practices reflect, whereas the second appeals to the human good the practices realize" (534). Thus Sandel opposes "the autonomy the practices reflect" to the human goods they realize. This opposition presupposes that autonomy is *not* a human good, and this presupposition is problematic. Instead of opposing both categories, it is better to envision autonomy as a human good that contributes to define other human goods. For example, it is doubtful that the human good expressed, say, in personal relationships, can be realized without assuming the autonomy of the participants. A forced marriage could contribute to procreation and even to a stable family, and some people may consider it a human good. But this good would be realized at the expense of two individuals who found themselves in a marriage without having exercised an autonomous choice. Can human goods be realized without autonomous individuals? See Sandel, "Moral Argument and Liberal Toleration."

33. "Justice as Fairness," 233; "The Priority of Right," 270.

34. "Dewey Lectures," 529.

35. "Idea for a Universal History," in *Kant's Political Writings*, 45–46.

36. This view does not deny the important differences between Plato's idea of the individual, which is guided by a transcendental conception of the human good, and Rawls's understanding of justice, which relies on the political culture of a democratic society.

37. Plato, *The Republic*, Book IV, 434d, 435e, 441a, 441c,d.

Chapter 6. What Is Political about Rawls's Political Liberalism

1. Mouffe, *The Return of the Political*, 47.

2. Honig, *Political Theory and the Displacement of Politics*, 128–61.

3. Connolly, "Identity and Difference in Liberalism," 59–85.

4. See "Justice as Fairness."

5. See "Overlapping Consensus."

6. See "Justice as Fairness," 231.

7. Ibid., 247.

8. Ibid., 229.

9. This view was first formulated in the "Dewey Lectures" and developed in "Justice as Fairness."

10. *Political Liberalism,* 224.

11. "Justice as Fairness," 236–37.

12. Rawls writes: "Most traditional doctrines hold that to some degree at least human nature is such that we acquire a desire to act justly when we have lived under and benefited from just institutions. To the extent that this is true, a conception of justice is psychologically suited to human inclinations" (456).

13. *Political Liberalism,* 86.

14. Ibid., 77–78.

15. "Basic Structure," 63.

16. Even in *Political Liberalism,* Rawls repeats a claim first advanced in the "Dewey Lectures," namely, that people's full autonomy is realized only by acting on the principles of justice.

17. "Justice as Fairness," 224 n. 2.

18. Ibid., 228.

19. "Overlapping Consensus," 14 n. 22.

20. "A Well-ordered Society," 12.

21. See *Political Liberalism,* 298.

22. "Justice as Fairness," 228.

23. Ibid., 229.

24. I elaborate these views in my *Hermeneutics, Citizenship, and the Public Sphere,* Chapters 2–5.

25. *Political Liberalism,* 235; see also 232. In Rawls's views only the court is expected to provide reasons that are not connected to comprehensive doctrines. As he says: "public reason is the sole reason the court exercises."

26. Galston, "Moral Personality and Liberal Theory," 519 n. 14.

27. The Rawlsian discourse clearly states that there is no sharp divide between the spheres; the principles of public consensus follow and define the individual in his or her private endeavors. Yet this narrative also suggests that some areas of an individual's private subjectivity cannot be part of a public quest for moral consensus.

28. Compare Rawls's distinction between the public and the private realms, in which the "highest interest" of justice ought to be present in the public domain, with Rorty's more flexible account: "Another central claim of this book [*Contingency, Irony, and Solidarity*] . . . is that our responsibilities to others constitute *only* the public side of our lives, a side which competes with our private affections and our private attempts at self-creation, and which has no *automatic* priority over such private motives. Whether it has priority in any given case is a matter for deliberation, a process which will usually not be aided by appeal to 'classical first principles.' Moral obligation is, in this view, to be thrown in with a lot of other considerations, rather than automatically trump them" (194).

29. "Dewey Lectures," 544.

30. Ibid., 545.

31. Rawls admits that citizens "might regard it as unthinkable for them to view themselves without certain religious and philosophical convictions and commitments" (Ibid.).

32. "Fairness to Goodness," 537.

33. Walzer criticizes this philosophical method in "A Critique of Philosophical Conversation."

34. "Overlapping Consensus," 11, 13 n. 21.

35. "Dewey Lectures," 542.

36. "Overlapping Consensus," 6. See also "Justice as Fairness," 229.

37. In this regard the Rawlsian domain of consensus appears to be the counterpart of MacIntyre's philosophy, in which the community has one conception of the good life, and both public and private reasons are justified by the criteria provided by it. In the Rawlsian account there is one conception of justice which provides criteria to justify institutions. Rawls also says that "more than one political conception may be worked up from the fund of shared political ideas" of democratic societies ("Overlapping Consensus," 7).

38. Ibid., 13, 17.

39. "The Priority of Right," 267.

40. Ibid., 268.

41. Ibid.

42. For a similar argument, see Neal, "A Liberal Theory of the Good."

43. "Overlapping Consensus," 6.

44. For a discussion of liberal virtues within the Rawlsian model, see "Overlapping Consensus," 17.

45. "Dewey Lectures," 525.

46. "Overlapping Consensus," 11.

47. "Dewey Lectures," 533.

48. Ibid., 548, 533.

49. Ibid., 553.

50. See, for example, "Justice as Fairness," 245ff.

51. "Overlapping Consensus," 3.

52. "The Priority of Right," 263.

53. Galston argues that in Rawls's recent theoretical developments, "justice as fairness has verged on a kind of democratic perfectionism." See his "Pluralism and Social Unity," 718. I will suggest, however, that his theory is not on the verge of, but already within, the boundaries of a perfectionist paradigm.

54. Yet it is possible to *argue* that Rawls's theory is also driven by a *telos*. This *telos* is neither happiness nor moral perfection, but political stability and social unity. Shapiro identifies another strand of teleology in Rawls's paradigm. According to Rawls, teleology assumes that "the good is defined independently from the right, and then the right is defined as that which maximizes the good" (*Theory*, 24). Shapiro replies: "Rawls's argument for the priority of right must rest on the converse of the independence thesis he identifies in 'teleological theories': he defines the right independently of the good and the good as that which maximizes the right. It might be objected that Rawls's ac-

count of the priority of right is derived from his 'thin' theory of the good, but we saw that if *this* is his position it is teleological in exactly the sense that he regards as objectionable" (*The Evolution of Rights in Liberal Theory,* 256). Shapiro attempted to prove this point earlier: "If the two principles are held to be nonteleological, however, as neutral among different conceptions of the good, they cannot be used as a basis for rejecting a particular conception of the good on the grounds that it violates the two principles, unless it is held a priori that only conceptions of the good consistent with the two principles are rational. If *this* is the claim, Rawls's argument is irreducibly teleological (ibid., 217).

55. *Political Liberalism,* 315; emphasis mine.

56. Ibid., 316–17.

57. Ibid., 317–18.

58. Ibid., 317.

59. Mouffe, *Return of the Political,* 51.

60. *Political Liberalism,* 239.

61. Wolin, *The Presence of the Past,* 182.

62. See Ibid., 180–207.

Chapter 7.   Envy, Nature, and Full Autonomy

1. In a well-ordered society, Rawls believes, social and economic inequalities "are not likely to generate animosity." His project seems to be an attempt to overcome resentment arising from economic disparities. People are called to accept the economic and social inequalities allowed by the Rawlsian order, and the public structure is expected to address inequalities arising from other sources through the priority of equal liberties (*Theory,* 545).

2. See *A Discourse on the Origins of Inequality* and *The Social Contract* in Rousseau, *The Social Contract and The Discourses,* 32.

3. As he writes: "Infringements of fair equality of opportunity are not justified by a greater sum of advantages enjoyed by others or by society as a whole. The claim (whether correct or not) must be that the opportunities of the least favored sectors of the community would be still more limited if these inequalities were removed. One is to hold that they are not unjust, since the conditions for achieving the full realization of the principles of justice do not exist" (302).

4. It is not clear what Rawls's position would be if the elimination of that arrangement and the transformation of the economy improved the prospects of the most disadvantaged in the long run.

5. See also *Political Liberalism,* 328.

6. And if we take men as they are, which is the old Rousseauian dictum defining Rawlsianism, it is not unreasonable to claim that some people might even prefer to make sacrifices for "the whole"—whatever this notion might be in their minds—but not necessarily for a particular group.

7. "Social Unity," 170.

8. I assume that, in the light of Rawls's arguments, this "foreseeable situation" must be reasonable. As Rawls says: "This division of responsibility relies on the capacity of

persons to assume responsibility for their ends and to moderate the claims they make on their social institutions in accordance with the use of primary goods" ("Social Unity," 170).

9. "Social Structure," 55.

10. Ibid.

11. *Political Liberalism,* 213.

12. "Reply to Habermas," 135.

13. "Justice as Fairness," 244.

14. *Political Liberalism,* 370.

15. Ibid., 340.

16. "Dewey Lectures," 521. Rawls claims that "the public affirmation" of those principles "by citizens of a well-ordered society in every-day life enables them to be fully autonomous" (ibid., 522; see also 528).

17. *Political Liberalism,* 77.

18. Ibid., 318.

19. Ibid., 319–20.

20. Ibid., 365.

Chapter 8.   Farewell to Rawlsian Justice

1. For a discussion of how Kantian liberalism is predicated on dubious assumptions about society's shared identity, see Bernard Yack's excellent essay, "The Problem with Kantian Liberalism."

2. It is worth noticing that the political character of Rawlsian parties depends on the political irrelevance of their attributes.

3. These two intuitive ideas are: the freedom and equality of moral persons, and society as a fair system of cooperation. See "Justice as Fairness."

4. Recall that cooperation, a goal that antecedes the deliberations in the original position, is a central component of the intuitive ideas Rawls uses to derive the principles of justice.

5. *Political Liberalism,* 329. See also "Social Unity."

6. *Political Liberalism,* 327.

7. Ibid.

8. Ibid., 328.

9. Ibid., 330. Rawls includes the fair value of the political liberties in the first principle not because civic participation is a paramount good, but because such inclusion "is essential in order to establish just legislation and also to make sure that the fair political process specified by the constitution is open to everyone on a basis of rough equality" (*Political Liberalism,* 330). In other words, even if society is regulated by a political conception of justice which all citizens recognize as reasonable and rational, the political process is exposed to the dangers of partiality, a danger Rawls tackles by giving all citizens the opportunity "to influence the outcome of political decisions."

Still, his arguments are problematic. First, the claim that the fair value of the political liberties is "essential . . . to establish just legislation" suggests the centrality of citizens' involvement in political affairs, and this is not present in justice as fairness. Rawls does not advocate an active citizenry participating in the political process. In a well-ordered society, he says, only a few people will engage in politics.

Second, justice as fairness could be read as a circle whose point of departure and final destination resemble the original position, which is why Rawls claims that at the judicial stage, "the constraints of the reasonable" are strongest. "While the constraints of the reasonable are weakest and the veil of ignorance thickest in the original position, at the judicial state these constraints are strongest and the veil of ignorance thinnest" (*Political Liberalism,* 340). The judiciary becomes the final anchor of justice as fairness, and Rawlsian justices are the highest evolutionary forms of the parties to the original position. The legislative process, by contrast, is a stage in which narrow interests and partisanship may taint the enactment of laws. Since Rawls, then, does not stand for many citizens participating in the political arena, the guarantee of the fair value of the political liberties exists as an important remedy should citizens' representatives act contrary to the principles of Rawlsian justice.

When we put these considerations together we are left with three possible options to explain the relationship between citizens' participation and stability in a Rawlsian society:

1. The public structure guarantees compliance with Rawlsian justice.
2. Citizens adopt the values of civic republicanism; by acting permanently in the political realm, they prevent public institutions from violating the agreement on Rawlsian justice.
3. Citizens may act, episodically, to correct any deviation from the two principles of justice.
4. The judiciary will ultimately uphold the Rawlsian contract.

Option 1 is unpersuasive since public institutions are administered by individuals whose judgments might be wrong. Option 2 is explicitly rejected. It is reasonable to conclude that in the light of Rawls's own arguments, the stability of a well-ordered society will depend on options 3 and 4.

10. *Political Liberalism,* 315.

11. Ibid., 166.

12. *Political Liberalism,* 329. Rawls also claims that the difference principle takes care of a fixed bundle of primary goods, but this argument is not persuasive. The difference principle is concerned with a social minimum.

13. Ibid.

14. See also *Political Liberalism,* 144.

15. We can alter the lexical ordering depending on social circumstances, but the principles of justice stay the same.

16. As is well known, Rawls is not inflexible about the lexical ordering of his principles. Historical circumstances may alter it. See, for example, *Theory,* 89, 543–44.

17. *Political Liberalism,* 297.

18. See problem 5 in the Bidding Farewell section. Rawls can say that the right of property can be restricted for the sake of liberty, which, in this case would be necessarily the liberty of some people to have their "basic wants fulfilled" (544). "The denial of equal liberty can be accepted only if it is necessary to enhance the quality of civi-

lization so that in due course the equal freedoms can be enjoyed by all" (542). It is clear that the quality of civilization is dubious when people lack shelter or food or medical care, not to mention education. Faced with a society committed to bringing about Rawlsian justice but lacking in material conditions, liberty can be restricted for the material gains of others, in this case the most disadvantaged whose basic needs are not yet satisfied.

19. *Political Liberalism*, 54.

20. Rawlsian reconciliation is predicated on the assumption that the state can be a moral agent with the capacity to moralize the social order, whereby 1) the Rawlsian state turns out to be an agent of public morality which 2) distributes benefits and injustices. 3) It is also the agent of social change and stability through distributive policies of property and wealth; but 4) it does not seek to transform civil society or to abolish inequalities, but to compensate for those inequalities (309). 5) State-regulated compensations seek to reconcile persons with the contingencies of the human condition.

21. *Political Liberalism*, 254.

22. Rawls does claim that "if justified civil disobedience seems to threaten civic concord, the responsibility falls not upon those who protest but upon those whose abuse of authority and power justifies such opposition. For to employ the coercive apparatus of the state in order to maintain manifestly unjust institutions is itself a form of illegitimate force that men in due course have a right to resist" (*Theory*, 391). This claim is explicitly contradicted by Rawls's insistence that civil-disobedient minorities should not destabilize public order. Moreover, the central assumption of the Rawlsian view of civil disobedience is that the context is one of a nearly just society, one in which, presumably, important liberties are recognized, and those liberties might be endangered by public disorders. This citation, however, refers to manifestly unjust institutions, which is not his description of a nearly just society. My position is thus warranted: in a nearly just society the burden of stability rests with minority groups who might engage in acts of civil disobedience.

23. *Political Liberalism*, 229–30.

24. Ibid., 232.

25. There is a way out available to the Rawlsian paradigm: the courts will determine whether the difference principle is being honored in a proper way; in making this determination, the courts are allowed to invoke only political values, which are the backbone of Rawls's understanding of public reason, "the sole reason the court exercises" (ibid., 235).

26. Ibid., 230.

27. Ibid., 229.

28. Ibid., 230.

29. Ibid.

30. Ibid.

Bibliography

Alejandro, Roberto. 1993. *Hermeneutics, Citizenship, and the Public Sphere.* Albany, N.Y.: SUNY Press.

Arendt, Hannah. 1958. *The Human Condition.* Chicago: University of Chicago Press.

Barber, Benjamin. 1984. *Strong Democracy.* Berkeley: University of California Press.

Barry, Brian. 1989. *Theories of Justice.* Berkeley: University of California Press.

Beiner, Ronald. 1992. *What's the Matter with Liberalism?* Berkeley: University of California Press.

Cohen, G. A. 1993. Equality of What? On Welfare, Goods, and Capabilities. In *The Quality of Life,* ed. Martha C. Nussbaum and Amartya Sen, 9–29. Oxford: Oxford University Press.

Connolly, William. 1984. The Dilemma of Legitimacy. In *Legitimacy and the State,* ed. William Connolly, 222–49. Oxford: Blackwell.

———. 1990. Identity and Difference in Liberalism. In *Liberalism and the Good,* ed. R. Bruce Douglass, Gerald M. Mara, and Henry S. Richardson, 59–85. New York: Routledge.

———. 1991. *Identity\Difference: Democratic Negotiations of Political Paradox.* Ithaca: Cornell University Press.

———. 1995. *The Ethos of Pluralization.* Minneapolis: University of Minnesota Press.

Doppelt, Gerald. 1988. Beyond Liberalism and Communitarianism: Towards a Critical Theory of Social Justice. *Philosophy and Social Criticism* 14:271–92.

Douglass, R. Bruce, Gerald M. Mara, and Henry S. Richardson, eds. 1990. *Liberalism and the Good.* New York: Routledge.

Dworkin, Ronald. 1981. What Is Equality? Part 2. Equality of Resources. *Philosophy and Public Affairs* 10:283–345.

———. 1983. In Defense of Equality. *Social Philosophy and Policy* 1:24–40.

———. 1987. What Is Equality? Part 3. The Place of Liberty. *Iowa Law Review* 73: 24–50.

Galston, William. 1982a. Moral Personality and Liberal Theory: John Rawls's "Dewey Lectures." *Political Theory* 10:492–519.

———. 1982b. Defending Liberalism. *American Political Science Review* 76:621–29.

———. 1989. Pluralism and Social Unity. *Ethics* 99:711–26.

Green, Philip. 1985. Equality since Rawls: Objective Philosophers, Subjective Citizens, and Rational Choice. *Journal of Politics* 47:972–97.

Griffin, James. 1991. Modern Utilitarianism. In *Contemporary Political Theory*, ed. Philip Pettit, 73–100. New York: Macmillan.

Gutmann, Amy. 1985. Communitarian Critics of Liberalism. *Philosophy and Public Affairs* 14:308–22.

Hamilton, Alexander, James Madison, and John Jay. 1961. *The Federalist Papers.* New York: New American Library.

Hart, H. L. A. 1975. Rawls on Liberty and Its Priority. In *Reading Rawls,* ed. Norman Daniels, 230–52. New York: Basic Books.

Hobbes, Thomas. 1994. *Leviathan,* ed. Edwin Curley. Indianapolis: Hackett.

Honig, Bonnie. 1993. *Political Theory and the Displacement of Politics.* Ithaca: Cornell University Press.

Jefferson, Thomas. 1984. Letter to William S. Smith, November 13, 1787. *Thomas Jefferson: Writings,* 911. New York: Library of America.

Kant, Immanuel. 1964. *Groundwork of the Metaphysic of Morals,* trans. H. J. Paton. New York: Harper and Row.

———. 1970. *Kant's Political Writings,* ed. Hans Reiss. Cambridge, U.K.: Cambridge University Press.

———. 1996. *The Metaphysics of Morals,* ed. Mary Gregor. Cambridge, U.K.: Cambridge University Press.

Kateb, George. 1989a. Democratic Individuality and the Meaning of Rights. In *Liberalism and the Moral Life,* ed. Nancy L. Rosenblum, 183–204. Cambridge, Mass.: Harvard University Press.

———. 1989b. Individualism, Communitarianism, and Docility. *Social Research* 56: 921–42.

Kymlicka, Will. 1988. Liberalism and Communitarianism. *Canadian Journal of Philosophy* 18:181–204.

———. 1990. *Contemporary Political Philosophy.* Oxford: Oxford University Press.

———. 1991. *Liberalism, Community, and Culture.* Oxford: Clarendon Press.

Larmore, Charles. 1988. *Patterns of Moral Complexity.* Cambridge, U.K.: Cambridge University Press.

———. 1990. Political Liberalism. *Political Theory* 18:339–60.

Laslett, Peter, and James Fishkin, eds. 1979. *Philosophy, Politics and Society.* New Haven: Yale University Press.

Macedo, Stephen. 1990. *Liberal Virtues.* Oxford: Oxford University Press.

Machiavelli, Niccolo. 1983. *The Discourses,* ed. Bernard Crick. London: Penguin Classics.

MacIntyre, Alasdair. 1984. *After Virtue.* Notre Dame, Ind.: University of Notre Dame Press.

————. 1984. Is Patriotism a Virtue? Lindley Lecture. University of Kansas.

Marx, Karl, and Frederick Engels. 1970. *The German Ideology,* ed. C. J. Arthur, 52–57. New York: International Publishers.

Mill, John Stuart. 1974. *On Liberty.* Middlesex, U.K.: Penguin Books.

Moore, Margaret. 1993. *Foundations of Liberalism.* Oxford: Clarendon Press.

Mouffe, Chantal. 1993. *The Return of the Political.* New York: Verso.

Neal, Patrick. 1987. A Liberal Theory of the Good. *Canadian Journal of Philosophy* 17:567–82.

————. 1990. Justice as Fairness: Political or Metaphysical? *Political Theory* 18:24–50.

Nickel, James W. 1990. Rawls on Political Community and Principles of Justice. *Law and Philosophy* 9:205–16.

Nussbaum, Martha. 1990. Aristotelian Social Democracy. In *Liberalism and the Good,* ed. R. Bruce Douglass, Gerald M. Mara, and Henry S. Richardson, 203–52. New York: Routledge.

Nussbaum, Martha C., and Amartya Sen, eds. 1993. *The Quality of Life.* Oxford: Oxford University Press.

Okin, Susan Moller. 1989a. *Justice, Gender, and the Family.* New York: Basic Books.

————. 1989b. Reason and Feeling in Thinking about Justice. *Ethics* 99:229–49.

Plato. 1985. *The Republic,* trans. Richard W. Sterling and William C. Scott. New York: W. W. Norton.

Rawls, John. 1963. The Sense of Justice. *Philosophical Review* 72:281–305.

————. 1971. *A Theory of Justice.* Cambridge, Mass.: Harvard University Press.

————. 1974. Reply to Alexander and Musgrave. *Quarterly Journal of Economics* 88: 633–55.

————. 1975. Fairness to Goodness. *Philosophical Review* 84:536–54.

————. 1978. The Basic Structure as Subject. In *Values and Morals,* ed. Alvin I. Goldman and Jaegwon Kim, 47–71. London: D. Reidel.

————. 1979. A Well-ordered Society. In *Philosophy, Politics, and Society,* ed. P. Laslett and J. Fishkin. New Haven: Yale University Press.

————. 1980. Kantian Constructivism in Moral Theory: The Dewey Lectures. *Journal of Philosophy* 77:515–72.

————. 1982. Social Unity and Primary Goods. In *Utilitarianism and Beyond,* ed. Amartya Sen and Bernard Williams. Cambridge, U.K.: Cambridge University Press.

————. 1985. Justice as Fairness: Political Not Metaphysical. *Philosophy and Public Affairs* 14:223–51.

————. 1987. The Idea of an Overlapping Consensus. *Oxford Journal of Legal Studies* 7:1–25.

————. 1988. The Priority of Right and Ideas of the Good. *Philosophy and Public Affairs* 17:251–76.

———. 1993a. *Political Liberalism.* New York: Columbia University Press.

———. 1993b. Themes in Kant's Moral Philosophy. In *Kant and Political Philosophy,* ed. Ronald Beiner and William James Booth, 291–319. New Haven: Yale University Press.

———. 1995. Reply to Habermas. *Journal of Philosophy* 92:132–80.

Riley, Patrick. 1982. *Will and Political Legitimacy.* Cambridge, Mass.: Harvard University Press.

Rorty, Richard. 1989. *Contingency, Irony, and Solidarity.* Cambridge, U.K.: Cambridge University Press.

Rosenblum, Nancy L., ed. 1989. *Liberalism and the Moral Life.* Cambridge, Mass.: Harvard University Press.

Rousseau, J. J. 1993. *The Social Contract and the Discourses,* trans. G. D. H. Cole. New York: Everyman's Library.

Sandel, Michael. 1982. *Liberalism and the Limits of Justice.* Cambridge, U.K.: Cambridge University Press.

———. 1989. Moral Argument and Liberal Toleration. *California Law Review* 77: 521–38.

Sen, Amartya. 1993. Capability and Well-being. In *The Quality of Life,* ed. Martha C. Nussbaum and Amartya Sen, 30–61. Oxford: Oxford University Press.

Shapiro, Ian. 1986. *The Evolution of Rights in Liberal Theory.* Cambridge, U.K.: Cambridge University Press.

Taylor, Charles. 1989. Cross-purposes: The Liberal-Communitarian Debate. In *Liberalism and the Moral Life,* ed. Nancy L. Rosenblum, 159–82. Cambridge, Mass.: Harvard University Press.

Tocqueville, Alexis de. 1994. *Democracy in America.* New York: Everyman's Library.

Walzer, Michael. 1989–90. A Critique of Philosophical Conversation. *Philosophical Forum* 21:182–96.

Williams, Bernard. 1988. Consequentialism and Integrity. In *Consequentialism and Its Critics,* ed. Samuel Scheffler, 20–50. Oxford: Oxford University Press.

Wolff, Robert Paul. 1977. *Understanding Rawls.* Princeton: Princeton University Press.

Wolin, Sheldon. 1960. *Politics and Vision.* Boston: Little, Brown.

———. 1989. *The Presence of the Past: Essays on the State and the Constitution.* Baltimore: The John Hopkins University Press.

Woottons, David. 1993. Introduction. *Political Writings of John Locke.* Middlesex, U.K.: Penguin Books.

Yack, Bernard. 1993. The Problem with Kantian Liberalism. In *Kant and Political Philosophy,* ed. Ronald Beiner and William James Booth, 224–44. New Haven: Yale University Press.

Index

Library of Congress Cataloging-in-Publication Data

Alejandro, Roberto, 1955–
    The limits of Rawlsian justice / Roberto Alejandro.
        p.   cm.
    Includes bibliographical references and index.
    IBSN 0-8018-5678-7 (alk. paper)
        1. Justice.   2. Law—Philosophy.   3. Rawls, John, 1921–
    I. Title.
    K240.A43   1998
    340'.1—dc21   97-165585
                                                                               CIP